WOODWORKER'S
GUIDE TO
MASTER
CRAFTSMAN
TECHNIQUES

WOODWORKER'S
GUIDE TO
MASTER
CRAFTSMAN
TECHNIQUES

Editors of
WOODWORKER
Magazine

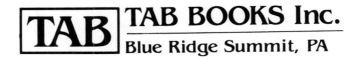

TAB BOOKS Inc.
Blue Ridge Summit, PA

FIRST EDITION
FIRST PRINTING

Copyright © 1989 by Davis Publications, Inc.
Printed in the United States of America

Reproduction or publication of the content in any manner, without express permission of the publisher, is prohibited. No liability is assumed with respect to the use of the information herein.

Library of Congress Cataloging in Publication Data

Woodworker's guide to master craftsman techniques / by the editors of
    Woodworker magazine.
        p.   cm.
    Includes index.
    ISBN 0-8306-9061-1   ISBN 0-8306-9361-0 (pbk.)
    1. Woodwork. 2. Furniture finishing. I. Woodworker (New York,
N.Y. : 1980)
TT180.W645 1989
784.1′04—dc19   88-37661
                                                            CIP

TAB BOOKS Inc. offers software for sale. For information and a catalog, please contact TAB Software Department, Blue Ridge Summit, PA 17294-0850.

Questions regarding the content of this book
should be addressed to:

    Reader Inquiry Branch
    TAB BOOKS Inc.
    Blue Ridge Summit, PA 17294-0214

Contents

WOODWORKER'S
GUIDE TO
MASTER
CRAFTSMAN
TECHNIQUES

Introduction

WOODWORKING IS A TIME-HONORED CRAFT that takes plenty of patience and years of practice to master. But there are tricks of the trade that master craftsmen employ to simplify certain methods without sacrificing quality. The articles presented here, selected by the editors of *Woodworker Magazine*, are perfectly suited to the novice who feels overwhelmed by the skill level required to complete many woodworking projects. The more advanced craftsman will also find this book valuable as a reference of time-tested techniques and a source of new ideas to help him further develop his craft.

All of the basics are covered—from hand and power tool use and joinery methods to achieving "special effects," like antiquing new wood for a truly authentic look. Handy techniques such as bending and inlaying wood are also included. Methods of reupholstery are simplified and the secrets to creating professional-quality dovetail joints are laid out in step-by-step fashion. Furniture refinishing is treated at length, along with specific instructions on what to look for in used furniture and how to turn each piece into a beautiful heirloom.

We at TAB BOOKS are pleased to present this book for your use and enjoyment and feel confident that, no matter what your level of ability or skill, you will find in it something new and helpful.

Section I
Tool Use
and
Maintenance

Hand Tools
For Your Shop

ONE RESULT of the growing trend to self-maintenance and improvement of our homes has been to get the pliers, wrench, and screwdriver out of the kitchen catchall drawer and organize them for greater convenience. As the variety of hand tools owned increased with confidence in our handyman capabilities, the good sense of the "place for everything and everything in its place" axiom became more obvious. The end result has been an efficient workshop, equipped with the right tools for the common jobs around the house, and arranged to eliminate "stop and search" delays (Fig. 1-1).

If you are in the early stages of planning or outfitting your shop, these few observations might be helpful. First, select tools of good quality for best and long-lasting service. Use the right tool for the job at hand. These suggestions apply to basic as well as special-purpose or occasional-use tools. It is just as important to have good screwdrivers, pliers, and soldering equipment at your workbench as it is to use durable, high quality construction materials for home improvement projects. If you "cut corners" on either, the finished work will show it. Even worse, your sense

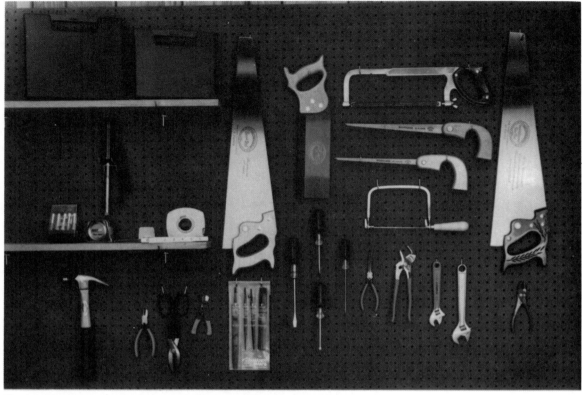

Fig. 1-1. The better-organized your tools, the more efficient your workshop will be.

of satisfaction that follows a job well done will suffer, and chances are there'll have to be a redo in the not too distant future.

SELECTING HAND TOOLS

Expert tool makers offer these general guides to the selection of some of the hand tools you'll be looking for at your nearby hardware store or home center.

• Hand tools are designed to make a job easier and enable the homeowner-handyman to work efficiently and safely. Knowing your tools and how to use and care for them is essential.

• Hand tools must be comfortable to use—balance, weight, size, and handles are factors to consider. For example, many Crescent and Xcelite pliers and wrenches are made with Cushion Grip, a red fiber-impregnated handle surface that ensures a positive and safe hold to prevent slips and skinned knuckles. Screwdrivers have oversize handles for better grip and turning power. Nicholson handsaws have comfort-engineered grips; Weller soldering tools feature heat-resistant handles; and Lufkin measuring tapes are compact and easy to hold and read, some even having position-lock blades to permit one-hand use.

• Look for precision-machined tools with component parts that are perfectly mated to each other. Materials and finishes are important too. Drop forged alloy or carbon steels, chrome plating for resistance to humid or corrosive atmospheres, modern and durable plastics, U.L. wiring tags, firm and positive action of interchangeable tips or blades are some of the signs of quality design and manufacture not always present in the ordinary ''garden variety'' of tools.

Basic hand tools can be grouped into seven broad classifications: cutting, gripping, measuring, soldering, filing, fastening, and striking.

CUTTING TOOLS

In the cutting group are saws, tin snips, wire cutters, and combination cutters/strippers.

The saw family, practically a classification in itself, includes seven types to meet most if not all wood, metal, or plastic cutting needs.

The most common and essential home-use saw is the *crosscut*, designed primarily for cutting straight across or at an angle to the grain of the wood. A practical model for fine cuts will have a 10-point (teeth per inch), 26-inch blade. Its counterpart is the 5½-point *ripsaw* for ''ripping'' or cutting with the grain. In a pinch. a crosscut can be used to do a fair job of ripping, but expect only the poorest results from crosscutting with a ripsaw.

The *coping* saw, sometimes called a jigsaw, is the most versatile of the saw family. It can work its way along a straight line, turn a right angle, or cut curves and circles. Its blade is removable and can be set at any desired angle. This feature permits cutting of an opening or design in a light wood panel inside the edges, to the limit of the depth of the saw frame, with only one drilled starting hole.

For making curved or straight cuts in heavier wood or wallboard beyond the normal capability of a coping saw, reach for either your *compass* or *keyhole* saw. While nearly twins, the keyhole saw is smaller with a narrower and sharper blade end, enabling it to cut openings, such as for an electrical outlet, where the compass might not go.

The *backsaw* is a crosscut with steel reinforcing strip along the top of the blade to keep it rigid (Fig. 1-2). Used in a miter box, it gives accurate straight cuts at 45-degree or 90-degree angles, handy when cutting decorative wood moldings for wall panels, cabinet doors or room entry doors.

Finally, there's the *hacksaw* to complete the saw inventory—an essential for cutting metal. Also a versatile tool, blades are interchangeable for cutting various metal thicknesses, and can be inserted in the frame in four different positions—with the teeth downward, upward, or facing either side depending on the clearance problem. It's also handy in the kitchen for cutting frozen foods or meat bones!

In the wire cutting category are combination *cutter/strippers* with an adjustable stop which prevents core damage when stripping the insulation off different size wires to install new light switches, and standard 6-inch solid joint *cutting pliers* for heavier wire diameters.

GRIPPING TOOLS

A workshop's elementary gripping tools should include the adjustable wrench and at least three types of pliers—tongue and groove, standard slip joint, and needle nose.

This last one is handy for getting at those hard-to-reach places—a difficult job to do.

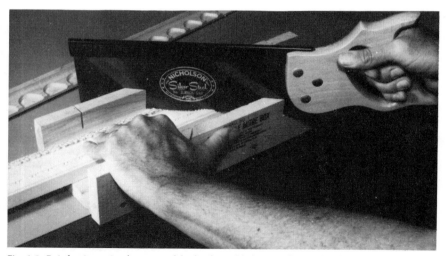

Fig. 1-2. Reinforcing strip along top of the backsaw blade provides rigidity for this crosscut. Used with a miter box, it will provide you with true 45- or 90-degree angles for picture framing, decorative moldings, etc.

Two of these tools are unique. The prime feature of the wrench is its ability to fit any size nut or bolt up to the limit of the adjustable jaw opening. In the case of an 8-inch-long wrench, that would be 1/16 inch shy of 1 inch. Sizes range from 4 inches to 24 inches with openings from 1/2 inch to nearly 2 1/2 inches.

An adjustable wrench and tongue-and-groove pliers are frequent companion-use tools—one to hold, one to turn—for removing a flat-siding fitting from a round pipe, as on a tank nozzle. You'll find the same type of pipe combination under a sink.

The other all-around utility tool is the tongue-and-groove plier. Its extra-long handles make it an easy-to-use and powerful gripping tool that doesn't require excessive hand pressure. Like the Crescent wrench, the opening can be adjusted and fixed. The aligned jaw teeth give a secure grip on round objects such as pipe or conduit. Sizes range from 7 to 14 inches long, with opening capacities of 1 1/4 to 3 1/4 inches.

MEASURING TOOLS

Every properly equipped workshop must include the capability for accurate measurement. There's nothing so disappointing as a new counter top that has been measured yet made a fraction short, or a shelf that turns out to need an eighth-inch shaved off to fit.

In this group of measuring tools are a 25-foot power tape, handy 6-foot pocket tape, a 50-foot-long tape, and the trusty old carpenter's standby, a 6-foot folding rule.

SOLDERING TOOLS

Soldering tools for permanently joining metals together, such as electrical wiring, come in two forms—pistol-grip guns and pencil-type irons. Both are made in various heat capacities and available even in kit form, complete with solder, interchangeable tips and plastic cases. Newest in the field is the cordless iron, rapidly becoming *the* home soldering unit because of its dual function as an in-workshop tool and at any job-site lacking an electrical power source.

FILES

Files are made in a wide variety of styles and sizes, and are handy for dozens of different uses in the shop and around the house. Their primary function is to shape, smooth, or sharpen—

applications like smoothing edges of paneling, reaming out or enlarging a door knob or lock hole, sharpening garden tool edges, knives and rotary lawn mower blades, edging a damaged or paint-filled screw slot, and many more.

A convenient answer to these multiple needs is a Handyman's Home File Pak. The pouch contains a file for sharpening, a tapered round file for hole enlarging, a triangular file to smooth angled surfaces, and a 4-in-Hand that is half file, half rasp with flat and half-round sides to work a variety of surfaces.

FASTENING TOOLS

Screwdrivers for normal household uses are made in two styles, with standard flat blade tips for the common single-slot screws, and Phillips for the special four-way types (Fig. 1-3).

Because screw slots vary in thickness and width according to the overall sizes of screws, and blade tips must fit closely to avoid slippage or overlap of the screwhead, workshops need several sizes of screwdrivers in lengths from 3 inches to 8 inches. For comfort and muscle saving positive hold, select screwdrivers with Cushion Grip handles of nitrile rubber as opposed to often slippery plastic.

Another handy fastening tool is the midget nutdriver, ideal for holding a nut while turning its bolt or for getting at a nut in cramped quarters. They are available in a number of plastic case

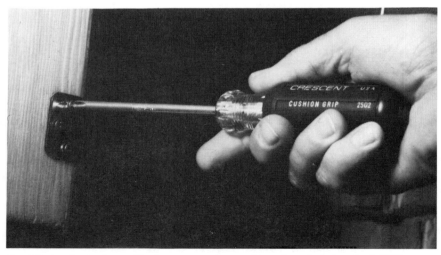

Fig. 1-3. Any home shop will, of course, need screwdrivers in varied sizes, both Phillips type shown here and the standard single-slot. In selecting them, pay close attention to handles; plastics can be slippery.

bench sets or singly, with "piggyback" torque amplifier handles that slip over the nutdriver handle for a larger gripping surface, extended reach and increased driving power.

OTHER WORKSHOP TOOLS

As confidence grows in your home maintenance, repair and improvement capabilities, so will your workshop inventory. Some other tools you will find use for are a bench vise, hand drill, wood chisels, a carpenter's square, level, shop knife, and plane. And the earlier the better, protective gloves for handling rough materials and plastic safety goggles.

CARE OF TOOLS

• Keep your shop clean and clutter-free, on the bench and on the floor. Organization of tools on pegboard is the best method yet devised, and there are fixtures made for securely hanging any hand tool you'll ever need.

• Protect tools from rust with a light oil or silicone spray coating.

• Keep all tools clean and cutting tools sharpened.

• Remove nicks from screwdriver tips with a file.

• Keep measuring tape blades clean to avoid inside-case dirt or sawdust accumulation.

• Keep files in their plastic case or wrapped to avoid damaging their teeth.

How to Use a
Table Saw Like a Pro

THE TABLE SAW is an efficient and effective tool. It saves you a tremendous amount of hard labor. It can turn out work that is straighter and more precisely dimensioned than you could possibly get otherwise. And it can be operated with complete safety year after year.

A table saw (often called a bench saw or circular saw) is a power tool, not a toy. *Use the saw correctly.* If you use the tool correctly, you are also using it safely.

Operating a table saw is simple and safe. The entire unit is solidly planted where it belongs. There's just a small blade rotating, most of it under the table and out of the way. Only a very small segment is exposed, usually only about an inch in height. But small as it is, the blade can wreak plenty of havoc when used carelessly or improperly.

PROPER USAGE

Here are the essentials of good woodworking practices:

• Have a saw of good quality and of ample size for the work to be done. The larger the table size, the better. Extra side extensions help to stabilize the wood stock as it is fed into the blade. A small table provides only a small area to hold a board steady while it is being cut. The saw fence should be of sturdy construction, with a dependable locking device, and preferably of the self-aligning type so the fence is square with the blade each time it is set.

• Have sufficient clearance on all sides of the tool to handle boards without hindrance. If you're running an 8-foot-long board through the blade, you need at least 16 feet of clear space, plus the width of the blade and room for yourself. If the space is long and narrow, you can mount the saw on casters to turn it sidewise for crosscutting. An extra table or roller platform at the back of the saw will support the board as it comes through, making it easier and safer to handle.

• Keep the shop floor clean, and have ample lighting. Sweep up sawdust and wood chips that might cause you to slip. Lights should be in a non-glare fixture, preferably fluorescent, and cover a large area. Don't let sawdust accumulate under the saw.

• Use a blade guard and splitter whenever possible. Have a push stick handy at all times for feeding narrow stock. Use only sharp and clean blades; dull blades require excessive pushing and make rough cuts. Keep the saw mandrel properly aligned with the blade so the stock will cut true and won't bind against the fence.

• Wear proper clothing—no dangling sleeves or tie. Always stand at the side of blade when running stock, not directly in back of it. And never reach to remove waste pieces of stock when the blade is running.

POSSIBLE MISHAPS

It's best to be informed of possible hazards and prevent them. When something goes wrong it happens instantly—without warning. There's no time to correct errors then. Here is a list of such situations and protective measures.

1. *Out-of-line ripping.* When feeding a board, it should be kept in contact with the fence until the blade has made a deep

cut into the stock. If the board is moving in without side support, an open space between the stock and the fence becomes larger. The board then wobbles so that the cut suddenly swerves out of line. If your fingers are nearby holding down the stock, they might get pulled into the blade. Never rip stock that does not have a straight edge to go against the fence, and keep fingers wrapped tightly around the fence top.

2. *Kickback*. This happens most frequently when ripping and the work is fed too quickly, or when it binds in the blade. The wood is thrown back with great force. Never stand directly in line with the blade. Hold work down firmly and use the splitter to keep kerf open.

3. *Binding*. This, occurs when crosscutting with a blade that is dull or rusty. If the saw belt is of the right tension, the motor will stall, and it should be shut off instantly.

4. *Narrow stock*. Always use a push stick to feed narrow stock along the fence. When fingers must be used to hold down the wood, hook the other fingers over the top of the fence, and slide them along as the work goes through the blade.

Each sawing job calls for a special method, which should be followed scrupulously. There will be plenty of times when your inventive talents will be called on to solve special problems. That means planning and setting up jigs that hold the work securely, particularly when you cut tenons, lock miters, bevels, and irregular shapes.

HANDLING LARGE PANELS

A common problem is that of cutting large plywood panels. A ¼-inch wallboard panel is light enough, and can be handled on a saw of average size provided you set up a table nearby for extra support, or have a roller-topped extension stand. Even with the ¼-inch stock, it's difficult enough to run the panel through and keep it always firmly against the fence.

A ¾-inch plywood panel is usually too unwieldy for a single person. It's best to have an assistant to help carry it into the workshop as well as align it properly on the saw.

The assistant should stand alongside the saw as the panel end approaches the blade, pressing in from the side against the fence. Both persons should then slowly guide the panel along until it is halfway through, then the assistant should go to the back to support the panel as it emerges. In the final stage, the person feeding moves to the side and continues pressure at the side to hold the panel edge at the fence so the cut is straight and true all the way. The feeder supports the free side of the ripped panel, while the assistant pulls the other part until it clears the blade.

An easier way to handle a full-length ¾-inch panel is to precut it roughly to width with a portable circular saw or jigsaw. The straight factory-cut edges on each side are retained to go against the fence for final ripping to precise size. Precutting is also helpful for getting the panel into a basement workshop when the entranceway presents difficulties. Only the large, professional model saws can cut to the center of a 4-foot-wide panel, so usually this must be done with a portable saw.

METHODS OF RIPPING

Ripping is cutting in the same direction as the grain, and is always done against the fence. When ripping, always use the blade guard and splitter. The splitter prevents the wood from squeezing together at the saw kerf and thus makes it easier to feed the stock smoothly.

When setting the fence for the cutting width, use a folding ruler to measure the distance from the fence to the inside tip of a saw tooth that is set toward the fence. Thus you will have the width that the blade will cut, and will avoid including the thickness of the kerf. That is, if the stock you want is on the fence side and the waste stock outside.

But it can be reversed; the outside piece can be the desired size. In that case, measure from the outside edge of a saw tooth to the edge of the wood, and the kerf will now be on the waste stock toward the fence.

To rip duplicate pieces to uniform width, use the fence side of the blade. This will eliminate need for measuring each time, and the dimensions will be uniform.

Adjust the blade height so that it is just above the thickness of the wood. Lock the fence, making certain it won't shift. Swing the blade guard into place. Hold the board flat on the table, and advance it toward the blade. As it moves into the blade, place your free hand so that the thumb and forefinger are pressing down on the stock just before the blade, holding the wood against the fence.

Your other fingers should be bent around the fence. In that way, if the blade should suddenly cause the wood to veer, your hand will remain safely gripping the fence, out of danger. This should be standard practice, even when the blade guard is used.

When ripping a board that is more than 6 feet long, provide support at the free end of the saw for the stock as it comes through; otherwise, you'll find that the free weight pulls it down and makes it difficult to run the last part through smoothly. It is possible to walk around to the back while holding the board in place, and pull the rest of the board from there, but this is awkward and could cause problems.

When ripping narrow stock, with less than 3 inches between the blade and the fence, always use a push stick instead of your fingers to run the wood alongside the blade near the end of the cut. When ripping thin strips at the fence side, stand well away as the strip will suddenly shoot back at your side of the table.

Taper Ripping

It is possible to rip a board at an angle to make one end wider than the other. This is done with the aid of a tapering jig, consisting of two hinged boards, with a stock block on the open end of one side. The jig is opened to form an angle that will give the desired taper. It is set against the fence and the stock placed so a corner is at the stop block. The entire unit—jig and stock—is pushed through. Because of the offset formed by the open jig, the blade cuts through the stock at an angle, wider at the front than at the back. Such a jig can prove extremely handy on a wide variety of construction projects.

Miter cutting is normally done with the miter jig, which can be adjusted to any angle by loosening a thumbscrew. But there's a tendency for the wood to creep slightly while it is cut, so wherever possible, the work should be held with a C-clamp.

Even so, the results might not be perfect on small work. A better method is with a large sliding panel which has two runners that move in the table slots. The work is easily held against large, correctly-positioned blocks set at 90-degree angles.

CROSSCUTTING TO LENGTH

The miter gauge is used when sawing work across the grain to obtain the desired length. The miter gauge should be tested occasionally to make sure it is square with the blade. The work is set against the gauge, which is moved toward the blade until the cut is made. In crosscutting, the blade guard may be a hindrance and you might be tempted to remove it entirely. This should be done only after you have acquired experience.

If the saw table is quite small, situations may arise when you want to cut 12-inch-wide stock and there's insufficient clearance for the wood between the front edge of the blade and the miter gauge.

One solution is to lower the blade so the wood can move forward over the blade plate. While holding the stock down, start the motor and raise the blade so it cuts through; then you can push the wood through with the gauge to complete the cut.

If you want to cut a number of pieces to the same length, adjust the stop rods on the miter gauge to correct position. Then each piece is moved against the bent end of this rod and will be cut to the same length.

Another way is to clamp a stop block at the front end of the fence so that the wood can be placed on the gauge in correct position. As the wood passes the stop block, it remains in the same position for cutting. But never use the fence itself—or stop block clamp near the blade—as a jig. This will cause the wood to bind and swing around out of your grasp, perhaps pulling your fingers into the blade.

RABBETING AND TENONING

There are many woodworking jobs that require rabbet joints, such as drawer fronts and cabinet doors. This entails setting the blade at precise height for each of two cuts. The first cut is made with the board held vertically against the fence. Place the board flat on the table with the cut end down, edge against the fence, and run through a second time, thus removing the square strip (See Fig. 2-1).

The blade height for each cut should be set first by measurement, but then tested for accuracy by running through a few pieces of waste stock. When vertical and horizontal cuts mate at the precise position to clear the edge stock, the setup is right to go ahead.

Dadoing across the grain, and grooving along the grain, are best done with an adjustable dado cutter, or a set consisting of several blades of different thickness placed together for a cut of the correct width.

Adjust the blade height by making test runs to cut the groove of the desired depth. When running the stock, hold it down firmly over the cutter, as the wood tends to bounce slightly which results

Fig. 2-1. To make a rabbet, hold board upright against fence for first cut, then lay flat, cut side down, for the second cut.

in an uneven cut. When using dado blades, the table insert plate must be changed for one that has a slot wide enough for the cutter.

For tenoning, a special jig makes the job easier, as the stock usually is long and must be fed into the blade along the narrow edge. Clamps on the jig hold the stock firmly and safely.

Half-lap joints, used for making frames for boxes or screens, bring two parts together, each of which has been cut to half the thickness of the wood so the corners match evenly and flush. The cutting is done against the miter gauge, either with a dado blade or a regular crosscut blade.

It is essential that the blade height be precisely at half point. As the dado blade will not be of the correct thickness, the work must be shifted while making several passes across the blade to obtain a sufficient width of cut. Because of this, you should use a regular blade.

First place the two pieces to be joined so that the corners are square to each other. With a pencil, mark lines at the inside edge on each part. After the blade is set to correct height, half the thickness of the work, make the first cut on the inside of the marked line. Then move the stock about ⅛ inch closer to the blade and repeat the pass, thus widening the kerf. Repeated passes, while moving the stock about ⅛ inch each time, will complete the lap cutting.

Repeat this with the other part, and fit the two pieces of stock together. In most cases, the cleared section must be smoothed with the edge of a chisel to clean out loose fibers. The half-lap joint must fit perfectly flush on all sides.

16

Fig. 2-2. Beveling is done by tilting the blade to the required angle. The position of the fence will control depth of the cut.

Beveling and chamfering are done by tilting the saw (or the table) to the required angle. Position of the fence will control the depth of the bevel cut (See Fig. 2-2). If you desire a full 90-degree angle as for a mitered cabinet top, clamp a strip of wood to the fence to provide a soft facing. Then raise the tilted saw blade while it is running, until it just begins to bite into the extra fence facing.

If the fence is positioned correctly, the blade just misses the top edge of the board, or the veneer if it is plywood. A few test cuts will be necessary to make the final adjustment to both fence and blade height so the mitered corners will fit precisely.

GETTING A STRAIGHT EDGE

It's not the fancy cuts that will give you trouble, so much as the ordinary, everyday situations. You might have perfectly good pieces of solid maple stock that would be just right for a desk frame, but that have rough, uneven edges. How do you get them straight enough so they can be ripped on the table saw? This is a common problem because many are sold that way.

The solution is easy if you have a jointer—in fact, that's a prime purpose of the jointer. Simply run the board through the rotary cutters until the sides are perfectly straight and smooth.

Another way, which is much slower and more difficult, is to plane the board by hand, checking with a square until it is true. Or you might try tacking the maple to another thin, straight board, setting the edge a little distance from the fence, so that as the bottom board moves along, the blade also cuts into the hardwood and forms a new straight edge.

SAWING PLASTIC VENEERS

When sawing plastic laminate sheeting (Formica, Micarta, etc.) on a table saw, always keep it face up to prevent chipping of the plastic coating at the edges. When cutting the thin plastic itself, feed slowly while holding the stock down close to the blade with a flat piece of wood to prevent bouncing. It is easier to saw when the plastic has already been laminated to a plywood backing.

When cutting plastic with a portable power saw, turn it face down, as this type of saw revolves the opposite way. The saw teeth must cut from the finished side down.

When sawing the plastic, or tempered hardboard, use a carbide-tipped blade or special hardened metal-cutting blade. A regular blade can be used, but it will quickly become dull.

CORRECTING SAW TROUBLES

Burning, which scorches the sides of the stock and sometimes causes smoke, is due either to a dull blade or green wood. Some of the hardwoods, particularly birch, are very difficult to cut on small-diameter home saws. If your saw has variable feed pulleys, set the belt for lower rpm. If gum or resins accumulate on the blade and make it sticky, wash it with turpentine or another solvent. Raising the height of the blade about ¾ inch above the thickness of the stock often will make cutting easier.

When the blade binds in the kerf, use the splitter to keep the kerf open. Binding may occur near the end when ripping a long board, because of the weight at the far end or possible twisting as a result of misalignment. Supporting the board with a table will correct this problem.

FOUR JIGS TO MEET ALL YOUR NEEDS

The mentioned jigs are highly versatile and will probably fill your needs for everyday use. Since you are going to depend on the jigs for making accurate saw cuts, it will be worth the time and effort to make the jigs accurately.

The Sliding Table

Also called the miter jig, this is the jig you will depend on for cutting miter joints. Once the jig is made, it will always pro-

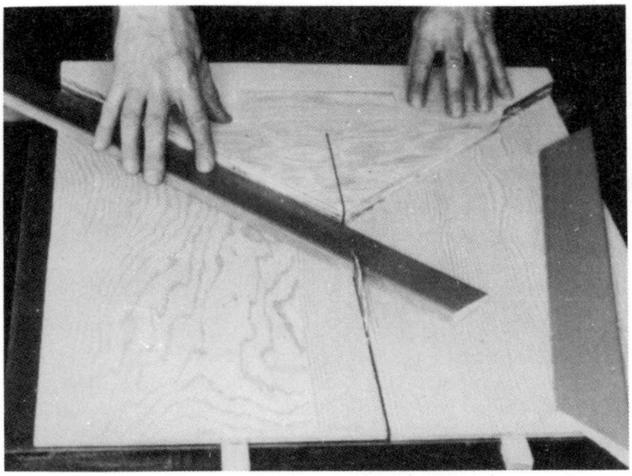

Fig. 2-3. One of the four jigs is the sliding table or mitering jig, which will always produce a saw-cut piece at exactly the same angle, and permits both right and left hand sawing.

duce a saw-cut piece at exactly the same angle and thus eliminate the possibility of an off-angle cut due to setting and resetting the miter gauge you received with your saw (Fig. 2-3). The chance of the stock "creeping" when making a cut with the standard miter gauge is also eliminated.

The miter jig will fit most 8- and 10-inch table saws and can be modified to suit other sizes of saws. Measure the width and depth of the miter gauge grooves on your saw and cut two 26-inch-long slide bars that will slide smoothly in the grooves. Use maple or some similar hardwood for these. Then cut the table or top from ¼-inch plywood and place it on the saw over the slide bars in the miter gauge grooves. Since the saw blade kerf is not cut until later, lower the saw blade below the table top when doing this. Temporarily fasten the table to the slide bars with small brads to establish location, then mark their position and reassemble with glue and ½-inch nails.

You can now cut the saw kerf in the plywood table and assemble the support block stop to the table. Be sure the stop piece is located at exactly 90 degrees to the saw kerf cut in the sliding table.

The inside and outside miter support blocks are not fastened to the sliding table so that they may be quickly set in position on the table for sawing inside and outside miter cuts when the stock cannot be flipped over (Fig. 2-4). Since the 45-degree angle-cut edges on the support blocks must be determined from the saw blade kerfs, fit the blocks to the block stop and make these saw kerfs first; then lay out and cut the 45-degree edges (See Fig. 2-5).

Fig. 2-4. Inside and outside miter support blocks are quickly changed since they aren't permanently attached. Gauge gives best duplication if work is first cut to overall length.

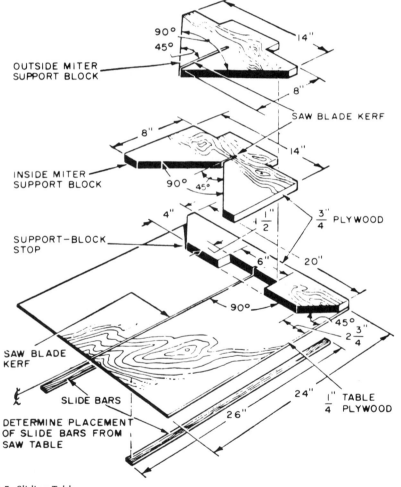

Fig. 2-5. Sliding Table.

The Tenoning Jig

The tenoning jig slides smoothly on the ripsaw fence and will enable you to safely and accurately cut tenons and deep rabbets, mitered spline grooves, and slots for "feathering" (Fig. 2-6).

When making the tenoning jig, be sure to measure the width and height of the rip fence on your particular saw first, and then make the fence guide pieces accordingly. Assemble them to make a sliding fit on the rip fence, or just snug enough to eliminate rocking.

When cutting the dado for the tenoning guide piece, set the bottom edge against the miter gauge so that the dado will be exactly 90 degrees with the bottom edge. Do not permanently fasten the 3/4- x -1-inch tenoning guide in the dado, since it must be removed to use the splining and feathering guides. Fasten the 3/16- x -3/4-inch pieces to the splining and feathering guides with glue and nails, but do not use any nails within the total depth of saw cut area since this would be in line with the saw blade when making a cut.

The Tapering Jig

The tapering jig (Fig. 2-7) will hold any work piece at an angle and enable you to saw duplicate long, tapering cuts at precisely the same angle each time. By making a mark 12 inches from the hinged end of the jig, you can open it at that point to establish the taper-per-foot that the work requires. After setting the jig, you merely adjust the rip fence to accommodate both jig and work, and then proceed like you were making a normal rip cut.

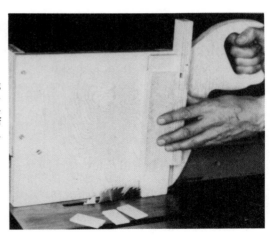

Fig. 2-6. A second jig is the tenoning jig, which supports work perpendicular to the saw table, enabling the safe and accurate cut of tenons, rabbets, mitered spline groves, and slots.

Fig. 2-7. The third table saw jig is the tapering jig, which will hold any work piece at an angle and enable you to saw duplicate long tapering cuts at precisely the same angle each time.

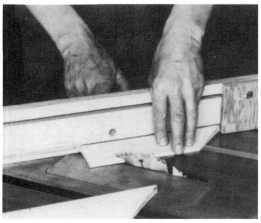

Fig. 2-8. The fourth jig is the miter gauge extension with adjustable stop block, which provides extra support for the work piece and a way of accurately duplicating cuts to specified length.

If a taper is required on opposite edges of the work, open up the jig two times the original setting, reset the rip fence, and make the second cut. If a taper is required on four edges, the first setting is used to cut two adjacent sides. The second setting is for the remaining two sides. Use straight grain, well dried lumber that will not warp.

The Miter Gauge Extension

This extension (shown in Fig. 2-8) is an attachment for your existing miter gauge that will provide both extra support for the work piece and a means of accurately making duplicate cuts to a specified length. The extension will not interfere with setting the miter gauge for angle cuts. In fact, it will help prevent

Table 2.1. Table and Gauge Settings for Compound Angle Cuts.

Work Angle	4-Sided Butt Joint		4-Sided Miter Joint		Hexagonal Joint		Octagonal Joint	
	Blade or Table Tilt	Miter Gauge	Blade or Table Tilt	Miter Gauge	Blade or Table Tilt	Miter Gauge	Blade or Table Tilt	Miter Gauge
5°	½	85	44¾	85	29¾	87½	22¼	88
10°	1½	80¼	44¼	80¼	29½	84½	22	86
15°	3¾	75½	43¼	75½	29	81¾	21¼	84
20°	6¼	71	42	71	28¼	79	21	82
25°	10	67	40	67	27¼	76½	20¼	80
30°	14½	63½	37¾	63½	26	74	19¼	78¼
35°	19½	60¼	35¼	60¼	24½	71¾	18¼	76¾
40°	24½	57¼	33¾	57¼	22¾	69¾	17	75
45°	30	54¾	30	54¾	21	67¾	15¾	73¾
50°	36	52½	27	52½	19	66¼	14¼	72½
55°	42	50¾	24	50¾	16¾	44¾	12¾	71¼
60°	48	49	21	49	14½	63½	11	70¼

Note: Figures are in degrees and are for direct setting to tilt scale and miter gauge. Scale providing tilt starts at 0° and miter gauge at 90° in normal position.

''creeping'' when making angle cuts because you can hold the work piece firmly against the slide stop.

Make the extension using a dado head to cut the ¼-inch slots and ½-inch groove in the bar. Turn the bar over when cutting the slot to clean out the uncut ends, and use a file to square the slot ends with the bar. Fasten the slide to the bar with a wood screw or carriage bolt and wing nut through the ¼-inch slot so that the slide can be positioned and locked on the bar. Then fasten the bar to your saw miter gauge with two screws through the holes already drilled in the miter gauge head (See Fig. 2-9).

When assembling any of the four jigs, be sure to sand smoothly all parts that will be sliding contact with your table saw. Give the entire jig a coat of penetrating sealer and, after it has dried, sand lightly again. Then apply paste wax to the sliding surfaces.

TWIN BLADE CUTTING

Most tablesaw arbors are long enough to accommodate more than one saw blade and you can take advantage of this feature to speed up common cutting jobs, or to make special setups for particular operations.

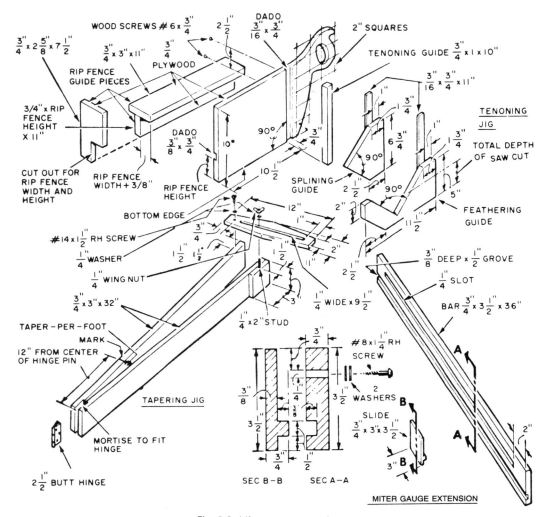

Fig. 2-9. Miter gauge extension.

The secret behind this trick of power-tool woodworking is nothing more than the placement of washers between two saw blades mounted on a single arbor (Fig. 2-10). Thickness of the washers regulates the width of the cut. When the saw blades have set teeth, you must allow for the set in determining the spacer thickness. This isn't necessary when using hollow-ground blades.

Industry uses this idea for gang-cutting of duplicate pieces. Of course industrial users are not limited to a single arbor; still it's surprising how much use you can get from the idea with the ordinary table saw.

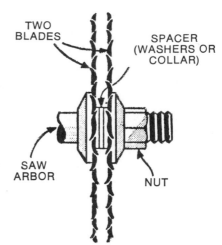

TWO BLADES

SPACER (WASHERS OR COLLAR)

SAW ARBOR

NUT

Fig. 2-10. Thickness of washers placed between the two saw blades regulates the width of the cut.

Fig. 2-11. Two blades double the speed with which a series of kerfs can be cut. Note special wood insert used to accommodate two blades rather than one, and pencil mark guide.

Two saw blades can speed up the job of kerfing wood for bending (Fig. 2-11). Spacing between the kerfs is set by the thickness of the washers placed between the saw blades on the arbors. Usually it is best to make a special insert for the saw table to reduce open area around the blades. This provides full support for the wood, ensures uniform depth of cut, and guards against the work being pulled down into the machine.

25

To make a special insert for your saw table, select plywood or hardboard which equals the thickness of the regular insert. Use the regular insert as a template and then cut and sand the substitute to fit. Lower the saw blades beneath the table surface, place the special insert in the slot, and raise the saw blades with the saw running so the blades cut their own slots. Hold the special insert down firmly with a length of scrap wood until the saw blades are through.

Multiple saw blades make it easy to do decorative cutting. Once the rip fence is set, it's just a matter of lowering the work over the turning saw blades. You can work with stop blocks clamped to the fence to gauge the beginning and end of the cuts, or you can work to pencil guide lines drawn on the work.

If you've ever tried single-blade cutting of the checks for a tenon, you'll recognize the value of the twin-blade technique. The distance between blades governs the thickness of the tenon while the spacing from the fence centers the cut in the stock. Any number of tenons can be cut this way on matching pieces of wood with the assurance that all will be the same size. Hollow-ground blades will give the smoothest cuts (Fig. 2-12). When making the cut, it's a good idea to use the follow-up block to keep the work vertical and (especially) to keep your fingers away from the blades.

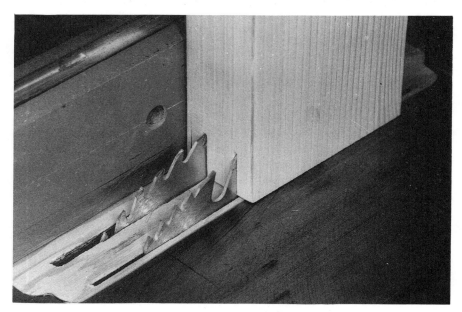

Fig. 2-12. Two sides of tenons are cut with one pass. Hollow-ground blades give a smooth cut.

Ever run into the problems involved in making pieces of equal thickness for laminating into a project like a cutting board, or of cutting a lot of strips the same width? Even when working with a jointer it's difficult to smooth the edges and still keep them square to the top surfaces. If the width of the pieces required can be handled within the limits set by the arbor length, twin-blade cutting will remove much of the frustration next time you try jobs like this. Using hollow-ground blades will give the strips a smoother finish.

Give the hollow-ground blades maximum projection above the table to guard against burning.

The two-blade technique is not limited to blades on a vertical plane; you can tilt them, too. A little experimenting along these lines will lead your imagination in many different directions.

Saw blades can even be mounted in two bunches on the arbor. This way you can use multiple blades as dado assemblies to cut the twin grooves, for example, sliding cupboard doors. This eliminates much rip fence resetting which is needed when cutting the grooves separately and guarantees accuracy.

Two blades, each cutting a ⅛-inch kerf, make a perfect ¼-inch groove or dado. When bunching the blades be sure to place

Fig. 2-13. Drawer fronts can be cut and rabbeted in one pass by using blades of different sizes.

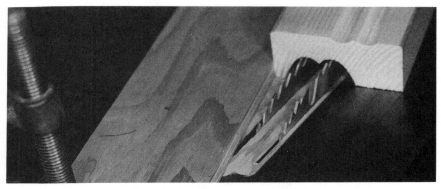

Fig. 2-14. When you use twin blades for cove cutting, you can achieve variations in the shape of the cove. A wide blade separation produces the double effect shown above.

the set teeth of one blade opposite the gullets of the next blade. Rabbets as well as grooves or dadoes can be cut in this fashion. Note that the special table insert has a wide slot to accommodate the whole assembly. If the distance between bunched blades is not too much, you can sometimes use a molding head insert to eliminate the chore of making a special one.

One multiple-blade application for a special operation is the cutting off and making the shoulder cut for a rabbet in one pass (Fig. 2-13). This is particularly useful when you need a quantity of drawer fronts. If the drawer sides are going to be made of ¾-inch stock, then the distance from the inside face of the larger blade to the outside face of the small blade will have to be ¾ inch. A second pass with a single blade and with the stock on edge will complete the rabbet cut.

If you combine the larger blade with a dado assembly, or a bunch of smaller blades, you could form the entire rabbet when you cut off. The stock must be turned end-to-end after each pass.

Using two blades for cove cutting accomplishes two things—since you are cutting on two lines you get a more flat-bottomed cove than you would with a single blade and, since one blade is following the other, you get a smoother cut. As with all cove cutting, blades with set teeth do the job best—and depth of cut for each pass shouldn't exceed ¹⁄₁₆ inch.

Two blades will also cut twin spirals. This idea can be used for decorative cuts (with the spirals left as is) or for outlining a spiral that you will finish by hand. All you have to do is file away the material outlined by the twin-spiral grooves to finish the job.

All About Radial Arm Saws

ONE OF THE MOST versatile power tools you can install in your workshop is a radial arm saw. In addition to making any cut a table saw can, it can also be pressed into service as a borer, router, shaper, disk or drum sander, or grinder—even as a power source for flexible shaft tools.

The radial saw yields to the table saw on one count. It cannot make cuts in the center of very wide stock. But, when cutting most lumber, the radial saw is more convenient than the table saw.

Essentially, the radial saw is a motor with an arbor carrying a circular saw blade. The motor is slung by a yoke beneath an arm. The saw and yoke slide on the arm back and forth over the work. The arm is mounted on a pivot.

OPERATING YOUR SAW

As you face the saw, the arm should be pointed at you. The work table has a fence at the back that runs crosswise from one side of the table to the other. The saw, at the start position, is on the other side of the fence at the far end of the arm.

To make a simple crosscut, hold the work against the fence with your left hand, keeping it well out of the path of the saw, grasp the saw by the handle with your right hand and pull it toward you, cutting through the work. Push it back and the operation is completed.

The versatility of the saw lies in the fact that the position of the arm and of the saw and motor unit are adjustable. The simple 90-degree crosscut, for example, was made with the saw riding through the work perpendicular to the fence. But, the arm can swing on the pivot. If you swing the arm to the left or right and lock it in place and make a cut, the result is a miter (Fig. 3-1). Most saws have a detent mechanism that makes it easy to stop the arm at most of the common miter angles.

Instead of swinging the arm, you can leave it at 90 degrees and tilt the saw blade itself to almost any angle. The result of a cut made this way is a bevel or chamfer, depending on where the work is held.

If you swing the arm and tilt the blade simultaneously the result is a compound miter cut, sometimes used in cabinet work like picture frames.

Safety note: When making any cut with a radial arm saw always keep your hands away from the saw blade. If you are working with small material, clamp or tack it to the table (Fig. 3-2).

Fig. 3-1. Miter cut with radial: Stock is held while blade moves. This beats moving a lengthy piece against blade as with a table saw.

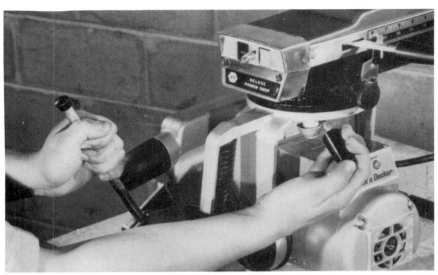

Fig. 3-2. This model has a yoke clamp which, when pulled, frees the yoke so motor can swivel about its horizontal axis to any desired angle. Pushing the clamp locks the unit.

RIPPING

Ripping is done with the saw and motor swiveled so the blade is parallel to the fence. Slide the saw in this position along the arm until it is the correct distance from the fence. You can use the rip gauge on the side of the arm to make this adjustment.

When ripping, always feed the stock against the rotation of the blade. The bottom portion of the blade should be moving toward you and the handle of the saw should be on the side away from you.

Never rip without engaging the anti-kickback fingers. Every saw has this device. Usually these fingers are at the end of an arm that can be adjusted upward or downward to accommodate different thicknesses of stock. Make sure these fingers extend about ⅛ inch below the surface of the stock before you start to rip.

As you feed the work past the saw and under the fingers, the fingers flip up and rest on the surface. If the blade kicks the stock back toward you, the ends of the fingers dig into the wood like ratchets and prevent the stock from moving.

Feed the work to the saw evenly, but don't force it. Also, remember to keep your hands clear of the saw blade. When working with narrow material, use a wooden pusher near the blade, rather than your hand.

In addition to ripping square cuts, the saw can be tilted while in the ripping position to make long bevels or chamfers. Do not

Table 3.1. Radial Arm Saw Trouble-Shooting Chart

Condition	Possible Cause	Remedy
Saw will not make a square cross cut or a good 45° miter cut	1. Arm is not perpendicular to guide fence	1. Adjust crosscut travel with guide fence
	2. Arm has excessive play	2. Tighten adjusting screws
	3. Column is loose in base	3. Make proper adjustment
	4. Too much play between arm and column	4. Make proper adjustment
	5. Roller head too loose in arm	5. Adjust roller head correctly
	6. Yoke too loose when clamped to roller head	6. Adjust yoke clamp handle
	7. Sawdust between lumber and guide fence	7. Keep table top clean
	8. Table not parallel with arm	8. Make proper adjustment
	9. Guide fence not straight	9. Replace fence
	10. Rear edge of fixed board not straight	10. Sand or replace
Lumber has a tendency to walk away from fence when ripping or ploughing	1. Saw blade is not parallel with fence	1. Make heel adjustment
	2. Arm not perpendicular to guide fence	2. Adjust crosscut travel with guide fence
	3. Dull blade or cutters	3. Sharpen or replace blade
	4. Fence not straight	4. Replace fence
	5. Feed rate too fast	5. Slow feed rate
	6. Wrong blade	6. Use correct blade
	7. Column too loose in base	7. Make proper adjustment
	8. Too much play between arm and column	8. Make proper adjustment
	9. Roller head too loose in arm	9. Make proper adjustment
	10. Yoke loose when clamped to roller head	10. Adjust yoke clamp handle
	11. Sawdust between lumber and fence	11. Keep tabletop clean
Saw stalls when ripping or ploughing	1. Saw blade is not parallel with fence	1. Make heel adjustment
	2. Arm not perpendicular to guide fence	2. Adjust crosscut travel with guide fence
	3. Dull blade or cutters	3. Sharpen or replace blade
	4. Fence not straight	4. Replace fence
	5. Feed rate too fast	5. Slow feed rate
	6. Wrong blade	6. Use correct blade
	7. Column too loose in base	7. Make proper adjustment
	8. Too much play between arm and column	8. Make proper adjustment
	9. Roller head too loose in arm	9. Make proper adjustment

	10. Yoke loose when clamped to roller head	10. Make proper adjustment
	11. Sawdust between lumber and fence	11. Keep table top clean
Saw blade scores lumber, not giving a good finished cut	1. Saw blade is heeling	1. Make heel adjustment
	2. Column too loose in base	2. Make proper adjustment
	3. Too much play between arm and column	3. Make proper adjustment
	4. Roller head loose in arm	4. Make proper adjustment
	5. Yoke too loose when clamped to roller head	5. Make proper adjustment
	6. Bent blade or dull	6. Replace blade
	7. Not feeding saw properly	7. Draw saw blade across lumber with a slow and steady pull
	8. Using improper blade for finish cut desired	8. Change blade
Saw blade or dado blades tend to push lumber to one side when crosscutting	1. Saw blade is heeling	1. Make heel adjustment
	2. Column too loose in base	2. Make proper adjustment
	3. Too much play between arm and column	3. Make proper adjustment
	4. Roller head too loose in arm	4. Make proper adjustment
	5. Yoke too loose when clamped to roller head	5. Make proper adjustment
	6. Fence not straight	6. Replace fence
	7. Dull blade or cutters	7. Replace or sharpen blade
Cut depth varies from one end of stock to the other	1. Table top not parallel with arm	1. Adjust table top parallel with arm
	2. Column too loose in base	2. Make proper adjustment
	3. Too much play between arm and column	3. Make proper adjustment

attempt to rip a chamfer or bevel on very narrow stock. Make your cut on a wider piece, then use a vertical rip to cut it to the correct width.

CUTTING GROOVES AND DADOES

The same techniques can be used to cut grooves and dadoes. Just raise the saw blade the correct distance from the table to provide the desired depth of cut and proceed as you would for an ordinary crosscut, miter, bevel or rip. Or the saw can be rotated so the blade is parallel to the table for cutting kerfs and rabbets in the edge of thin stock.

Every radial saw has a handle that the user rotates to raise and lower the arm—and with it the motor and saw. Usually, the handle or crank is calibrated so that the amount of rotation equals a given amount of travel up or down—⅛ inch per turn, for example.

You can use a dado head or simply make a series of parallel cuts with a saw blade to remove material. When using a dado cutter, remember that the saw must remove much more material per inch of travel than it does with an ordinary blade, so feed the work more slowly.

OTHER USES

Without a saw blade, the machine can be thought of simply as a source of rotary power that can be set at almost any angle. The motor can be used to turn sanding drums or disks, twist drills, shapers, router bits, and abrasive grinding wheels.

To sand a miter with precision, for example, set the machine up in the same way as for sawing, but use a sanding disc instead of a saw blade. Then, pass the sanding disk across the miter cut as if you were sawing it. This will provide an accurate flat surface with no risk of removing too much material at the edges, as you could with a sanding block or a hand-held power sander.

The machine can also be used as a drill press by swiveling the motor so the arbor points at the fence and chucking on a drill bit. Instead of boring vertically, the radial saw bores horizontally. If you need to drill angled holes, simply swing the arm to either side to the desired angle, as you would for a miter cut.

Generally, the saw motor is tilted so the arbor is vertical when it is used to turn a shaper, although varying the angle can be used to obtain a variety of profiles from the same set of shaper blades.

When the radial arm saw is used with a grinding wheel, set the motor in the same position as for the basic crosscut with a saw blade and construct a rest for the work out of a few pieces of scrap. Use this rig just as you would an ordinary grinder to sharpen tools and the like.

To achieve the accuracy that a radial saw is capable of, check the adjustments when you install and periodically after that. All the key assemblies of a radial saw are adjustable, although the way these adjustments are made vary from saw to saw. See your owner's manual to see how each is made.

CHECKING LEVELNESS

The table top and the radial arm must be on parallel planes. There are two ways to check this. The first is to remove the blade and the blade guard and tilt the motor so the arbor is vertical. Lower the motor until the tip of the arbor barely touches the table. Then, bend over so your eye is at table level and move the saw around the table. Watch to see that the arbor is barely touching the table at all points. If there is space between the arbor and table, the table is too low at that point. If the arbor presses against the table hard, the table is too high.

The second method is to make a similar test with the saw blade and guard in place and the blade vertical. Place a flat piece of plywood on the table and lower the saw to make a skimming cut. Move the saw over the flat plywood and observe the depth of cut. It should be the same skimming depth at all positions.

To make sure the arm is precisely perpendicular to the fence when it is in the 90-degree position, mark a 90-degree cut on a wide piece of stock with a square. If the arm is properly adjusted, the blade will follow the line from the start of the cut to the end.

Also use a square to determine whether the blade is perpendicular to the table. Remove the blade guard and place one leg of the square on the table and the other against the saw blade. Make sure the square is in the gulleys of the saw blade between the set teeth.

Test for heeling by making a crosscut in a wide piece of stock about 2 inches thick and then looking for pronounced radial marks left on the cut by the back teeth of the saw. If you find them, it means that the saw is slightly swiveled in relation to the arm and the back teeth are not following the same path as the front teeth through the cut. You can also feel heeling during cutting. The blade seems to drag, and you will notice that cut edges are rougher than they ought to be.

Getting the Most from Your Circular Saw

A PORTABLE CUTOFF SAW will save you time and effort. A 2 x 4 that takes 45 seconds to cut off with a handsaw takes 3½ seconds to cut with a cutoff saw; a square cut across a 1- x -12-inch pine board, requiring 30 seconds with a handsaw, can be cut in 4 seconds with a cutoff saw. Difficult 40-degree x 40-degree compound miter cuts on a 2 x 4 take 190 seconds by hand—27 seconds with a cutoff saw. A 4- x -8-foot sheet of plywood, hopelessly unmanageable with a conventional bench-type circular saw, is reduced to handling size in 2 or 3 minutes with a cutoff saw.

An electric motor supplies the power for the actual sawing, all you do is lift and guide the saw across the boards. As far as accuracy is concerned, regardless of your skill with a handsaw, the built-in guides and protractor on a cutoff saw will assure you of a straight and square cut, or a beveled cut every time.

SIZES OF CUTOFF SAWS

Several sizes of cutoff saws are available. An easily handled little saw with a 5½-inch blade having a 1¾-inch depth of cut and weighing just under 12 pounds is an ideal size for the homeowner. It will cut through all thicknesses of hardboard, plywood, and solid lumber up to a 2-inch (actually 1⅝ inches) thickness. It's a good size for building a basement room, cabinets and shelving, fitting storm windows, building a fence or similar light jobs.

Larger cutoff saws weighing up to 19 pounds with 7½- to 8½-inch blades will miter cut 2-inch stock at a 45-degree angle. This is a building contractor's size and will handle all lumber used in building a house or garage. The 8½-inch blade has a 3-inch depth of cut and will sever a 6- x -6-inch timber by making cuts on opposite sides. These larger saws can also be used on lighter work because the weight of the saw on the most cutting operations is supported by a piece being cut.

PRECAUTIONS

There are two precautions to observe when using portable electric tools. One is the matter of extension cord size. The compact motors draw quite a lot of current, requiring rather heavy cords; the longer the cord used, the thicker the gauge of the wire should be. Most machines have the amperage marked on the case.

The second precaution is grounding, a must if the machine is used outdoors when the ground is damp. Many saws are equipped with three-conductor cords, one conductor for grounding the tool to guard against electrical shocks. Follow directions given by the manufacturer. Three-conductor extension cords and plugs are available.

The saw blades are guarded above by the housing and beneath by an automatically telescoping guard which can be drawn up with a handle when necessary to get it out of the way. The base plate is pivoted sidewise for making square and angular cuts, and is also hinged on the front end or otherwise designed for regulation of depth of cut. An adjustable gauge guides the saw for ripping length of predetermined width. Some machines have clutches that slip if the blade is overloaded or strikes an obstruction, thus preventing damage to the motor.

BLADES

Many types of saw blades are available (Fig. 4-1). The combination blades, either fast- or smooth-cutting types, are best for all-around work requiring ripping and crosscutting. The specialized types are reserved for long runs of crosscutting or ripping.

For difficult-to-saw materials, use carbide-tipped and deep-hardened blades. Blades for sheet metal are also available. In general, set the blade only deep enough to project the teeth on the underside of the board for easy sawdust venting.

USING YOUR CUTOFF SAW

To cut a long piece from a board on sawhorses, shift the board until the horse at the right is near the center of the section to be cut, but with a little extra length at the end. Hold the near board

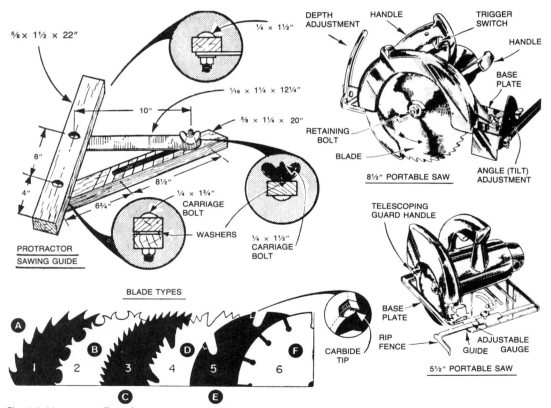

Fig. 4-1. Your saw will produce accurate cuts when you use various guide attachments available, top. Accurate miter cuts can be had using protractor guide, middle. Blade types are: (A) fast cut combination, (B) reversible, (C) crosscut, (D) smooth cut combination, (E) carbide-tipped, (F) slitted friction. Turn your saw into a table model, bottom.

with your left hand. As the piece is sawed through, the cut end will gently rise, thereby preventing jamming or splintering.(See Fig. 4-2).

You can crosscut a board on a pile by sliding it endwise to clear the part to be cut. Hold the projection with your left hand while the piece is being severed. If the piece is long, block up the far end. When cutting to a line, set the guide notch on the line and follow it. By leaning to the right you can see both blade and line, a help in getting started.

Use the saw for bevel cutting as shown in Fig. 4-2. Loosen the wing nut at the tilt quadrant and slope the base as required, and read the degrees on the scale. Tighten the nut and handle the saw as in plain crosscutting.

Mitering or other angle cutting across the face is a matter of following the guideline. Accuracy is improved by the use of an adjustable protractor guide, the stock of which is held against the edge of the board. Details for making a guide with a strip of coarse sandpaper glued to the contracting edge to make it slip-proof is shown in Fig. 4-3.

To saw a plywood panel, lay the smooth- or face-side down on horses since most of the splintering occurs in the upper side. If necessary, pad the horses to prevent scuffing the face side.

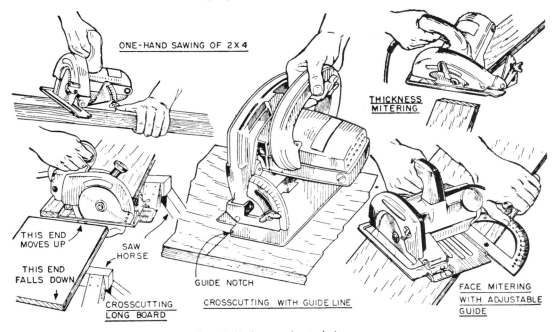

ONE-HAND SAWING OF 2 X 4

THICKNESS MITERING

THIS END MOVES UP

THIS END FALLS DOWN

SAW HORSE

CROSSCUTTING LONG BOARD

GUIDE NOTCH

CROSSCUTTING WITH GUIDE LINE

FACE MITERING WITH ADJUSTABLE GUIDE

Fig. 4-2. Various sawing techniques.

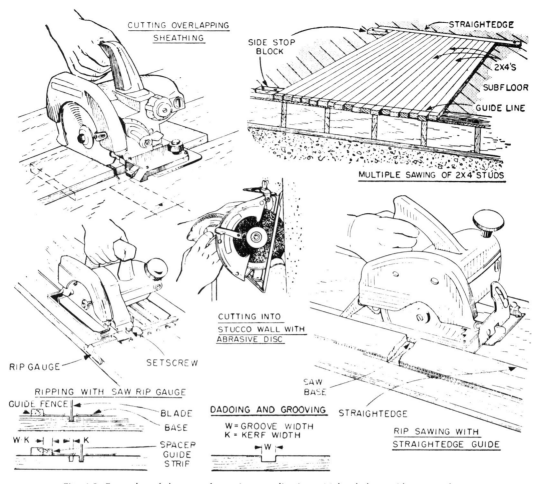

Fig. 4-3. Examples of shortcuts for various applications. Make dadoes with repeated cuts.

Hardboards and similar sheets coated with finishing materials should also be cut with the finished or polished sides down and resting on suitable pads.

When cuts across the horses must be made, block up the panel with scrap 1- × -2-inch stock to clear the horses. For ripping, set the gauge by calibrations, or by measuring from the inner face to the far-set tooth. Slide the fence along the edge of the wood when ripping.

For rough cutting, follow guidelines; for careful work use a straightedge against which to slide the saw base. To locate the straightedge, add to the width of the piece to be cut the distance from the right edge of the base to the tip of a blade tooth set toward the left.

When the part to be sawed off is too narrow to carry the straightedge, subtract the distance from the left edge of the saw base to the left set tooth of the blade from the width and clamp the straightedge, again placing the kerf to the right of the line. Slide the left edge of the saw base against the straightedge.

To saw inside holes, such as an opening in a drainboard apron to receive a breadboard, or a rectangle in a plywood door for a grill, set the blade for a deep cut, draw the guard back, and lower the rotating blade into the work as the saw is steadied on the forward end of the base. Start the cut enough forward of the end mark to avoid slitting beyond it. If the pocket is narrow, chisel out the ends and finish with a wood file; if wider, bore a corner hole and use a compass saw or portable jigsaw.

Plywoods and hardboards dull saw teeth rapidly. If there is much work to be done in these materials, a carbide-tipped blade is economical, because it will stay sharp 20 times as long as an ordinary blade. The saving in sharpening time and loss of time due to changing blades more than offsets the greater cost. The hard-pointed "throw-away-blades" can be touched up two or three times by grinding on an ordinary energy wheel before they become worthless.

Dadoing and grooving can be done with a cutoff saw by setting the blade to the required depth of cut, and then cutting the sides of the groove. Clearing the groove can then be done with saw cuts between the sides or with a chisel.

If the blade can't be fully retracted, rest the saw bottom on a piece of thin hardboard to saw through. Clamp a guide fence for cutting one side of the dado, then lay a second strip against it, of width equal to the dado minus the kerf width, and make the second cut. Grooving cutters are available for some saws.

SAW ACCESSORIES

A homemade stand for converting a portable saw into a stationary one is shown in Fig. 4-4. Use ¾-inch, 5-ply plywood. Use a stiff metal plate rabbeted flush into the top against which the bottom of the saw is clamped. One edge of saw bottom should be held by a stationary block, the other by a sliding block locked with a wing nut.

The miter gauge and rip fence are built of wood. The head of the miter gauge is locked with a wooden knob into which the

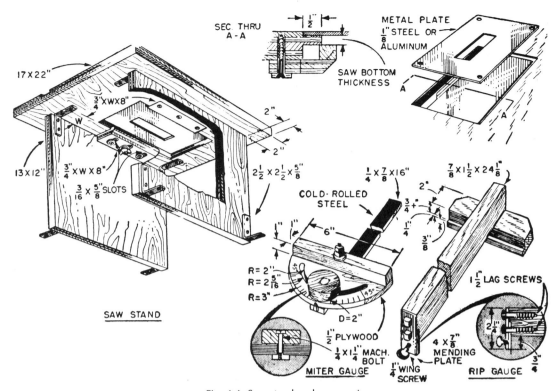

Fig. 4-4. Saw stand and accessories.

bolt head is sunk. Drill and tap the cold-rolled steel guide for the bolts. Countersink the underside and rivet end of pivot bolt after it is screwed in place.

Fasten the square-head of the rip fence with glue and wood screws. Make the clamping mechanism from a 4-inch mending plate sawed into 2¼- and 1¾-inch pieces. Notch the short piece into the near end of the fence. Attach them to the end of the rip fence with two lag screws. Only the lower screw should pass through the short metal piece.

Drill and tap the long piece for a wing screw, which bears against the short metal piece, exerting pressure against the edge of the saw table when the screw is tightened. The telescoping guard on the saw emerges through the slot in the plate, guarding the blade. While a pull cable and catch can be rigged to operate the saw trigger switch, it is simpler to mount a plug-in receptacle with switch on the stand into which to plug the saw cord.

CUTTING DUPLICATE LENGTHS

In house and garage building, a good deal of duplicate length pieces must be cut. A setup for sawing studs to uniform length is shown in Fig. 4-3. Lay a number of 2 × 4s edge-to-edge on a subfloor with the squared ends against a fixed straightedge and the far piece stopped against blocks which hold the group square with the straightedge. The ends to be cut project beyond the floor. A guideline is then chalked or penciled, or a straightedge tacked in place across the studs.

Single pieces of subfloor and sheathing are cut by holding the piece in hand, like the 2 × 4 in the drawing. Where two join end-to-end, they are tacked in place with ends overlapping, as in the drawing, and the blade allowed to cut through both pieces over the joist or rafter.

When cutting an opening in a wall for installing a door or window, the process is similar to cutting an inside hole in a board. If an abrasive disc is substituted for the saw blade, an opening in a stucco wall can be neatly sawed. Be sure to wear goggles to protect your eyes.

The abrasive disc can also be used to cut metal tubing or rods. Clamp the work in a vise or hand-screw and cut off the projecting ends. Cut sheet metal with slitted blade the same way as sawing wood.

Saber Saw Techniques

MAKING CURVED SAW CUTS in large plywood panels too bulky to handle on a band saw or conventional bench-type jigsaw is a typical job where the portable electric saber saw proves its worth. The wide variety of types and sizes of saw blades available makes it possible to saw metal, plastics, sponge rubber, all kinds of composition board and, of course, wood.

Because of its compactness and light weight, from $4\frac{1}{2}$ to $6\frac{1}{2}$ pounds, portable jigsaws are used by the building trades for quickly cutting holes in walls for electrical outlet boxes, heating and cooling ducts, pipes, ventilators, etc.

TYPES OF SABER SAWS

Portable saber saws can be classified into three types and sizes. The inexpensive machines are satisfactory for intermittent home workshop use. Some models, however, are limited to a cutting thickness of 1 inch. The medium-price saws will handle 2-inch-thick dressed lumber (actually $1\frac{5}{8}$ inches) and some models have

Fig. 5-1. Saber saw can be tilted as much as 45-degrees on its baseplate for bevel cuts. Baseplate acts as straightedge with guide block.

a tilting base for bevel cuts (Fig. 5-1). Heavy-duty saws are built for continuous duty as required by the building trades.

The cutting action of the blade on the various machines differ. Some have a straight up and down stroke, while others have an orbital or canted blade action, which backs the blade away on the downstroke and moves it forward on the cutting or upstroke. This backward movement of the blade on the downstroke frees the kerf, or cut, of sawdust or metal chips and reduces power-wasting drag on the downstroke. The blade roller supports and guides the blade while cutting.

BLADES

Since the primary purpose of a portable saber saw is to make inside scroll and straight cuts that are beyond the range of other types of power tools, the type of blade used can hinder or hasten the work (Fig. 5-2). A good rule-of-thumb is this: *the narrower the blade and the wider the set of the teeth, the sharper the turns of corners that can be sawed.*

For fast but rough cutting of wood use a blade having 6 or 7 spring-set teeth per inch. For smooth finish cuts use a hollow-ground blade. Although you cannot cut as small a radius with a hollow-ground blade as you can with a spring-set blade, often this can be overcome by boring relief holes to match small turns in design.

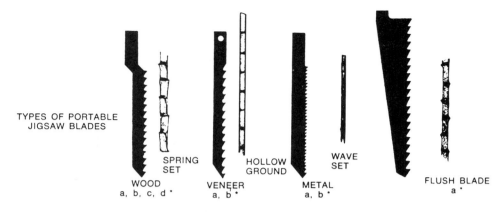

TYPES OF PORTABLE JIGSAW BLADES

WOOD
a, b, c, d *

SPRING SET

VENEER
a, b *

HOLLOW GROUND

METAL
a, b *

WAVE SET

FLUSH BLADE
a *

| Material | Blade | Teeth per in. | Length | Spring Set | Wave Set | Use | | | | Cut | | | Hollow Ground |
						Straight	Curve	Scroll	Pocket	Finish	Med.	Rough	
Wood	a	7	3″	X			X	X	X			X	
	b	10	3″	X			X	X	X			X	
	c	8	3″				X		X		X		X
	d	6	4″			X					X		X
Veneer	a	6	4″			X				X			X
	b	6	3″				X		X	X			X
Metal	a	14	2⅞″		X	X					X		
	b	32	2⅞″		X	X					X		
Flush	a	7	4″	X		X					X		

Fig. 5-2. Choose saw blades carefully. They can either hinder or hasten work.

Because portable saber-saw blades are much wider than the blades used on a stationary, bench-type jigsaw, don't expect to be able to do the intricate scroll work you can with the stationary type of machine. Instead, design the scroll work with radii large enough for the portable saw blade to follow.

CUTTING WITH A SABER SAW

The ability of a portable saber saw to make its own starting hole for inside or pocket cuts eliminates the need for drilling a hole as must be done for a stationary jigsaw. To make such a "plunge" cut, tilt the machine forward on the tips of the base (Fig. 5-3). Then slowly feed the blade into the wood, keeping the base tips firmly in place on the workpiece. When the blade pierces the work, swing the machine down and proceed with the sawing in the normal way.

Feed the saw along the line of cut at a uniform rate of speed so as not to exceed the cutting speed of the saw teeth. Remember,

Fig. 5-3. Starting a plunge cut: Tip saw forward so blade clears work, start saw, slowly lower blade tip to wood, continue until it passes through.

the saw cuts on the upstroke only, which tends to pull the saw downward firmly against the workpiece. Feeding the saw too fast will place the blade teeth in contact with the forward end of the kerf on the downstroke which will tend to lift the saw and cause vibration.

Making Curved Cuts

Since the cutting edge of the saw is in full view, with a little practice you will soon develop the skill needed to freehand-guide the jigsaw along curved pattern lines. Although circle cuts can be guided freehand, most jigsaws are equipped with an adjustment radius-rod attachment that can be used to guide the saw around a perfect circle (Fig. 5-4). No guidelines on the workpiece are needed. Simply adjust the radius rod so the distance from rod pivot point to a tooth on the blade corresponds to the radius of the circle desired.

Measurements to the inside or outside of the blade tooth will depend upon whether the circle or the area around it is the waste piece. Hold the pivot point firmly in place with your left hand as you feed the saw around with your right hand.

Making Straight Cuts

For ripping or straight-line cuts parallel to an edge, and a short distance from it, insert the jigsaw fence attachment, measuring

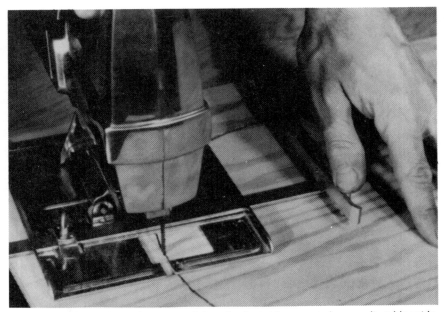

Fig. 5-4. A circle cutting attachment, consisting of a pivot stylus mounted on an adjustable guide, produces perfect circles every time.

from its head to a near tooth, and saw with the fence head sliding along the edge. To prevent the wood grain from turning the blade to one side and the other producing a weaving cut, use a wide blade, and for smoothness, one with little set. A hollow-ground blade will hold splintering to a minimum when sawing plywood and fir.

Cutting Wide Boards

When cuts are too far from the edge to use the rip fence, or at an angle with the edge, use a straightedge tacked or clamped to the work (Fig. 5-5). Position the straightedge away from the line of cut the distance the saw base edge is from a near blade tooth. Slide the saw base against the straightedge when cutting.

When crosscutting square with the edge of a board, follow a pencil line or slide the saw base against a T-square made by nailing a strip of wood to a block for a head. A notch cut in the T-square head allows for blade projection at the start of the cut. Metal adjustable protractor guides can be purchased for use in making square or oblique cuts. When using such guides, make allowance for cutting offset by marking blades position on the guide head.

Fig. 5-5. To make a long straight cut on a board too wide for a guide, clamp a straightedge to the work and keep the base plate snug against it.

Making Rafter and Wall Stud Notches

For house or garage building, the portable saber saw is the only portable power tool that can be used to saw rafter notches. After notching the first rafter, nail register blocks to one end and the upper edge of it and use as a pattern for marking the others.

The portable saber saw will also make quick work of notching wall studs for gas or water pipes and electrical conduit. Saw into the stud horizontally for the top cut, swinging the saw downward to make the vertical cut. Then remove the saw and make the bottom cut of the notch as you did the top.

One model of jigsaw will make a cut flush with the front end of the saw. This feature makes it particularly useful in the installation of heating and air conditioning ducts. The saw has a retractable base that can be moved back so that the forward edge will be flush with the teeth of a flush-type saw blade. Jigsaws having tilting bases come in handy for cutting compound miters on the upper ends of valley and hip roof rafters.

Metal Cutting

With metal-cutting blades inserted in the portable jigsaw, you can cut any metal that a hacksaw will and to any width because the jigsaw does not have a C-shaped frame to limit the depth of cut as a hacksaw does. Use a blade having fine-enough teeth so that at least two full teeth are in contact with the thickness of the metal being cut. A coarse-toothed blade will straddle the thickness of the metal and the teeth will either be stripped or the blade will bend or break.

When sawing thicker metal, however, a coarse-tooth blade should be used to prevent the teeth from becoming clogged with metal chips. Be sure to grip the metal firmly in a vise when cutting so that vibrations will not pinch the blade and break it.

When sawing sheet metal, support the underside of it close to the saw blade to avoid buckling of the metal and binding of the blade. Intricate shapes can be cut from thin sheet metal smoothly and with little burr if the metal is nailed between two sheets of thin plywood or hardboard.

Accessories

Tables to convert the portable saber saw into a stationary jigsaw are available. Some tables are grooved for a miter gauge and rip fence, but this setup is usually used for freehand sawing of small pieces.

How to Keep
Saw Blades Sharp

IF YOU HAVE a treasured circular saw blade, or anything else that needs sharpening, it's wise to take the time to tell the saw sharpener what you expect done—and what you do not want done. All blades are not sharpened the same way.

You may want to sharpen the blade yourself. If you get the basic sharpening equipment and take the trouble to learn the proper techniques, you can. One of the big advantages of do-it-yourself sharpening is that you never get stuck with a dull blade when a pro sharpening is unavailable.

You can spend all kinds of money on saw sharpening equipment. The more elaborate jigs are great if you do much sharpening and can stand the initial cost. On the other hand, you can get along very well with much simpler, less costly equipment.

Your first acquisition should be a tooth-setting tool—for two reasons. First, the teeth of a newly sharpened saw should be set, you will need the tool in any case. Secondly, you can often bring a saw back to life without sharpening, just by resetting the teeth.

SETTING TOOLS

You can spend anywhere from about $20 to over $60 for a blade-setting tool. Basically, it is simply a device that permits bending alternate teeth on the saw left and right, uniformly, by some controlled amount that depends on the particular saw or saw blade. The set is necessary to prevent the saw from binding in the kerf. Softwoods are best cut with saws having more set than is needed for working hardwoods.

Many stores sell high-priced setting tools that handle circular saw blades from 4 to 16 inches in diameter. You might prefer, however, a much simpler hand-operated tool. One still works as well as it did when it was first available back in the 1920s. It's very much like a paper punch, except that it only bends the teeth and doesn't bend much of the saw. Somehow it seems—however unfounded it might be in fact—that bending the teeth by hand-squeezing action is a lot easier on saw teeth than pounding them over an anvil.

After acquiring a saw-setting tool, use it to check a saw blade that seems to be getting dull before taking it to a professional sharpener. You'll probably discover that the cost of the setting tool is recouped in short order by savings on actual sharpenings.

Of course, the time comes when setting the teeth is no answer. You can then have the full job done by a reliable pro—as some woodworking experts urge—or take a stab at it yourself. Here again, you can buy expensive or moderate cost sharpening equipment as your shop budget permits.

Sears offers two options. The more expensive (around $60) resharpens, reshapes, and joints saw blades when coupled with any 6-inch or larger grinder. It handles anything up to 16 inches inches in diameter. A lower-cost sharpener (around $35) attaches directly to a radial or table saw to handle resharpening, retoothing, and jointing of saws up to 12 inches in diameter. A 60-grit grinding wheel is recommended. Bear in mind that these tools are not disposable or carbide-tipped blades.

JOINTING

Incidentally, jointing is an operation that brings all saw teeth (except the raker teeth of a combination saw) to the same height so that they all do their fair share of cutting. The job can be done without special equipment. Mount the blade on your table saw arbor with the teeth pointing *backward*. With the blade lowered, mount an oilstone flat over the blade slot, then *very slowly* raise the blade until it barely *grazes* the stone. Take it easy, examine the results frequently, and stop when every tooth shows a small shiny area at the tip. Do not joint with an expensive oilstone.

SHARPENING THE TEETH

Actual sharpening of the teeth is, of course, a must following the jointing operation. Here's where you face the toughest part of the job, and a jig that ensures identical grinding of all teeth may well be worth its cost. However, hand filing is not out of the question, at least for rough-cut blades, if not for your best cabinet-making saws. It would be best to practice first.

The cardinal rule is never to put the saw blade into an ordinary vise, unprotected. Use a saw vise, or protect the blade between two slabs of plywood. If you provide the wood pieces with bolt holes, you can fasten the blade between them in such manner that it can be rotated easily to get at all the teeth. The objective is to restore the original shapes of the teeth while removing as little metal as possible.

Incidentally, if the saw has raker teeth that are lower than the cutting teeth, they are most conveniently sharpened while the blade is still on the table saw, following jointing. Place a mill file horizontally on a block of wood about two inches high, then raise the blade up to the file. Keep the blade from turning by jamming a piece of wood into a raker gullet, then just slide the file-bearing block of wood on the table surface to provide constant-height filing action.

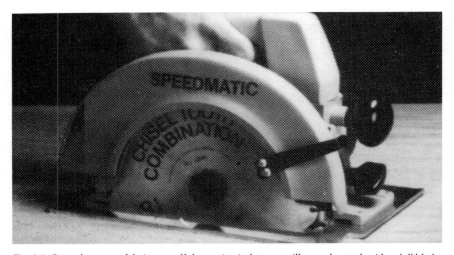

Fig. 6-1. One advantage of do-it-yourself sharpening is that you will never be stuck with a dull blade.

53

SHARPENING HANDSAWS

Old-timers got to be pretty skilled at sharpening their own handsaws with nothing more in the way of tools than a saw vice and a file. But these days most of us just would not have the time or patience to develop such skills. So the purchase of a saw sharpener is a good idea if you wish to do your own saws. This relatively simple device costs only about $25 even at carriage trade tool outlets. It consists of a guide and saw file in a frame that makes certain that you maintain the same angle of filing from tooth to tooth. Since this type of jig typically handles crosscut and ripsaws having up to 15 teeth per inch, it's fine for any handsaw except the finest dovetail saw. One company (Garrett Wade 161 Avenue of the Americas, New York, NY 10013) advertises that the firm's saw sharpener comes with full instructions that even take into account differences between right-and left-handed users.

KEEPING RECORDS

If you intend to try your hand at do-it-yourself saw sharpening, make matters easier by keeping a record of the tooth characteristics of every new circular saw blade you buy. Trace a few teeth carefully on a file card and jot down any additional descriptive information, such as the angle of set. This record keeping is not so important for handsaws because they tend to keep their own records—the teeth close to the handle. These normally suffer little or no wear, and therefore provide the best possible reference information.

Pro Ways with a Power Drill

THE REMARKABLE VERSATILITY of a good drill press is not self-evident to the uninitiated, but becomes increasingly obvious once the tool is available. If you have the shop space, and several hundred dollars to spend, by all means go for a well-made floor model because it provides the maximum benefits. If the prices seem too steep, shop around for a good used model, especially an industrial grade drill press that has not been abused.

CHOOSING A POWER DRILL

Even a used, heavy-duty industrial press can work better than a brand new job built mainly to sell to the home workshop trade. In any case, run the tool before buying, and especially watch for any evidence of spindle shimmy or wobble; if the chuck doesn't turn smoothly and accurately along the full extent of vertical travel, the tool isn't worth floor space even if you get it free.

If space is a real problem, and you must opt for a table model, you still will have a tool worth owning, although it will inevitably lack some of the versatility of a floor model. Unless you are really strapped for space and money, or if your crafts work is limited to very simple constructions, avoid those stands to which you clamp your portable power drill.

ACCESSORIES

You will need many accessories to enjoy the full benefits of a drill press, and these you can acquire gradually as the needs arise. But you absolutely must have good clamp-down devices immediately. There's nothing so dangerous as a piece of sharp-edged metal that gets stuck on a fast-moving drill bit and without warning begins to spin. It could make mince meat of your fingers.

On the other hand, so long as the work is securely held down on the table, the drill press will be one of the safest tools in your shop. The clamp-down accessories should include a good vise which, in turn, is locked to the table with bolts, as well as, a selection of C-clamps for holding down metal, and more convenient spring-type clamps to cope with wood which is less dangerous and easier to drill without jamming the bit. Incidentally, use only twist drills or flat-blade wood bits with the drill press.

If you are tempted to try old bits intended for hand augers (after sawing off the enlarged end), first file the threads off the cutting tip. Many hold-down problems are most conveniently solved with the aid of an accessory that mounts onto the drill press column; you just slide the device down until an arm presses the workpiece firmly to the table and then lock in place. It's a real timesaver, but could cost you in the neighborhood of $40.

Other woodworking accessories you may wish to add to your collection include a rotary planer, mortising kit, dovetail attachment, and shaper fence. Get each of these when and if you are convinced they would be used frequently enough to be worth the cost.

To increase the versatility of your drill press even more, you might want to acquire such special accessories as a milling attachment and/or rotary indexing table. The first enables such metal shaping operations as milling, facing, slotting, and precision drilling. The operations can of course also be applied to other materials such as plastic.

The indexing table is another great aid to facilitate lay-out work, indexing, holding, drilling, milling, routing, and shaping in general. The basic milling attachment will cost $60 or more, while the indexing table will probably put a dent five times greater into your shop budget.

After considering costs of that magnitude, you won't at all mind spending the relatively few bucks for sundry accessories that you will use over and over again. These include sanding drums and discs, various sizes and types of rotary files and rasps, some stirrers to make paint mixing easy, wire brushes, buffing wheels and compound, and grinding wheels. Just naming such accessories underscores the remarkable versatility of a drill press.

Sometimes specific accessories have applications that are not entirely evident to the uninitiated. For example, you would buy one or more wire brushes in order to clean rust and other soils from such things as metal. But you might never realize that the same brushes can be used to "sculpt" the surface of a board to create interesting three-dimensional free-form shapes. But one word of caution: whenever you use such accessories as wire brushes, buffing wheels, or any other tools that can throw particulate matter around, be sure to wear goggles or a face mask.

Pretty soon you will begin to invent many kinds of special accessories that you can build for yourself,often using scrap materials that cost little or nothing. For example, build a square box having an inside depth of 3 or 4 inches that will form a work table resting on top of the regular drill press table. Cut a round hole in the center that is a little larger than the diameter of your largest sanding cylinder. Lower the sanding device part way into the hole, and you will have a very handy table on which to sand-shape all kinds of irregular work.

Another accessory easily made from a scrap of thick plywood is a router table that also clamps onto the drill press table. It's essentially nothing more than a flat board with a rear fence along which you can guide the work to be routed. You can find endless ideas for other simple jigs by watching the pages of do-it-yourself magazines, and by reading books dealing with the use of power tools.

SPECIAL USES

By this time you should be convinced that a drill press would be a real workhorse in your shop. But it can be much more—a tool that will inspire the exploration of the fascinating potentials of creative design. It's easy to visualize such obvious shaping applications as making fancy edges on tables or manufacturing your own moldings. But would you also think of the drill press as a deluxe tool for making elegant *carvings?* Many different kinds of cutters—including router bits, fly cutters, and even rotary rasps—can be used to carve and cut symmetrical or free-form patterns of endless variety (Fig. 7-1).

You can even inlay wood with soft metals such as aluminum (Fig. 7-2). Just cut narrow grooves with a router bit or circle cutter, then hammer in snug-fitting aluminum strips to fill the grooves. No glue should be necessary. Then use the drill press and a sanding disc to even any surface irregularities, and proceed with finishing operations. The effect of inlaying wood with metal can be very attractive on many kinds of craft items.

There are even ways to use a drill press without turning on the power. For example, if you have tried to tap threads into a hole and found it difficult to keep the tap aligned properly, the drill press will be your salvation the next time the job needs to be done. Tapping is definitely a no-sweat job if the workpiece is clamped in the drill press vise and the tap is mounted in the chuck of the press. Do *not* under any circumstances turn on the power; in fact it is advisable to pull the plug during this operation. Lower the tap to the work and turn the chuck by hand; the turning is easier if you use a ''handle'' consisting of a metal rod stuck into one of the holes on the chuck. This way you will get the neatest tapping job ever.

Hole drilling is one of the most often-used of all basic crafts operations. Drilling holes is, of course, still a basic function of a drill press. It's the only truly reliable way to drill holes accurately into virtually any material, including metal, wood, plastics, and ceramics. Note I said *accurately*, not ''straight.'' That's because with a press you not only can drill holes that don't slant, but also holes that do slant properly when you want them to do so. Small objects are drilled handily when clamped in a special drill press vise that holds the work in line with, or perpendicular to, the travel of the bit. But the vise can also be tilted and locked to any desired angle for easy drilling of slanted holes, even into round stock such as metal rod. For larger workpieces, use clamps and jigs to hold the work at the proper angle on the drill press table or, better still, acquire an accessory table that can be locked into various tilt positions.

The drill press of your choice should have a wide range of speeds, say from about 380 rpm to 8,000 rpm, or higher. The odds are you will use the slow speeds most often and, in fact, at times wish the tool had still slower speeds. One example: when

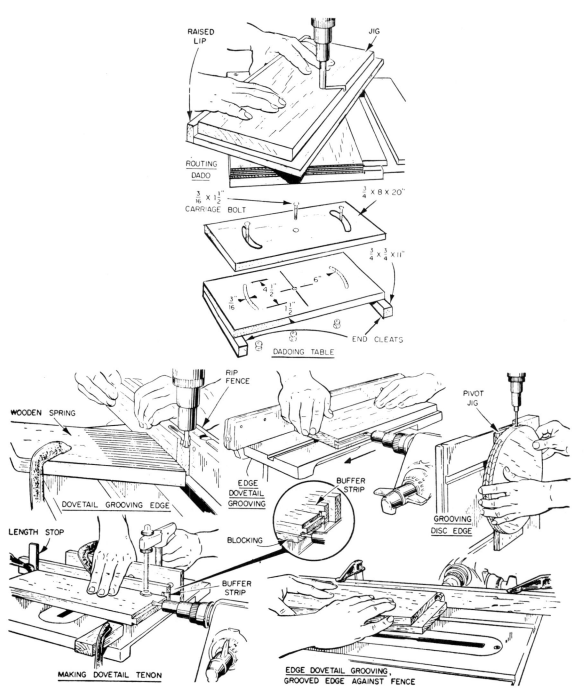

Fig. 7-1. Using a drill press or braced power drill to create dadoes, tenons, dovetail grooves and joints by attaching router bits.

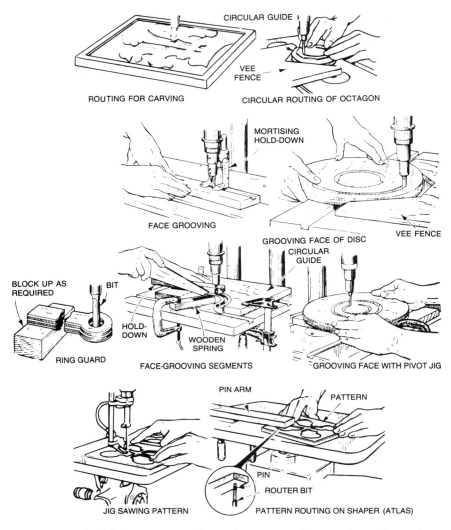

CIRCULAR GUIDE

VEE FENCE

ROUTING FOR CARVING

CIRCULAR ROUTING OF OCTAGON

MORTISING HOLD-DOWN

FACE GROOVING

GROOVING FACE OF DISC

VEE FENCE

BLOCK UP AS REQUIRED

BIT

HOLD-DOWN

WOODEN SPRING

RING GUARD

FACE-GROOVING SEGMENTS

CIRCULAR GUIDE

GROOVING FACE WITH PIVOT JIG

PIN ARM

PATTERN

PIN

ROUTER BIT

JIG SAWING PATTERN

PATTERN ROUTING ON SHAPER (ATLAS)

Fig. 7-2. Using the drill for carving, to make circular grooves and rings. Delicate inlay work can also be accomplished.

attempting to cut holes several inches in diameter with an adjustable fly cutter. On the other hand, safety and good work mandate the use of very high speeds in such applications as routing.

SPECIALTY BITS

Many novice do-it-yourself craftsmen harbor the mistaken notion that the only hole-making equipment needed is a power drill, a set of twist drills for making small holes, and a few spade bits for boring holes larger than a quarter inch in diameter. However, experienced shopmen know that manual drilling and boring still has its place, and that special bits for use with either manual or power drilling enable completing jobs faster as well as more expertly.

Only three basic reminders need be made about the most commonly used twist drills: buy only top quality drills to do good work and save money in the long run; learn to adjust drilling speeds to suit the size of drill being used and the nature of the material being drilled; buy and use a good drill sharpener because only a very experienced craftsman can manually sharpen drill bits without doing more harm than good. If you still think that a twist drill has a conical tip, you definitely need an automatic drill sharpener.

Every well-equipped home workshop should include a good auger and at least one set of auger bits (Fig. 7-3). So-called Jennings bits are preferred if you can tolerate the relatively high costs because they cut best by virtue of double helical chip lifters and two edge-cutting "spurs" that help make smooth holes. The threaded lead screw at the center is what *pulls* the bit into wood as it is turned; the rate of feed depends on the fineness or coarseness of the lead screw thread.

A bit having a coarse-threaded screw works fast, takes out big chips of wood, but is sometimes hard to turn and doesn't provide the smoothest hole. A bit having a fine-threaded screw makes small chips to produce the best hole, but you could become impatient with the slow boring action. Thus, for general shop applications, a medium-threaded lead screw is a good compromise.

A set of thirteen Jennings bits, for boring holes from a ¼ to 1 inch in diameter, might cost about $96 or $110 or more if purchased separately over a period of time. If that seems too steep, consider Irwin "solid center" auger bits that sell for less than half that price.

You can recognize an Irwin type bit because the central shaft seems to run all the way through the fluting to the cutting tip, whereas the shaft on a Jennings bit stops where the fluting starts. The Irwin bit has only one helical chip lifter instead of two intertwined lifters as in a Jennings bit. Irwin bits work almost as well as Jennings bits, and also are less likely to bend if you must

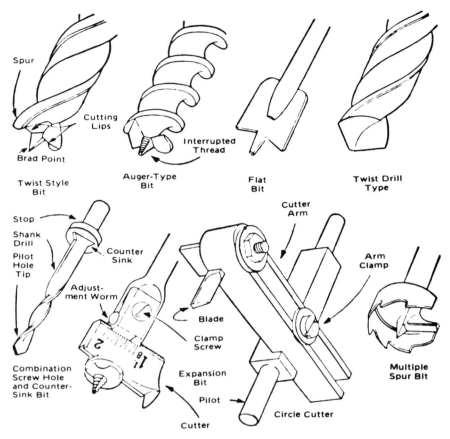

Fig 7-3. Every good workshop worthy of its sawdust is equipped with a variety of bits. And remember that each drill bit may require a different speed on your drill.

exert more than normal pressure to get through especially hard wood.

Standard auger bits bore slightly oversize holes that are not best for very exactly dowel-joining work. If you anticipate doing much fine cabinet work, shop around for auger bits specially sized to produce holes in which dowels fit tightly (Fig. 7-4). A set of five bits, to make holes from ¼ to ½ inch in diameter, can be had for about $22, compared to $15 for five comparable standard bits that bore oversized holes (Fig. 7-5).

Conventional auger bits having screw leads are not of course suitable for use with power drills. However, the dowel-size bits are also available, at the same cost, with unthreaded points and without the square tangs needed for chucking in augers; these are for use with drill presses and portable power drills.

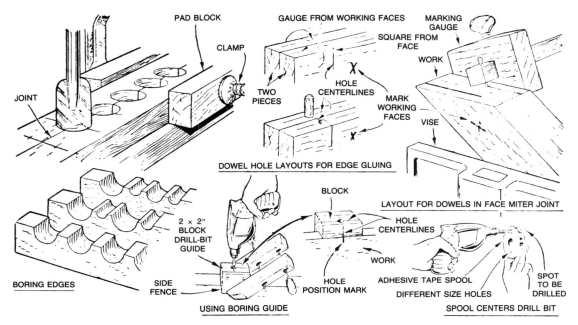

Fig. 7-4. Your power drill can assist in creating decorative edging and precisely centered holes for doweled joints. You may need a boring guide.

Fig. 7-5. The wide variety of bit attachments available include large hole cutters which give you accuracy as well as a clean cut.

Incidentally, if you inherited a set of auger bits from your dad, but can't use them because the screw threads are too worn, don't throw them away. File off smooth points, and hacksaw off the remaining screw threads to form square tangs at the other ends, so that the bits can be used with power drills. Another tip: shop at garage and tag sales for good buys in usable auger bits.

Also keep your eyes peeled for those old-fashioned gimlets that are so hard to find these days. A gimlet can be recognized by a flute that starts as a very compact helix at the tip and then expands gradually into a much wider flute. The other end of the bit has a horizontal handle since it is a hand-drilling tool that is not intended for use with an auger or drill. Gimlets are just great for occasional hole-making because you can have a job done in a fraction of the time it takes to get a drill, find a suitable bit, put them together, then disassemble and store them.

If you already own a set of standard auger bits, you may prefer to invest in ''brad point'' dowel drills instead of another set of dowel-sized auger bits. These are ideal for very accurate doweling work because the sharp brad points enable accurate centering and prevent the drill from wandering during the start of drilling.

A big timesaver, when assembling projects with flat-head screws, is a set of five Stanley Screw-Mate brand drills that make pilot holes for five different sizes of screws. A single drilling action provides the proper-size hole for the threaded part of a screw, a larger-diameter hole above it for the unthreaded part, and a countersink hole for the screw head at the surface of the work. This type of accurate pilot hole drilling also ensures maximum holding power.

You might prefer taper point drills that just make tapered holes for various sizes of screws, without simultaneously countersinking. Or if your shopwork calls for frequent mounting of hardware such as hinges, a ''Vix'' bit can be a timesaver. This latter type of pilot drill is mounted inside a centering sleeve, and comes in two sizes suitable for making pilot holes for five different sizes of screws.

There also are bits for many kinds of special jobs. For example, carbide-tipped drills are used for making holes in masonry, and extra long (30-inch) auger bits are available for drilling long holes when making lamps or woodwind musical instruments. Sometimes make-shift techniques work, but they rarely are good substitutes for the right tools, especially if the same hole-making problems are encountered repeatedly.

MAKING THE MOST OF YOUR PORTABLE DRILL

The portable electric drill with the various accessories available is, without a doubt, the most useful and versatile portable power tool there is today. Originally intended as a portable power tool for drilling holes, it has developed into a power pack for operating such attachments as: a circular saw, jigsaw, belt or disc sander, grinder, buffer and polisher, and wood lathe. It even operates an air compressor for paint spraying.

New time- and labor-saving attachments for the portable electric drill are being developed every day to make it even more useful and versatile.

Sizes of Drills

The size of a portable drill indicates the maximum diameter of drill bit the chuck will take and bore a hole through mild

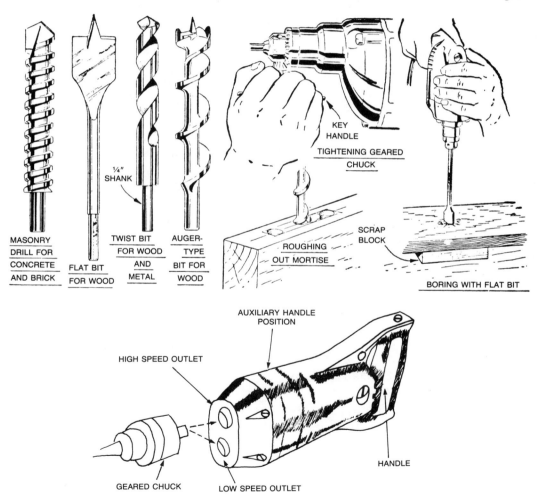

MASONRY DRILL FOR CONCRETE AND BRICK

FLAT BIT FOR WOOD

¼" SHANK

TWIST BIT FOR WOOD AND METAL

AUGER-TYPE BIT FOR WOOD

KEY HANDLE

TIGHTENING GEARED CHUCK

ROUGHING OUT MORTISE

SCRAP BLOCK

BORING WITH FLAT BIT

AUXILIARY HANDLE POSITION

HIGH SPEED OUTLET

GEARED CHUCK

LOW SPEED OUTLET

HANDLE

Fig. 7-6. Above are various bits for different drilling jobs. Below is a heavy-duty drill having two speed outlets.

65

steel. Larger diameter drill bits for boring holes in wood have ¼-inch shanks to fit the popular ¼-inch portable drill. Home workshop electric drills are available in ¼-, ⅜-, and ½-inch chuck sizes and are duty rated as *light-, standard-,* or *heavy-duty.* The price of a drill varies with its duty rating and this rating depends largely on the design of the equipment's motor.

Light-duty drills are for intermittent use only. Since their motors are wound with small-diameter wire on the field and armature coils, these drills tend to "heat up" if overloaded or used continuously for long periods of time. Overheating eventually breaks down the insulation and the drill motor shorts out. When used intermittently they are entirely satisfactory since the motor has a chance to cool between jobs, thus prolonging the life of the drill.

Standard and heavy-duty drill motors are wound with larger diameter or gauge wire than the light-duty drills, which in turn require larger aluminum cases to house the motors. Heavy-duty drills also have larger ball bearings, hardened gears and shafts, and more rugged construction throughout. All this adds up to higher cost. The standard-duty drill, however, will run continuously under an average load with small temperature rise and take short overloads without harm.

The standard-duty drill is probably the most satisfactory for home workshop use because of its construction, price, and ability to operate drill attachments for longer periods of time than required to merely drill a hole. The heavy-duty drill, although satisfactory for home use, would be uneconomical for occasional use because of its higher price.

Drill Speed

The type and speed of the drill chuck must also be considered when purchasing a drill. Choose a geared-type chuck operated by a key if the drill is to be used with attachments. Drill-chuck speeds vary from no-load speeds to 500 rpm for ½-inch drills to 1600 to 2800 rpm for ¼-inch drills. The correct speed for a particular drilling job depends upon the size of the drill bit and the type of material being drilled (see Table 7-1). Most ¼-inch drill attachments operate best at a speed of about 1500 to 2500 rpm. Drill speed will drop 200 to 300 rpm when a load is placed on the drill bit or attachment.

Since it requires two drills (a ⅜-inch or ½-inch slow-speed and a ¼ high-speed) to handle all the jobs around the house, some

Table 7-1. Drill Speeds for High Speed Steel Drill Bits

	Mild Steel	Tool Steel	Hard Cast Iron	Copper Bronze Brass	Steel Forging	Wood	Masonry Concrete Stone
1/16	6000	3000	4000	8000	3700	12000	
1/8	3000	1500	2200	5000	1800	7000	
3/16	2000	1000	1500	4000	1200	4000	
1/4	1500	750	1000	3000	900	3000	700
5/16	1250	600	900	2800	750	2500	600
3/8	1000	500	700	2600	600	2000	500
7/16	875	425	600	2400	500	1800	400
1/2	700	400	500	2200	400	1600	300

Note: For carbon steel twist drills, reduce speeds by one half.

manufacturers make a two-speed drill for home workshop use. The drill-speed reducer is another way of making a ¼-inch drill do the work of a large slow-speed drill. Variable-speed drills are also available.

Bits

Drill bits are available in a wide variety of types and sizes for boring holes in almost any material (Fig. 7-6). The common twist drill can be used for both wood and metal and is especially useful where there is danger of boring into hidden nails or screws, as frequently occurs in building repair.

Auger-type bits have shanks of a fixed size in a set regardless of hole-boring size. These cut fast and clean and can be accurately centered by inserting the points at intersecting lines or in dimples made by indenting the wood with a center punch or awl. Flat bits also extend the diameter capacity of a drill. To prevent splintering the underside of the wood when the drill bit breaks through, rest or clamp a block of scrap wood under the workpiece. Flat bits are excellent for fast rough boring. When drilling holes larger than ¼-inch with a ¼-inch drill, keep the drill-feed pressure light and "nurse" the drill through the material to prevent overheating the motor.

Boring is adaptable to ornamental as well as utilitarian work where gallery edgings are being made. Clamp two strips of wood together, using the joint for a center line. Various patterns are possible with variation of bit size and spacing. Bore a series of holes with an auger bit to rough out a mortise.

Other Attachments

A hole saw saws out discs instead of reducing the material to shavings as a boring bit and makes it possible to cut 2½-inch diameter holes with a portable drill. The nested blades are removable so that the one of the diameter selected can be used alone by inserting it in its groove and locking with a screw. The hole saw is guided and held on center with the pilot bit. Apply pressure until the cutter has sawed through the board. As the saw is withdrawn, the center spring ejects the disc (Fig. 7-7).

A side-cutting drill bit converts your power drill into a router-like tool that will cut intricate curves, making a ¼-inch wide kerf. First bore a hole with the side-cutting bit, then force it along the layout line with the bit in the waste wood. Adding a push and pull, or sawing action is helpful, when cutting diagonal to the wood grain. The sides of the hole can be beveled by tilting the bit at the appropriate angle.

First aid to driving screws is the screwdriver bit which bores a pilot hole for the threaded part of the screw, a shank hole in the piece that is to be screwed down, and countersinks the hole for a flat-headed screw all in one operation. Such a bit may have a stop adjustable for height so that the hole can also be counterbored for a wooden plug, either to be dressed flush to hide the screw, or to appear as a false dowel rising a little above the surface.

To use such bits, tack or clamp the parts together and bore in the usual manner. Bits are available for the various sizes of wood screws. To drive screws rapidly, the speed reducer can be used. Several types and sizes of screwdriver bits are available.

The most generally useful disc sander for portable drills is a flexible rubber back-up disc faced with an abrasive sheet which is held with a screw sunk into the depressed center. Insert the shank of the sanding-disc arbor in the drill chuck, and sand by pressing a part of the disc against the work while rotating. With the soft backing there is little tendency to gouge in, and the strokes feather off well, leaving no offsets.

Cross scratches can be removed by finishing with fine sandpaper. On broad work a better job of surfacing is done if the machine is mounted on a sliding base and locked at a slight angel. Stroke toward the raised side of the disc.

A flat sanding disc with a flexible joint is suitable for freehand use with a portable drill because the shank accommodates itself

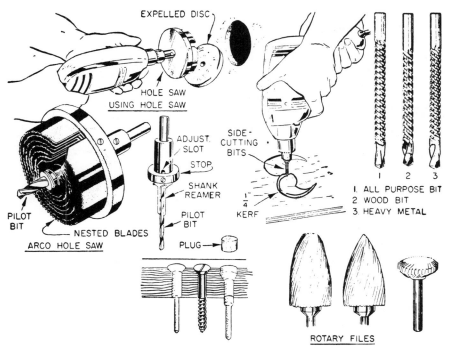

Fig. 7-7. Several attachments expand the range of uses for your drill.

to small variations from the vertical of the holding position. So used, the gouging is reduced and a flat surface is easily obtained. An oversize sandpaper disc used on the metal tends to reduce sanding laps.

Sanding-disc tables, adjustable for tilt and provided with small miter gauges, can be set for accurate sanding of small work, correcting miter joints and hopper cuts. Move the piece across the face of the disc while holding it firmly against the miter gauge head to avoid uneven cutting due to the more rapid travel of the sandpaper near the outside of the disc. Vibration-type sanders with straightline or orbital motion, are also available as attachments for drills. The rapidly moving pad sands smoothly and will work up into corners of panels and other recesses.

Many of the advantages of a drill press are obtained by clamping a portable drill to a bench stand. Held rigidly in the yoke, the drill is raised and lowered with a lever, the drill moving in a vertical line (Fig. 7-8). The depth of boring is regulated by clamping the yoke at the required height, or in some models by locking a collar below the yoke, on the column, to limit travel.

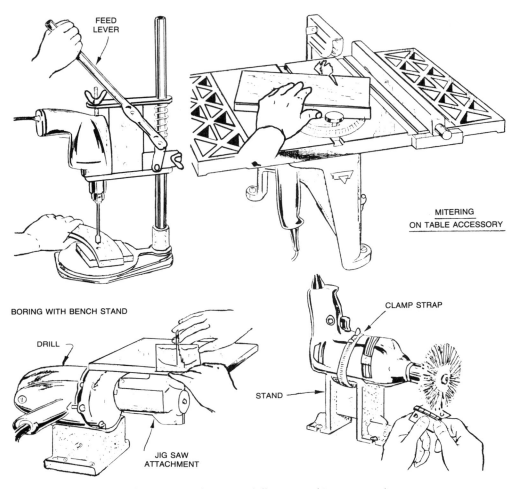

FEED LEVER

MITERING ON TABLE ACCESSORY

BORING WITH BENCH STAND

DRILL

JIG SAW ATTACHMENT

CLAMP STRAP

STAND

Fig. 7-8. Transform your drill into a multi-purpose tool.

Before drilling, press the switch-lock button to free both hands for holding the work.

The circular saw attachment has many of the features of a standard portable saw, and is used like it, guiding the indicator along the line, or tacking or clamping a straightedge to the work for the edge of the bottom of the attachment to slide against. By the use of a dado arbor, which has a tilted washer and socket joint arrangement for a wobble saw, a cutting blade is made to sweep from side to side, cutting a wide groove.

Saw tables, complete with rip fence, miter gauge, and table extensions, turn the portable drill with its saw accessory into a standard table saw. For this work the miter gauge, swiveled to the the required angle, guides the work past the blade. When setting the rip fence for cutting a board to width, measure the distance from the fence to a blade tooth which is set toward it.

What You Should Know About Routers

IDEAL FOR JOBS too large to be handled on stationary power tools, the portable electric router with its variety of cutter bits and attachments becomes a versatile power tool capable of routing, drilling, shaping, carving, planing, and even cutting through ¾-inch stock. Because of its extremely high speed of rotation (14,000 rpm and over), the router makes smooth cuts that in most cases require no sanding. While the weight of a portable router may run anywhere from 6 to 30 pounds, depending upon type and size, it is easy to handle because the work supports it.

With a shaper table, you can use the router as a standard shaper (vertically or tilted). With a special attachment and spiral cutter, the router becomes a portable planer useful for jointing edges of large jobs. Also, grinding jigs permit sharpening of cutters with grinding points mounted on a router.

RABBETING WITH A
PORTABLE ROUTER

Rabbeting is a typical use of a portable router. To set it up for this operation, insert a router bit or a special rabbeting cutter in the router chuck, stand the machine on the board to be worked, and adjust the bit to touch lightly on the wood. Set the calibrating sleeve or ring on the router to zero position, lock it, and lower the bit to depth of cut. When cutting large rabbets it is better to make two or more light cutting passes rather than one heavy cut.

Next, mount the guide on the router with the straightedge toward the cutter, measure the distance from the guide to the far edge of the cutter, and clamp the setting. For end rabbeting, press the guide against the end of the board, and feed from left to right at such a rate that the free motor speed is not slowed down more than about one-third. Too fast a feed overloads the motor; too slow a feed burns the wood, and may soften the cutter.

A close fit between the cutter and the guide opening is desirable when rabbeting, so that the beginning or ending corner will not enter the gap, causing the router bit to gouge. A wooden strip 8 or 9 inches long and ½ to 1 inch thick screwed to the guide will prevent such difficulty. (Refer to Fig. 8-1.) The cutter will its own recess in the facing as the bit is lowered to cutting depth.

Hold the board between the bench stops, by clamping to the top, or if thick enough, by gripping it in the vise, the end to be rabbeted projecting a little. A strip of scrap wood clamped to the following edge prevents splintering as the cutter emerges, and one at the other edge helps.

Where two or more pieces are to be rabbeted, line them up edge to edge. If an end and edge are to be rabbeted, do the end first, so that the edge cut will trim off the splinters. The board can be rabbeted all around in one continuous cut.

Rabbeting of an inside edge of a box or frame has many uses, as in making a window screen, where the frame can be joined with butted joints and dowels, and rabbeted for the screen mold afterward. Screw a 90-degree-angle guide block to the router guide if it has no pointed end and move around against the rotation of the cutter. Trim the rounded corners square with a hand chisel.

Stopped rabbets are made by feeding the cutter up to a marked point, or if stopped at the beginning of the cut by feeding in from that point. Accuracy is automatic if a block is clamped on the edge to contact the end of the guide, a precaution especially valuable to prevent kickback when starting a stopped rabbet.

73

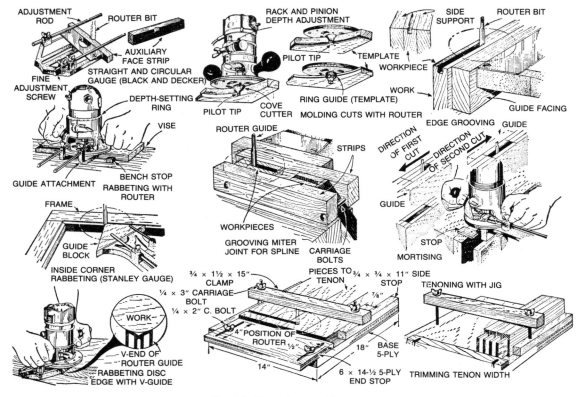

Fig. 8-1. Uses of a portable router.

To rabbet the edge of a disc, remove the straight guide from the fixture and use the V-end guide against the work. Instead of the V guide, a wooden guide facing shaped to the curve of the disc can be used. This type of guide will produce smoother work.

DADOING AND GROOVING

Dadoing and grooving are operations similar to rabbeting, the guide being used in much the same way. Choose a router bit of diameter equal to the width of the dado desired and set it for depth as in rabbeting. Anti-splintering strips at the edges should be used. (See Fig. 8-2.)

In heavy work, make two or more passes. If a groove wider than the cutter is needed, first cut one side, then extend the guide setting and make another cut, repeating until the needed width is gained.

Instead of using the guide fixture, a strip of wood clamped to the work for the router base to slide against can be used. This

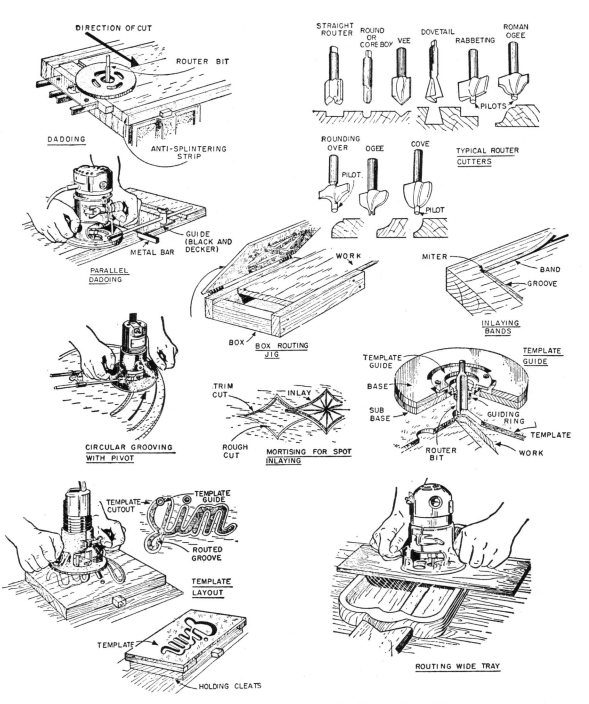

Fig. 8-2. Dadoing, circular and freehand grooving, and making templates with a router.

is necessary if the dadoes run at an angle to the edge of work. When a series of parallel dadoes are to be made, cut the first one, then shift the guide or the straightedge and cut the next one and so on.

Circular Grooving

Circular grooving of a disc is done with the V-guide or by means of a trammel point clamped to the guide rods and pressed into the work (Fig. 8-2). This pivot method is especially handy where the circles are not concentric, or if the piece is not round, providing no guiding edges.

The bottoms of grooves can be rectangular, V-shaped, or rounded, according to the type of cutter used. Narrow and shallow grooves are called veins, and veining is used for ornamental purposes. For inlaying wooden bands, cut rectangular grooves slightly shallower than the thickness of the band, so that the band will project a little when glued into place. Touching up with sandpaper will cut the band down flush with the surface, without need of sanding the whole surface.

Freehand Grooving

Irregular inlays, such as the sport ornaments often used in the centers of tables, are mortised in using the router freehand or with the use of templates (Figs. 8-2, 8-3). To cut the recess, trace around the inlay with a sharp knife point and rout out the work again a little shallower than the thickness of the inlay. Start the mortise near the center and trim toward the lines. Insert the inlay with the paper side up.

Freehand grooving is sometimes used for making signs and nameboards. The groove can then be filled with Plastic Wood or other composition to resemble inlaying, or the background painted a color contrasting with the lettering.

To rout out names or designs accurately, or if there is to be duplication, make a template from hardboard or ¼-inch plywood. The working size of the template depends on the bit and guide to be used. The template guide, through which the router bit is inserted, is a small cupped disc having a thin-walled ring slightly larger than the router bit to be used. A good bit to use for this work is a ⅛ inch diameter left-hand twist router.

Making a Template. When making a template, first draw the design on paper, and then sketch in a larger outline to allow for

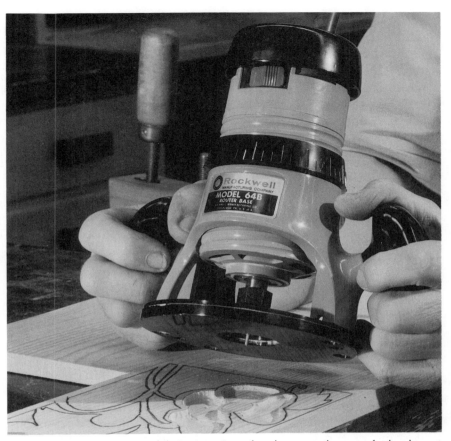

Fig. 8-3. To carve an ornamental design in a piece of stock, operate the router freehand to cut inside of the design.

the extra diameter of the guide ring. Transfer this to the template material and tack it to a scrap board which is clamped to the bench. Set the router bit for a projection of about ¹⁄₁₆ inch below the template, and trace around the inside of the design outline freehand with a rather rapid feed. Then, at slower feed, take a second cut, carefully trimming to the design line. Since any irregularity of the template is transferred to the work, the template edges must be smoothed with files and sandpaper.

Hold the template in place on the work by driving brads into waste parts that will be cut away, or if this is not possible, by nailing cleats under the template where they will clasp the work. Place the router on the template with the guiding ring bearing against the template edge and trace around the edges of the template. If the design has large routed areas, use a small router bit to outline and then change to a larger bit to clean out the remaining waste wood.

Cutouts, such as grills, are similarly made, the bit being extended through the thickness of the work. Mount the work on a waste board to avoid marring the bench top with the bit tip.

A box template is a convenience for production work. The piece is dropped or slid into the box and the template, hinged like a lid, is closed down over the work and clamped. Blanks of scrap wood cut out drop out of the way through the open bottom of the box.

Routers are excellent machines for quickly making carved wooden trays. First trace the design to the workpiece. Then, using the router freehand, work it into the pockets of the tray, using a router bit or shaping bit of suitable profile. Rough-cut to the design outline, and then go around again carefully trimming to the line.

Depth is obtained by making two or more passes or cuts, lowering the bit each time. In some cases it is best to leave the outside edges of the tray unfinished for easier clamping, until the inside is finished. If you are making a tray with a large pocket, too wide to support the router base, fasten a piece of plywood to the router base to carry the machine.

MAKING MOLDED EDGES

Because of the many cutter shapes available, the router can be used as a shaper for making decorative molded edges. Note that some of the cutters have a pilot or small cylindrical tip projecting beyond the end of the cutter (Fig. 8-4). When ⅛ inch or more of the lower edge of the workpiece can be left unshaped it can be used as a guiding edge for the pilot to bear against. Start routing a molded edge at the left corner of the work and feed from left to right, the pilot sliding along the unshaped part of the edge. As the tip is only ³⁄₁₆ inch in diameter, it follows small curves readily; however, it will also reproduce any jogs or irregularities in the edge. For this reason, the edge must be well smoothed before shaping.

To shape the entire edge of the work, tack a template on the underside of the work for the pilot tip to bear against. If may be the same size or larger or smaller, depending on the profile and projection of the cutter. Pilotless bits, or shaper cutters, use a template above the work. As in rabbeting, shaping on straight and evenly curved edges can be done with the guide fixture too, either directly against the edge or with guide strips.

Fig. 8-4. The round tip at the end of the cutter is called the pilot. When carving a molding edge, it keeps the cut true.

Edge Grooving

Edge grooving is a required operation for building panels and for joining boards edge to edge reinforced with a spline. This is identical to face grooving except that a provision must be made for steadying the base of the router. This can be done by clamping a 1-inch strip to each side of the workpiece flush with its upper edge, for the router base to slide upon, or by facing the guide fixture with a relatively wide strip which, held against the side of the work, will keep the base level during the cutting.

The spline, usually ¼-inch plywood cut across the grain, matching the ¼-inch router bit used for grooving, is equal in width to the combined depth of the two grooves cut in the pieces to be joined.

Splines are excellent fasteners for mitered joints too. Use a setup for grooving similar to that shown in the drawing (Fig. 8-1), where the two members of a joint are clamped between two strips bolted together. This forms a jig that can be used time and again. Center the bit accurately on the work. If the edges of the joined pieces are to show in the finished assembly, it is better to make stopped grooves so that the spline ends will not show.

MAKING MORTISE AND TENON JOINTS

Mortise and tenon joints are easily made with the router. Lay out the mortise centering it on the thickness; and using a router bit a little narrower than the mortise, cut the mortise to length as in grooving. Then, with the router guide bearing against the other side of the work, make a second cut, which will trim the mortise to width and exactly center it. The rounded ends can be squared with a chisel, or the ends of the tenons can be rounded to fit.

For making the tenons, set the router bit depth to make the tenon the same size as the mortise already made. Making tenons is a rabbeting operation, the shoulder being cut first and the waste trimmed away, working from the shouldered end to give maximum support for the router base. The tenoning jig detailed in Fig. 8-1 provides an adjustable end stop, router base guide, and clamp for workpieces, and will handle one or more pieces at a time. After making cheek cuts, turn the pieces on edge, reclamp, and trim the tenons to width.

A tenoning jig is particularly useful for production work, because the end stop can be returned to a marked position for turning out duplicate parts quickly and accurately at a later date, or the jig can be left in a locked position to serve as a step in a production-line setup.

Dovetailed Grooves

Dovetailed grooves have uses such as attaching a cleat to the end of a drawing board to lessen warping. Fastening, except at center, is not needed, the board being free to slide in the cleat as it shrinks or swells according to humidity. Use a dovetail cutter to make the groove (Fig. 8-5).

To make the tenon, cut two dovetail grooves, working partly in the side support strips, the part between the grooves forming

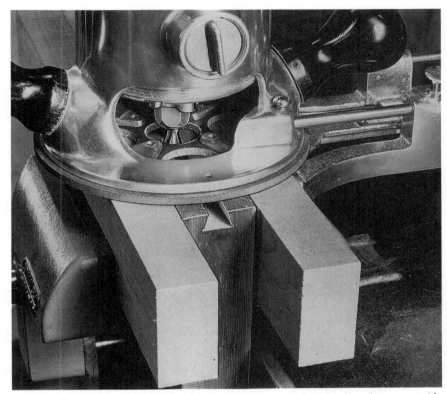

Fig. 8-5. When using a dovetail cutter, block the work into the vise and set the router guide accordingly. This assures a true cut.

the tenon. With accurate setup, the tenon is very slightly less in width than the mating groove, allowing for a push fit and a little glue room. This joint makes a strong connection between a rail and a stile, and can be left unglued for knockdown construction.

How to Choose
and Use a Lathe

ONE OF THE MOST PLEASURABLE moments any emerging crafts-man can experience comes when he puts a lathe chisel to spinning wood for the first time. There is something strangely exciting, almost magical, about the way the raw wood takes on beautifully symmetrical, rounded curves—even when the chisel is in the hands of a rank amateur.

A lathe is one of the safest of shop power tools, provided you observe a few simple basic rules. First, never wear loose clothing, in particular a free-dangling necktie, when operating a lathe. Secondly, study the operating manual so that you know how to position the tool rest for maximum safety and cutting efficiency. Third, start experimenting by using the lathe chisels as *scrapers* rather than, as *cutters*. You will do just as good a job, although somewhat more slowly, than a master wood turner who has developed the skill of actually cutting the wood away.

Perhaps the most satisfying aspect of wood turning is that you can often make the finished object without use of any other tools. A wood bowl, for example, can be turned from raw stock, smoothed, and given the final staining and other finishing steps right there on the lathe. As you explore the crafts potentials of a lathe, you may be surprised at the variety of jobs it can perform—certainly much more than just shaping table and chair legs, or making bowls. There are, for example, handy ways to use a lathe without turning the power on to spin the wood! But more about that later.

BUYING A LATHE

First, let's consider what type of lathe might serve your purposes best. Obviously, that is a question you must answer for yourself because only you know what type of craftwork you will wish to do. If you are mainly interested in model construction—ships, doll houses and furniture, and the like—then a large shop lathe would be virtually useless. What you need is a small "Kitchen table" version such as a small Dremel lathe. A special chucker features a nest of six removable square metal tubes to hold different sizes of turning stock on a chucker adapter that fits the spindle threads. This small lathe, fitted with the chucker, permits a user to turn intricate designs quickly and accurately for such crafts purposes as doll house furnishings, model ships, miniature cannons, model railroads, and model airplanes.

A full-size lathe is, of course, needed to make the kinds of objects you might want to decorate your own home. If all you have in mind is to turn a few table or chair legs, the do-it-yourself lathe

Fig. 9-1. This Dremel miniature "kitchen table" lathe is perfect for working on hobby crafts such as model ship building, doll house furnishings, model railroads and airplanes.

approach would be an absurdly costly solution. You can buy a lot of readymade legs for the price of a lathe. Besides, there sometimes are more practical, alternative solutions. For example, if you already own a router, consider a relatively inexpensive *Router Crafter* accessory sold by Sears for under 100 dollars. It obviously can't do all that a lathe can, but it can turn out such things as table legs quite easily.

These are practical second choices if your shop budget won't stretch enough right now to permit the purchase of a lathe plus all the necessary tools and accessories. Meanwhile, watch the newspapers for notices of auctions where you might luck out and pick up a good lathe at a bargain price.

If you shop for a new lathe, resist the temptation to purchase the first machine you find. Lathes are not all alike, and some have special features you could find especially valuable. For example, let's say you have a flair for designing unusual table lamps that can command good prices. You may wish to develop this talent into an income-producing sideline. Any good lathe can turn out the lamp bodies and bases, but a lathe having a *hollow dead center* would permit fast and easy drilling of the long, straight holes through which to thread the lamp cord. The work is mounted between the headstock spindle at the motorized end of the lathe, and the tailstock spindle at the other end. If the latter support is *hollow*, a long drill can be fed through it to the lamp base.

SIZES OF LATHES

A more important decision for most craftsmen is to decide the needed capacity of the purchased lathe; the larger the stock it can handle, the more it will cost. For example, in one line of lathes, a machine measuring about 2 feet between centers and having a 12-inch diameter maximum capacity costs close to $300 without a motor; go to the largest size (39½ inches between centers and a 16½-inch diameter capacity) and the price (also without motor) doubles.

Some lathes permit "outboard" turning of such things as bowls and tabletops that are of larger diameter than the normal maximum diameter which is determined by the distance from the spindles to the horizontal bed of the lathe. The work is mounted on the opposite side of the headstock, thus the maximum theoretical diameter is twice the distance from the headstock to the shop floor. However, outboard turning of large objects is to be discouraged because the high rim speeds make this type of work very hazardous, except with very heavy duty equipment specially designed for such applications. In fact, outboard turning on lathes other than "pedestal" latches is forbidden in Sweden where the fine *Luna* lathes are manufactured.

APPLICATIONS

The kinds of objects you can make with a lathe are limited only by your ingenuity as a craftsman. Some applications are quite obvious: bowls, cups, candlestick bases, circular picture frames, and the like. Less obvious examples are decorative "carvings" made by turning out a fancy spindle, then sawing it lengthwise down the middle so that the flat surfaces can be glued to other crafts objects.

And suppose you wish to restore a valuable piece of furniture, such as an antique dresser, but one or more of the original drawer knobs are missing and modern store-bought versions just would not look right. It would be an easy matter to turn duplicate knobs on a lathe. Remember, too, that the lathe provides a handy power source for such things as wire brushes and buffing wheels.

The uninitiated naturally "think round" when a lathe is mentioned. Yet, with the aid of simple jigs you can build from scrap lumber, a lathe can be used to do all sorts of surprising things. For example, you can convert it into a router by fitting a router bit to a chuck on the headstock spindle, and placing the work to be routed on a wood table fitted at the proper height above the lathe bed. With this setup you can rout rabbets, grooves, round-end mortises, and even do shaping and molding cutting by adding a vertical fence to the table. Similarly, accessory tables can support the work when disc or drum sanders are fitted to the lathe's headstock spindle.

Fluting long cylindrical objects with a router is easy if the work is mounted in a lathe, and the router is made to ride along a wooden accessory bed that is slightly higher than the top surface of the work. In this application the lathe is not turned on because it serves only as a convenient holder for the object to be fluted. If the lathe is equipped with an indexing head, positioning the work for the various parallel lengthwise cuts is particularly easy.

You are urged to consult basic woodworking reference books, such as those written by master craftsman De Cristoforo, to learn in detail how to build simple jigs that will help convert your lathe into a truly useful general-purpose tool.

All about Belt Sanders and Pad Sanders

BELT AND PAD SANDERS HAVE many advantages over disc sanders and, with proper care and use, can be an asset to any workshop.

BELT SANDERS

Anyone who has ever seen a belt sander in use knows that this extremely useful power tool belongs in every workshop. The main question is whether the sander should be a large disc/belt combination sander or a smaller, portable version. The answer: probably both, for most shops. The problem then boils down to deciding which type should be acquired first, if economic considerations preclude getting both at the same time.

Combination v. Portable Sanders

A combination sander is by far the more useful on average in shop work because its inherent stability frees both hands for handling the work. Also it can sand larger pieces faster and more accurately by virtue of the relatively large belt area.

On the other hand, if much sanding is to be done out of the shop, a portable sander is the one to choose. It can be used wherever an extension power cable will reach, for sanding anything from the edge of a sticking door to a wooden fence that needs a cleanup before refinishing.

In one sense the portable sander is the more versatile because it can handle in-shop sanding needs reasonably well besides doing all those other jobs to which a large combination sander cannot be taken. In general, then, the acquisition of a portable sander is likely to take priority in the minds of most shopworkers who also want to lighten construction and maintenance chores around the house. Others will choose a portable model for economic reasons; typical disc/belt sanders, that include both a motor and a stand, generally cost well over two times as much as the average portable belt sander.

Uses of a Belt Sander

The primary reason for acquiring either type of belt sander is the elimination of tiresome hand sanding. But even the most basic workshop boasts a portable power drill with a disc sanding attachment. So is a belt sander actually very important? Yes, it is. First, a belt sander works much faster. More importantly, it does an infinitely better job because it can sand with the wood grain and eliminate all those hard-to-remove swirl marks that a disc sander inevitably leaves. Also, the belt sander never bucks and chatters all over the stock as does a disc sander that is not held at exactly the right tilt. The disc sander comes into its own mainly when sanding curved surfaces, such as a puttied car fender.

Buying a Portable Sander

Selection of a portable sander is no real problem when buying name brand tools; you'll get what you pay for. For example, the lowest-priced model in a given line may have a ¾ horsepower motor which will not work as effectively as a 1 HP model. Moreover, the lightweight model may lack a dust pickup bag which I consider a "must" because sanding dust that floats around the room not only complicates shop cleanup chores but also poses a health hazard (Fig. 10-1). If your sander lacks a dust pickup, by all means wear a dust mask when using the tool.

Heft the various portable, models when shopping for a sander, bearing in mind that sanding vertical surfaces can be very tiring with a heavy sander. If you anticipate no extensive sanding of

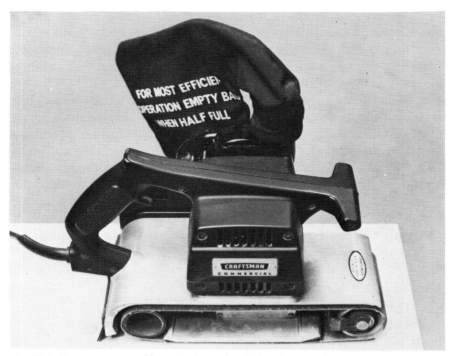

Fig. 10-1. Be sure your portable sander has a dust pickup bag to collect potentially hazardous dust expelled during use.

vertical surfaces, a somewhat heavier sander is acceptable, and even preferable because of its increased efficiency. Incidentally, do not bear down heavily on the sander, but let the weight of the sander itself do the work.

Increased versatility for a portable belt sander comes with the acquisition of a store-bought or self-made stand that in effect transforms the tool into a small-scale stationary sander. For instance, Sears stores carry a handy "Belt Sander Finishing Stand" that fits most Sears' portable sanders having 3- or 4-inch belt widths. The stand holds the sander horizontally for "heavy" sanding and vertically for "light touch-ups."

Making a Finishing Stand

It's not much of a trick to make one's own supports for a portable sander. Any means of firmly holding the sander upside down converts it into a horizontal sander. It's often possible to simply clamp one end of the sander into a bench vise to stabilize it; just avoid excessive clamping pressure, especially against any plastic housing parts.

Another trick is to lay the sander on its side, atop a piece of scrap ½- or ¾-inch plywood that measures about 2 feed on edge, and fit a shaped wood block against the handle side, or use some other convenience means of stabilizing the tool, so that work can be pressed against the moving belt.

Sharpening Tools

You might do at least as much tool sharpening with a belt sander as with a conventional grinder, partly because the belt has less tendency to overheat tool edges than does a grinder. Also, larger tools can be applied to an open belt much more easily than a typical grinder wheel.

The sander does a nice job on knives, axes, hatchets, rotary-mower blades, and even tin snips. When sharpening an axe, take care to orient the tool so that the belt moves away from, rather than toward, the tool edge. Slowly rock the blade back and forth to retain its normal curvature.

To sharpen a tool with a flat bevel, just hold it steadily against the belt. The easiest way to sharpen tin snips with a large, stationary sander is to flip the belt into vertical position and place the table at a tilt conforming to the bevel on the tool. Then just rest the tool on the table and slowly feed the blade to the belt. To finish the job, whet the flat side of each blade with a fine handstone to eliminate the burr that may form.

Choosing a Belt

Choice of grit is important, as for any type of sanding. The standard belt has aluminum-oxide abrasive on cloth. You can get belts in fine, medium and coarse grits for all belt sizes, plus extra-fine and extra-course for a few belt sizes. With the wide range of grits available, you're bound to find the right one for your needs. (For a premium price and a little searching you can opt for polyester-backed aluminum oxide belts.)

The main problem with any belt sander is the all-too-rapid clogging of the belt with wood particles. Shopsmith offers a special cleaning apparatus that is said to remove the entrapped crud efficiently to prolong the life of any belt or disc. The stick is simply rubbed against the moving belt or disc to effect cleaning.

Nothing messes a new belt faster than old paint. So use paint remover first, then finish the job with a sander loaded with a coarse or medium grit belt. Remember that many old paints are loaded with toxic lead compounds, so take every possible precaution to avoid breathing the paint dust or letting it float throughout the shop. Do such sanding outdoors with a portable sander, and wear a respirator, old clothing and hat.

PAD SANDERS

There are many good reasons why you should consider the purchase of a finishing pad sander, even if you already own a belt or disc sander. A pad sander does not produce the troublesome swirl marks characteristic of disc sander action; and because it is slower cutting than a belt sander, it can be controlled more easily to produce really fine wood-finishing jobs (Fig. 10-2).

The pad sander can save you hours of time by making many other around-the-house chores easier to do. It can be used to remove old paint and varnish before refinishing, for smoothing out spackle used to patch holes in walls, buffing the wax applied to the family car or to furniture, and even for polishing small metal and plastic objects.

Types of Pad Sanders

The most popular type of pad sander features a rotary motor that imparts an orbital motion to the sandpaper attached to the platen of the sander. The orbit may be circular or elliptical, but in either case the orbit is so small that you cannot see it in action. Orbital action removes wood much faster than linear (straight back-and-forth) action that is typical of a second, less expensive breed of pad sander that utilizes a magnetic vibrator to drive the platen.

Some deluxe pad sanders provide both orbital and linear sanding at the flick of a switch. If you are interested in ultra-fine finishing of good furniture, the extra cost of such a combination job may be justified; but for the average homeowner and craftsman, the orbital sander alone is sufficient.

Fig. 10-2. Because a pad sander has slower cutting action than a belt sander, it can be controlled more easily to produce really fine wood finishing jobs like tabletops.

Basic Sanding Procedures

Although many pad sanders have grips for two-handed operation, do not assume that this is because pressure must be applied. In fact, a pad sander works most efficiently if you apply no more pressure than that provided by the weight of the machine; use your hands simply to guide the machine over the work.

If your sander is double-insulated, it can be safely plugged into any wall socket that provides proper AC voltage. If the sander is not double-insulated, it should have a three conductor cord terminating in a three-pronged grounding plug. Use the grounded plug only in a suitable, properly grounded socket to ensure your personal safety.

If you must use a long extension cord, select one having No. 18 A.W.G. (American Wire Gauge) or larger conductors for distances up to 100 feet. If the wire is too lightweight, there may be enough of a voltage drop to damage the sander motor.

Most pad sanders utilize strips of sandpaper measuring about $3\frac{2}{3} \times 9$ inches which you can obtain by cutting (don't tear) a conventional sheet of sandpaper into three equal parts. Clips at the front and rear of the platen hold the sandpaper in place, over the sander pad. Stretch the sandpaper as tightly as possible before fastening under the second clip because loosely attached sandpaper will not perform efficiently. Start the sander and let it get up to proper speed before laying it down on your work, move it about slowly and evenly in overlapping arcs, and remove from the work before shutting off the motor.

Actually, no special skill is required to use a pad sander. You will get the hang of it within a minute or two after you first turn it on. But you won't obtain the best possible performance from the sander unless you become familiar with the various types of sandpapers that are available, and what they are used for. No one type or grade of sandpaper can possibly handle all your sanding jobs, and buying all available types and grades would be a waste of money.

Choosing the Right Sandpaper

You can scratch one type of sandpaper off your list immediately, as far as its use with any mechanical sander is concerned; it's the old-fashioned flint sandpaper having granules of quartz as the abrasive material. Flint sandpaper simply is not strong enough for machine use. This leaves you with three other basic types of sandpapers: *garnet*, *aluminum oxide*, and *silicon carbide*. In many instances their uses overlap, but not necessarily in reverse order. For example, you could use aluminum oxide papers for those jobs that a garnet paper could handle easily, but the garnet paper cannot equally well substitute for the aluminum oxide paper when the job calls for more abrasive toughness than is characteristic of garnet.

Aluminum oxide is a synthetic material that is somewhat harder and tougher than garnet, and significantly tougher than flint. But the slightly higher price of aluminum oxide paper is more than offset by the longer use you will get from it. Aluminum oxide paper is unquestionably the favorite among home craftsmen.

Garnet is superior to flint, but it is losing out to aluminum oxide so you may not even find it in all stores. If you do, and the price is right, it will serve very well for ordinary woodworking.

Silicon carbide is a very hard synthetic mineral (almost as hard as diamond) so it can tackle really tough jobs. It is usually applied to cloth or waterproof paper backings so that it can be wet with water or light oil for final smoothing and polishing operations. You are likely to see silicon carbide papers only in the finer grits. Both silicon carbide and aluminum oxide papers are suitable for working metal as well as wood.

Grit Ratings

The abrasive characteristics of sandpapers are rated in several different ways, but the two most common systems utilize grit numbers and/or a numerical grading scale. Grit numbers run from about 16 (very coarse) to 400 (very fine). The finer the particle, the larger is the grit number which actually indicates the number of openings per square inch of screening through which the abrasive particles could pass.

The numerical system works just the opposite: the smaller the number, the finer the grit size. In fact, the industry soon ran out of real numbers and had to go to a multiple zero numbering systems as finer grades of sandpaper were developed. For example, grade 4 paper is very coarse; the coarsest coarse paper is number 2; the coarsest medium paper is 1/2; the coarsest fine paper is 3/0 (an abbreviation of 000); and the coarsest very fine paper is 6/0 while the finest very fine paper is 10/0.

As a general rule, you should use a slightly coarser sandpaper on hardwoods to obtain the same degree of smoothness you could get on softwood with a slightly finer sandpaper. Use the coarsest sandpapers only for roughing which implies the removal of a considerable amount of wood. A medium-grit paper should be used for blending, which involves some material removal and the imparting of a fairly smooth finish. Fine sandpapers are used primarily to eliminate fine scratches made by coarser sandpapers. Very fine grits are used for final polishing and rubbing actions.

To start, you should try out the effects of the various grades of sandpaper (very coarse, coarse, medium, and fine) on both soft and hardwoods. But do not buy every grade within these basic categories until you see a specific need; and you would probably waste your money buying very find sandpaper unless you are involved in a finishing project that calls for extremely fine finishing. To get you thinking in the right direction, not only in the selection of papers for woodworking but for other applications such as processing of metals and plastics, here is a summary of the recommendations made by the manufacturer of one of the pad sanders illustrated:

Soft wood and wallboard. Use 2-1 grit garnet cabinet paper for fast material removal, 1/2-2/0 garnet for material removal with fair finish, and 3/0-5/0 garnet finishing paper for fine finish. Aluminum oxide papers of comparable grits can be used, but the toughness of aluminum oxide is not actually required when working with such soft materials.

Plastics. 60-100 grit aluminum oxide for material removal, 120-220 silicon carbide with paper ''C'' weight for material removal with fair finish, and 240-600 silicon carbide wet paper ''A'' weight for fine finish.

Hardwoods and hard composition materials. 36-50 grit aluminum oxide for material removal, 60-100 grit aluminum oxide for material removal and fair finish, and 120-180 aluminum oxide finishing paper for fine finish.

Paints and varnishes. 2½-1½ open coat garnet paper for material removal, 240-400 silicon carbide wet paper ''A'' weight for fine finish.

Fine finishing techniques. If you want the best possible finish on your woodworking projects, you must follow specific surface preparation procedures. Hasty or inexpert use of a sanding machine will lead to disappointment, in which case you should not be too ready to blame the equipment. Good finishing, even when using time- and laborsaving machines, requires patience.

The wood should first be sanded down to the smoothest and flattest possible surface using various selected grades of sandpaper. Do not jump from a coarse to a fine sandpaper and expect good results; prepare the surface in stages until you have the kind of smooth finish you want.

When working with hardwoods, you can obtain noticeable improvement in the surface as you go to finer grits, all the way down to a 9/0 paper. But such very fine paper would be wasted on softwood which just won't sand down to a comparable surface. About the finest sandpaper that is practical for softwood is a 6/0 paper. Also, it is rather pointless to work toward an ultra-smooth surface if you plan to apply an enamel coating which would fill in minor pores anyway. A 4/0 or 6/0 paper should be fine enough to prepare a wood surface for enameling.

If you intend to apply a clear-type coating, and especially if the wood is to be stained with a water stain, the sanded surface should be wet down with clear, warm water. This makes the wood swell and raises fine surface fibers so that they can be removed with a final sanding, using the finest sandpaper used in the preliminary sanding, *after* the wood has dried thoroughly, preferably by standing overnight. Do not skip this step if you are to use water stains. Some workers go one step further and apply a coat of thin shellac or a special sanding sealer after the fibers have been raised to harden them before the final sanding. This produces an even smoother final finish. Just be sure not to apply a sealer that might prevent a stain from being absorbed properly by the wood.

These tips provide only the rudiments of good finishing practice, and will be quite adequate for many average wood-finishing jobs. But if you plan to do very exacting finishing, or refinishing of fine furniture, you should refer to books that deal with such subjects in detail. There are many special tricks and techniques you should learn before attempting serious finishing work.

Other Applications

Your pad sander can be used for many purposes other than the basic job of preparing wood for finishing. An orbital sander will do a good job removing old paint and varnish provided that you pick the right kind of sandpaper. Ordinary closed coat sandpapers will soon clog up and become useless. What you need is a special ''open coat'' abrasive having the grit particles spaced relatively far apart so that they do not clog as easily.

It's also important to keep the sander moving constantly with broad, sweeping motions. If you stay in one place too long, the paint or varnish may become soft and gummy because of the frictional heating. If you use a liquid paint or varnish remover to speed the job, let the solvent dry completely before using your pad sander. In all such removal jobs, the loose paint or varnish should be scraped off with a putty knife before the sander is used, to make the sandpaper last longer.

The taped joints and spackled nail head indentations in a new gypsum wall can be smoothed quickly and easily with your pad sander by using a fine grit, open coat abrasive. Similarly, it's a cinch to repair cracks and nail holes (as from old picture hooks) in existing walls by spackling and then sanding smooth with a pad sander. *Caution*: Plaster dust is very abrasive, so do not let it accumulate on or inside your sander; use compressed air (vacuum cleaner) to blow the dust off frequently.

You will find many other practical uses for your pad sander around the house. Buffing the wax on your car is a cinch if you add a lamb's wood pad to your sander (Fig. 10-3). Mount the sander upside down in a vise and use it to buff and polish all sorts of small objects, such as metal jewelry. Experiment with different types of buffing pads, from thin cloth to scraps of carpeting. The use of buffing compound may help the process.

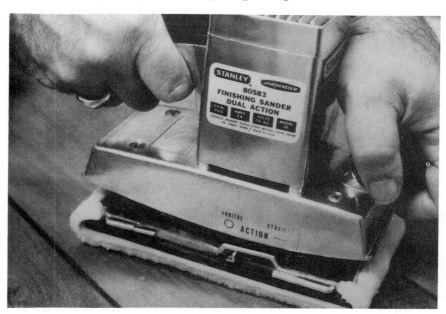

Fig. 10-3. If you add a lamb's wool pad to your sander, you will have a machine to buff and polish many kinds of surfaces and objects.

The sander is also excellent for tough rust-removal jobs. Just go over that decrepit old saw, or other tool, with your sander after fitting it with fine sandpaper. You may be surprised at the big improvement.

Undoubtedly, you will think of still more uses for this versatile tool if you experiment with it.

Section II
Woodworking Techniques

All About Adhesives

MATCH A MODERN ADHESIVE to the job and you can bond almost any material. Often the joint will be solid and waterproof in 5 minutes or less with a strength running to tons per square inch.

One versatile acrylic adhesive, for example, has been applied with a toothpick to mend a broken camera control and smeared on with a brush to bond an aluminum patch to the cracked iron hub of an earth moving machine.

TYPES OF ADHESIVES

Large hardware stores stock most of the modern glues. The remainder are available through marine suppliers or directly from the manufacturer. To pick the right one for the job at hand, you need only the basic facts. For these, let the following data serve as your guide (Fig. 11-1).

Fig. 11-1. With the great variety of adhesives available today, the craftsperson can choose the one perfectly formulated for the job at hand.

Acrylic Resin Adhesive

Acrylic resin adhesive is the fastest setting adhesive generally available. Based on the same formula used in high-strength white dental fillings (you'll recognize the aroma) it sets in as little as 5 minutes to a strength of 3 tons per square inch. It is a two-part type (liquid and powder) with setting time varying from 5 to 20 minutes, according to the mixing proportions of the two components.

Table 11-1. Brand Name Adhesives

Type of Adhesive	Brand Name
Acrylic resin adhesive	3-Ton Adhesive; P.A.C (plastic adhesive cement)
Aliphatic resin glue	Titebond
Buna-N adhesive	Pliobond
Epoxy glue	Ten-set Epoxy
Epoxy, water phase type	Dur-A-Poxy
Hide Glue	Franklin Liquid Hide Glue
Hot-melt resin glues	Thermogrip; Swingline
Polyester resin glue	Fibre-Glass-Evercoat
Polysulphide	Say-Cote
Resorcinol resin glue	U.S. Plywood Resorcinol Waterproof Glue
Rubber base adhesive	Miracle Adhesive

A stiff mix gives short setting time, a wet mix longer setting time. Acrylic resin bonds to most materials including wood, metal, and ceramics. It is completely waterproof and widely used in marine repair work. It is also well suited to many types of delicate repair work, as on cameras, record players, and so on. Clamping is no problem because parts can be hand-held while the adhesive sets. Sold in two-container packages consisting of two cans, or can and plastic jar combination.

Aliphatic Resin Glue

This leading furniture glue is a one-part, beige, liquid type that dries clear. It can also be colored with water-soluble dyes to match the wood finish to be used. It is unaffected by most common finishes.

Tackiness is similar to old-style hot animal glues, making it possible to stick gluing blocks in furniture frame corners without clamping. Where clamps are required, glue is usually firm enough for clamp removal in about an hour. Allow to sit overnight for a complete set.

This glue is moisture-resistant, but not waterproof. It is sold in squeeze bottles.

Buna-N Adhesive

Originally developed for aircraft use, this glue is a one-part, thick, beige liquid that will bond almost any material with a completely flexible and waterproof bond. It can bond fabric to metal or wood, metal to glass, even to bond patches to work clothes with greater strength than stitching.

Joints are usually pressed together while the applied adhesive is still wet.

In fabric-to-fabric bonding the dried adhesive-coated surfaces may be placed together and bonded by heating from the outside of one fabric piece, as with a flatiron. Sold in tubes and cans.

Casein Glue

This adhesive is strong, inexpensive, with good moisture resistance (not waterproof) and gap-filling qualities that are useful in woodworking. It is a cream-colored powder that must be mixed with water for use. It stiffens shortly after mixing, then becomes creamy on restirring.

Follow the manufacturer's instructions carefully, and *do not* add water at the pre-stiffened stage. No longer widely available, it is stocked by cabinetmakers' supply houses and large hardware suppliers under various brand names.

Cellulose Nitrate Cement

Often called household cement or model airplane cement, this is a one-part water-resistant adhesive that is usually clear. (Some forms are tinted to make coated areas visible during work.) Cellulose nitrate cement dries firmly enough for gentle-assembly handling in unstressed work after an hour or two. For regular handling, let stand overnight. It is sold largely in tubes.

Contact Cement

This cement was developed for bonding plastic laminates to plywood counters, and similar applications. Available in very quick-drying (flammable) types and in nonflammable form, it should be applied to both meeting surfaces to be bonded, and allowed to dry completely.

A wrapping paper "slip sheet" should then be placed between the coated surfaces so they can be aligned without touching each other. Next, the sheet should be slipped out while the parts are held in alignment, permitting the cement-coated surfaces to come into contact. A rubber roller is used to ensure firm, full-area contact and work any trapped air bubbles outward to escape at edges.

Contact cement is widely available through hardware stores under many brand names, mainly in cans, but occasionally in tubes.

Epoxy Glue

This two-part adhesive comprises a liquid resin and liquid hardener. Available in both clear and opaque types, epoxy is completely waterproof and will bond most materials.

The usual types set firm overnight and continue to increase in strength for a week or more. They are often used in marine fiberglassing and hull repairs. Quick-setting types are available with hardening times as short as 10 minutes.

As formulas vary widely, follow the manufacturer's instructions when mixing and using any epoxy. When buying, specify the characteristics you require (clear, opaque etc.). Epoxy is sold by hardware and marine suppliers under many brand names.

Epoxy, Water-Phase Type. This form of epoxy is relatively new to the retail market. It may be used either as a coating or as an adhesive, and, prior to setting, can be washed from brushes and tools with water. Once hard, it is completely waterproof.

This two-part adhesive is composed of two liquid components which are mixed in equal proportions for use. Complete setting time is around 8 hours. Unmixed leftovers last indefinitely if containers are tightly closed. It is made in clear, white, and colored forms, and can be tinted with the same dry colors used in cement work.

Water-phase epoxy can also be mixed with portland cement (follow instructions on the adhesive containers) to make a high-strength bonding filler for masonry repairs and similar jobs. The adhesive cement mix has a much shorter setting time than the adhesive alone, so plan to work accordingly.

Ideal for fiberglassing seams on plywood porches and decks, it also is used with mineral granules for non-skid surfaces around swimming pools. It is sold in twin cans.

Hide Glue

This adhesive is available mainly in liquid form through hardware stores, though some cabinetmakers' supply houses still stock the traditional flake-and-sheet form. The latter forms must be water-soaked, then heated for use. Known as ''hot glue,'' this type must be applied to joints and clamped before cooling.

In the common liquid form it is used like any other one-part liquid glue. Usually it will harden overnight into a bond that is stronger than wood, but it is not very moisture-resistant.

Hot-Melt Resin Glues

The polyethylene-base types are used in electric glue gun cartridges. They bond to most materials, and are waterproof and moderately flexible. Because they harden by cooling, they are in the fast-setting class and require quick assembly of the parts to be glued. They are sold in cartridge form to fit specific glue guns.

Multi-resin hot-melt glue is also available for special uses without a glue gun. These usually are sold in foil trays, and are melted on a heating device, such as a hot plate. Types like ''Hot Grip'' are used for bonding to plastics that will not accept other adhesives, such as polyethylene and polypropylene.

Neoprene-Base Adhesives

These glues are widely used in caulking guns to mount wall paneling. Now, combination-resin forms are also used in house frame construction to bond sheathing to framing. Characteristics vary with the brand, and the manufacturer's instructions should be followed carefully.

Polyester Resin Glue

Best known as a boat fiberglassing adhesive, this type is also a strong, quick-setting, waterproof wood glue that can be used clear or colored with pigments sold for the purpose.

It is a two-part type. A liquid resin and a liquid catalyst are mixed just before use. Typically, a specified number of drops of catalyst from a small squeeze bottle are stirred into a quart or pint can of the resin. A portion of the resin may be poured off and mixed with a corresponding portion of catalyst. The amount of catalyst is important; an excess will harden the resin before it can be applied.

Temperature of the working area is also a factor because hardening time shortens as the working area temperature rises. Temperature-hardening time charts are available from suppliers for many resin brands. Do not apply a chart for one brand to another brand of resin; formulas vary widely.

Polyester resin glue is sold in cans, usually with a plastic tube of catalyst in a plastic overcap, by boatyards, marine suppliers, and large hardware outlets. Shelf-life of unused resin varies with brand and storage conditions, so buy it fresh, as needed.

Polysulphide

Also known as Thiokol, this adhesive is widely used as a marine caulking compound, though it is also a strong, completely waterproof adhesive with great flexibility and unusual vibration-damping qualities. The two-part form requires the mixing of two thick pastes. The one-part form sets by reaction with moisture in the air. When set, polysulphide is actually synthetic rubber, so mixed leftovers may be formed into gaskets, tires for toy wheels, etc. Molds with oiled surfaces may be used.

Polyvinyl Acetate Glue

This glue is the familiar one-part "white glue." It is easy to use and stronger than wood, but its strength is affected by high humidity and high temperature. It is handy woodworking glue for joints that do not require the glue, alone, to sustain a prolonged load. (Most furniture joints are designed so the wood takes the load, the glue holds the joint together.) This glue should not be used on bare metal because of the possible corrosive effect. Acetate glue is sold in squeeze bottles under various brand names.

Resorcinol Resin Glue

This two-part adhesive is a two-part (liquid and powder) adhesive generally accepted as the best completely waterproof glue for wood. Originally developed for torpedo boat construction, it is stronger than wood, completely waterproof (even in prolonged boiling), and unaffected by gasoline, oil, mild alkalis, mild acids, or common solvents. A working advantage: before hardening, it can be washed from brushes and tools with water.

Hardening time depends on temperature. Once components are thoroughly mixed according to manufacturer's instructions, the glue will cure in about 10 hours at 70 degrees, or in as little as 3½ hours at 90 degrees.

Mix portions by volume are usually four-measures of the liquid component to three measures of the powder. *Important*: protect your eyes from both parts when mixing. And, before mixing, shake the closed can of powder thoroughly to "fluff" it. It tends to pack during storage, so volume measure is thrown off unless it is shaken up. Resorcinol resin glue is sold in twin cans by hardware stores and marine suppliers.

Rubber-Base Adhesive

A one-part waterproof type that bonds to most materials, this adhesive can be applied as a sealer even under water for emergency repairs. It should not be used where exposed to gasoline or oil, however, as both act on it as solvents. It is sold in tubes and cans by hardware stores.

Urea Formaldehyde Glue

Now usually called plastic resin glue, this one-part powder type is mixed with water for use. It is stronger than wood, and highly water resistant but not quite waterproof. It is not a gap-filler type, however, and requires well-fitted joints. Use this glue for general woodworking, especially where high humidity or high temperatures are likely, as it remains strong under both conditions. It is sold in cans under various trade names.

RULE-OF-THUMB

In woodworking, match the nature of the glue to the job. Thermoplastic adhesives can be softened by heat. Thermosetting ones can't. Thermoplastic glues (like white glue) shouldn't be used on joints where the glue alone must sustain a constant load, as in a simple lap joint. They are fine, however, in joints where the glue holds the joint together and the form of the joint takes the load.

Craftsman's Guide to Joints and Joinery

THE ART AND SCIENCE of woodworking is largely a matter of making joints since most of the things we build consist of two or more individually fabricated parts that are joined one way or another. Obviously, every serious shopworker must know how to make many types of joints well, and must be able to decide what type of joint is most suitable for any given construction project. But it's also fun, and instructive, to make joints as end products in themselves, if for no other reason than to improve one's skills.

TYPES OF JOINTS

Let's discuss the types of joints more commonly used to build everything from bird houses and toys to fine furniture. I suspect that most nonprofessional shopworkers would have to admit their skills in joinery could use improvement. What follows is not a complete guide to joinery instruction; view it as an introduction that you can expand upon by reading more comprehensive textbooks dealing with the subject.

The *butt joint,* which is used extensively in rough construction, is too familiar to require much elaboration. It is rather inelegant, and of itself weak, but adequate in applications where sufficient strength can be imparted through use of glue, nails and screws.

The *rabbet* joint is an improvement over an end butt joint because it provides additional gluing surface and looks somewhat neater. It's used for such things as shelving and cabinets (Fig. 12-1).

A *dado* joint is essentially the same as a rabbet, except that it is used anywhere except at the end of a board, as is the rabbet (Fig. 12-2). Because the end of one board fits snugly into a channel (dado) cut across another board, there is additional structural strength. Glue, nails, and screws can impart more strength when necessary. This is an excellent joint to use when making such things as bookcases without adjustable shelving.

The basic dado joint becomes still stronger, and more stable, when refined into a *dado rabbet* joint in which the dado is made narrower than the end of the board that is to be joined to it; the second board is rabbeted for proper fit, which leaves a shoulder.

Lap joints are of several varieties, but in each case the joint is almost always used on joined pieces of equal thickness. Half

Fig. 12-1. A shaper is a good tool for cutting rabbets. Bevel the edge of the guide strip so that it supports the stock when fed at an angle.

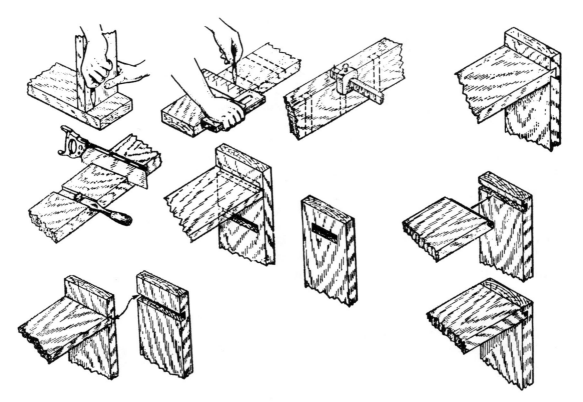

Fig. 12-2. Dado joints take many forms. The drawings at left show a housed dado, the simplest type. Various dodoes can be used for different jobs; a housed dado is good for a bookshelf, but where pulling force is present, a dovetail dado, top right, is a better joint.

the thickness of each member is cut away so that the cut sections can be "lapped" together to form a joint having the same thickness as the boards themselves.

An *end lap* joint has the cuts at the ends of both boards. A *half lap* joint has wood removed from the end of only one member so that the remaining stock fits into a wide notch cut into the other board. A *cross lap* joint uses two interlocking notches cut anywhere except at the ends of the members so that the joined boards actually cross each other. Any of these joints is very easy to make with a circular saw, or even with a handsaw and chisel. A properly made cross lap joint, when fitted together, will hold the parts from falling apart even before glue and other fasteners are added.

The familiar *miter* joints are found at the corners of picture frames, door frames and the like. These are essentially butt joints except that the ends of both members are cut at a 45-degree angle

109

to position the joined members at right angles to each other. In light work, such as small picture frames, the joint is held together with glue and brads (Fig. 12-3). Heavier frames require sturdier fasteners such as dowels, splines, corrugated fasteners, and even angle irons where they are not visually objectionable or are out of sight (Fig. 12-4). A good test of your crafts skills is to make a perfectly joined picture frame in which all four corners are square with joints that reveal no ill-fitting gaps (Fig. 12-5).

In applications that require especially good joint strength, the *mortise and tenon* joint comes into its own. It's one of the strongest general use joints you can make, and is ideal for such projects as chairs, fences and doors. Maximum strength is achieved if the tenon (a tongue-like projection cut into the end of one member) is made one-third the thickness of the stock to which it is to be mated. The mortise, which is the hole into which the tenon fits, should have the same amount of wood on each side of the hole. You can get much joinery practice working with the tenon and

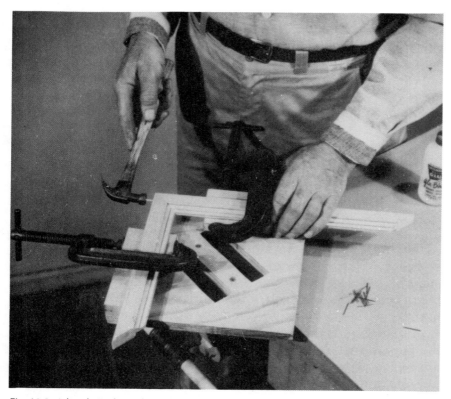

Fig. 12-3. A handy jig for making miter joints consists of two guides set at right angles to each other on a platform. Just clamp and nail.

110

Fig. 12-4. A frame jig will ensure precise alignment of spline slots in mitered frame pieces.

Fig. 12-5. The ubiquitous miter joint is found in virtually every door and picture frame, but is a good test of a craftsman's joinery skill since all four corners must be cut square with no gaps left.

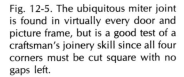

MITER WITH
CORRUGATED
NAILS

MITER WITH
FEATHER JOINT

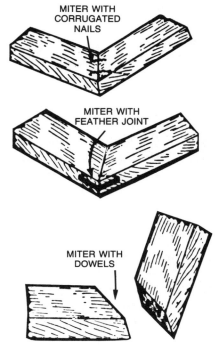

MITER WITH
DOWELS

111

mortise joint because it can be made in several different forms: miter tenon, blind tenon, haunched tenon and through tenon.

The *finger* joint, also called *box* joint, has a series of notches cut into the ends of two boards so that the fingers fit into opposing notches in much the same way that you can interlock the fingers on your own two hands. This is a much stronger way to join the ends of two boards, than with a butt or rabbet joint. Yet it is a relatively easy joint to make. If the fingers are not secured firmly with glue, but are joined by means of a metal pin dropped through a hole drilled through the series of interlocking fingers, you have a moveable joint that works like a hinge (the outer ends of the fingers, and the inner reaches of the notches should be curved slightly). This joint can be used in a fold-away support that holds up a table drop leaf, for example.

A much more elegant and stronger interlocking joint is the *dovetail* which derives its name from the shape of the fingers which resemble the tail of a dove. This joint can be part of your "final exam" in joinery skills provided you make it using only hand tools. If you lack that kind of patience, do it the easy way using a router and a commercially available dovetail template; you'll get a perfect joint on the first try (Fig. 12-6). Because the dovetail is a modified finger joint having wedge-shaped fingers, rather than straightcut fingers, it is much more resistant to being pulled apart. It is the type of corner you see in, for example, drawer construction in quality furniture.

You should become familiar with three different types of dovetail joints: the *through* dovetail in which the tails go all the way through the opposing member; the *blind* or *stop* dovetail in which the fingers stop short of going all the way through; and the *blind miter* dovetail which is cut so that, after assembly, you see not the slightest evidence of the dovetail structure. It's the kind of strong joint that will puzzle the uninitiated who will be hard put to imagine how it is held together so firmly with no evidence of screws, nails, or other fasteners. This joint provides another challenge for advanced craftsmen, rather than for beginners. Refer to woodworking texts for descriptions of this joint.

Many of the joints discussed can be made elaborate with variations. You can look into these on your own by reading up on such joints as: double-rabbet; gain joint; end dado rabbet; splined edge butt joint; doweled edge butt joint; stopped or blind dado joint. Also learn how to use dovetails to lock a straight member onto the side of a cylindrical shape.

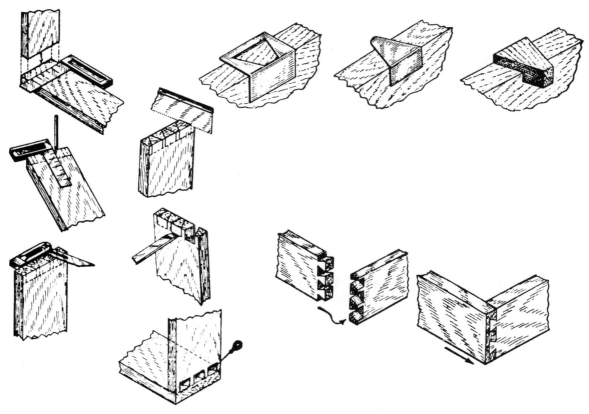

Fig. 12-6. Templates, or forms, above, are a handy way to ensure accuracy when laying out dovetail angles. The other drawings on this page, starting in the top left corner, show the exacting sequence for laying out and hand-cutting dovetails.

Now, a few comments about the use of dowels which can be applied in so many ways to strengthen different kinds of joints and which, in some instances, *are* the main components (in end and edge butt joints, for example): many novice shopworkers avoid using dowels, and stick with less efficient nailing, in the belief that fitting dowels perfectly is too tricky. The biggest problem is getting the holes in the opposing members aligned perfectly so that the parts are not pulled askew on assembly. Solve that problem by purchasing an inexpensive set of *dowel centers*. These are small plugs, with center points, that fit into standard dowel-diameter holes. There are usually four pairs of different sizes per package.

First drill dowel holes in one member to be joined, then place a plug of correct size into each of the holes. When the second member is mated with the first, in exact alignment, the center points on the plugs press tiny prick marks on the other piece of wood to mark the locations of the other set of dowel holes. If you have more than two holes to mate, and only two plugs that fit them, locate and drill out only two matching holes. Fit these with temporary dowels as you use the same plugs to match another pair of holes.

The only other requirement for obtaining a perfect dowel job is to drill the holes perpendicular to the work. A drill press makes this a cinch, or you can use a drilling aid such as Portalign. Lacking either of these conveniences, you can make a simple jig from scrap wood that will ensure that the drill goes in straight.

JOINT CONSTRUCTION

In woodworking, the making of well-fitted and properly constructed joints is of utmost importance. Although nails, screws, bolts, and other types of fasteners are used extensively in the construction and maintenance of a house, the home craftsman should also be familiar with the common joints used in woodworking and with the proper methods of making them before he attempts to construct, alter, or repair furniture or cabinets.

The common joints in woodworking are the lap, butt, rabbet, dado, mortise-and-tenon, dovetail, miter, and tongue-and-groove joints. (See Figs. 12-7 and 12-8.)

LAP JOINTS

The types of lap joints are the half lap, halved cross lap, end or corner lap, and middle half lap (Fig. 12-9). They are used in the construction of bookshelves, stretchers on chairs, easels, kitchen cabinets, and in similar projects.

The middle half lap joint is laid out by superimposing one piece of the wood upon the other to mark accurately the width of each cut. Then clamp the two pieces together in a vise, and with the tri square draw the lines for the width of this cut accurately square across both work edges. Remove the work from the vise, and again using the tri square, square the shoulder lines of both the face and the edge of the work. Gauge and mark the depth of the required notches with the marking gauge.

Again secure the work in the vise, and saw down to the required depth with the backsaw. Be sure to make the saw cuts on the waste part of the stock. If the notches are more than ¾ inch in width, make several cuts to facilitate the removal of the waste

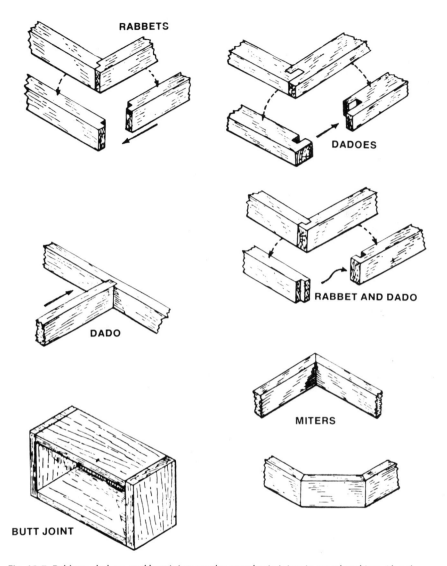

Fig. 12-7. Rabbets, dadoes, and butt joints are the most basic joints in woodworking. Also shown is the common rabbet and dado combination joint.

material. Chisel down to the gauge line on each side of the notch. To prevent breaking the grain of the wood and to produce a clean, smooth cut, the chisel should be slanted outward very slightly. The final step in the making of the middle lap joint is to finish the cut to a uniform depth (Fig. 12-10).

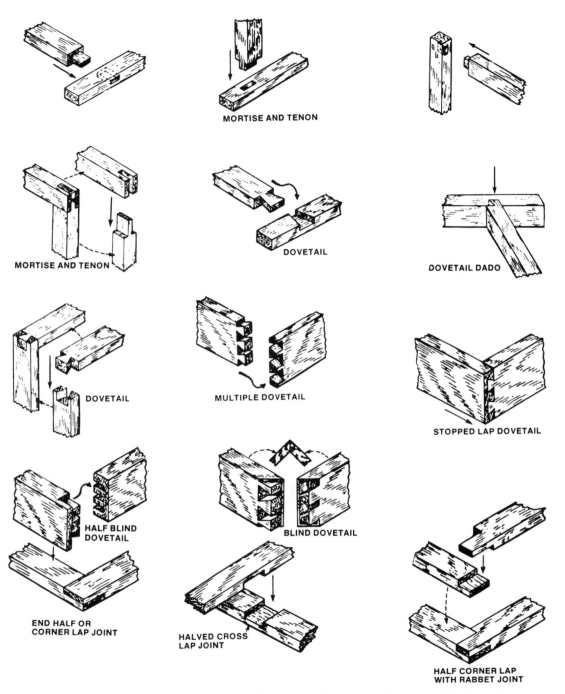

MORTISE AND TENON

MORTISE AND TENON

DOVETAIL

DOVETAIL DADO

DOVETAIL

MULTIPLE DOVETAIL

STOPPED LAP DOVETAIL

HALF BLIND DOVETAIL

BLIND DOVETAIL

END HALF OR CORNER LAP JOINT

HALVED CROSS LAP JOINT

HALF CORNER LAP WITH RABBET JOINT

Fig. 12-8. The dovetail joint is an advanced technique by which woodworkers gauge their level of skill. Several variations are shown above.

116

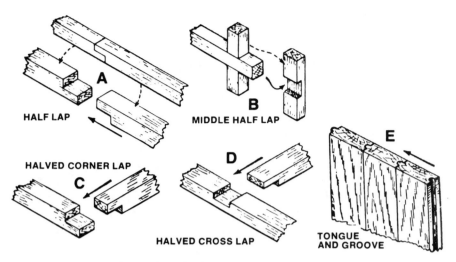

Fig. 12-9. Lap joints are frequently used in the construction of chairs, easels, bookshelves, cabinets, and the like.

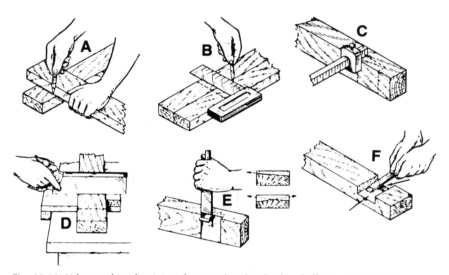

Fig. 12-10. When making lap joints, be sure that the depths of all cuts are accurate.

BUTT JOINTS

The butt joint is the simplest joint and is the only one in which nails or screws must be used. It is used only for rough construction. Though it is extremely simple to make, test the edges to be joined for absolute squareness with the try square before the pieces are fitted together.

117

RABBET JOINTS

Rabbet joints are formed by recesses or rabbets, cut out on the edges of the work so that they may be fitted into each other or secured further with a spline fitting into them (Fig. 12-11). Rabbet joints are used in the construction of cabinets, table tops, and similar projects. The rabbet joints commonly used are the rabbet on end and the rabbet on edge. The shiplap and the rabbet and fillet are two variations of the lap joint.

To make a rabbet on end, lay out the joint by squaring a line for the side or shoulder of the joint across the face of the board and down the edges. This line should be as far from the end of the board as the thickness of the joining piece. Then gauge the required depth of the rabbet, and mark the lines on the two edges and on the end with the marking gauge. Cut out the material.

DADOES

Dado joints are grooves cut across the grain of the board into which a second piece of wood is fitted accurately. They are used in the construction of end tables, cabinets, bookcases, and similar projects. A housed dado joint is one in which the entire end of the second piece fits into the dado, or groove. In a stopped or gained dado joint, the dado does not extend entirely across the

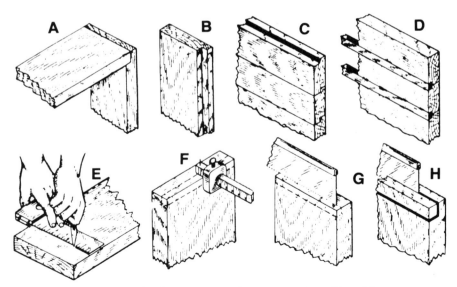

Fig. 12-11. Rabbet joint with spline (D) can combine construction with an inlay.

face of the work. Other types are the dovetail and shoulder-housed dado. (See Fig. 12-12.)

To lay out a plain dado, set the board to be housed on end on the face of the board in which the dado is to be cut, and mark the width of the dado accurately on the face of the board. Square lines with a tri square across the face of the board through the marks and down both edges. Then mark the required depth with a gauge, connecting the two marked lines. Using a backsaw, make the necessary cuts; remove the waste wood with a chisel.

A stopped dado is laid out in the same manner as a plain dado, with the exception that it does not extend across the full width of the board.

The dovetail, housed, and grooved types are three other variations of the dado joint.

A combined dado-and-rabbet joint is laid out and made in the same manner as a plain dado, except that a rabbet, or a recess, is cut on the end of the housed piece.

MORTISE AND TENON

The mortise and tenon joint is used extensively by skilled woodworkers. When properly laid out and accurately made, it is strong and dependable (Fig. 12-13). To ensure maximum strength and rigidity, it must be fitted very accurately. Mortise and tenon joints are used in the construction of desks, tables, chairs, and cabinet furniture that will be subject to hard usage. While there are several kinds of these joints, the directions given here are for the type known as the blind mortise and tenon joint. The description and drawings of the procedure in making this joint will help the woodworker to lay out and make any of the other types.

The tenon section should be made first. Cut and square both pieces of the work to the desired dimension and plainly mark both faces of each piece for easy identification. From the end of the piece in which the tenon is to be cut, measure back a distance equal to the length of the tenon, then square the shoulder line and mark it around this piece.

For general purposes, the tenon in this type of joint should be one-quarter to one-half as thick as the entire board. To lay out the thickness of the tenon correctly, locate the exact center of one edge, accurately measure with a rule one-half the thickness of the tenon each way from the center, and mark these places with the point of a knife-blade or a brad awl. Set a marking gauge to these

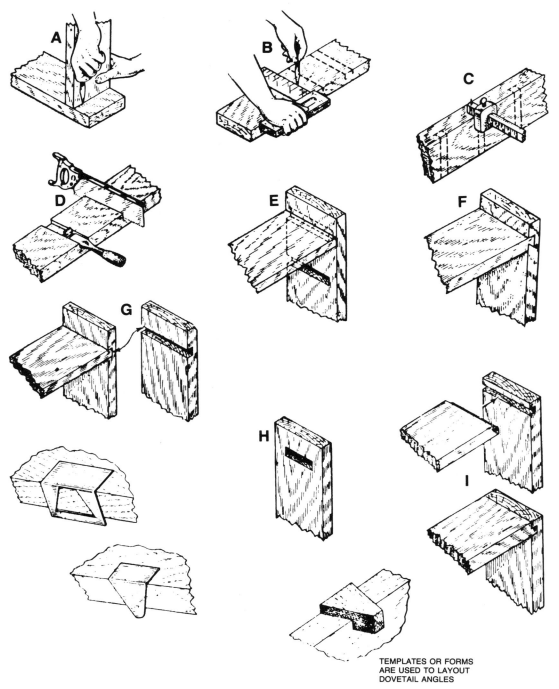

TEMPLATES OR FORMS
ARE USED TO LAYOUT
DOVETAIL ANGLES

Fig. 12-12. Dado joints take many forms. Drawing G is a house dado, the simplest of dado joints. In selecting the type of dado in G is fine for a bookshelf, but a dovetail dado as in F should be used where a pulling force tends to separate the joint.

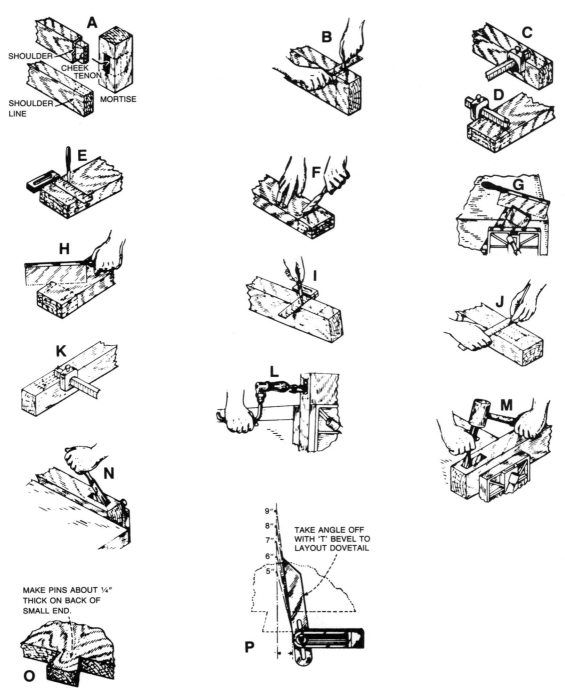

Fig. 12-13. The mortise-and-tenon (A-N) is as it appears—a very strong joint giving rigid support to a variety of furniture on wood projects that are subject to hard usage. Layout technique for dovetails is shown in O and P.

points, and mark both lines across the end and down both edges to the shoulder line previously marked around the board. All gauging must be done from the face side of the work.

The width of the tenon also must be laid out very carefully, and the lines gauged through these points across the end and down both sides to the shoulder line. With the tri square as a guide and using the point of a sharp knife, score the shoulder line repeatedly, to a depth of about $\frac{1}{16}$ inch.

Fasten the work securely in the vise, and using a very sharp chisel, cut a narrow triangular groove along the outside of the scored line on the waste material. Fasten the work at an angle in the vise, and with a backsaw proceed to cut the cheeks of the tenon to the shoulder line.

Change the position of the piece in the vise so the next cut will be made square with the face of the work. Now proceed to cut the shoulder of the tenon to the required dimension with the backsaw.

The length of the mortise must equal the width of the tenon. To determine the position of the mortise, square lines with the tri square across the work. Locate the exact center of the piece, and measure each way from the center exactly one-half the thickness of the tenon to lay out the correct width of the mortise on the other board. Mark these points now, and carefully check the width of the mortise to make sure that it is equal to the thickness of the tenon. Gauging from the working face, mark through these points, stopping at the end of the mortise. A center line should also be gauged lengthwise of the mortise.

Secure the work firmly in a vise. Select an auger bit $\frac{1}{16}$ inch smaller than the width of the mortise, and adjust the bit gauge to bore holes $\frac{1}{8}$ inch deeper than the length of the tenon. Place the spur on the bit on the center line, keeping the bit exactly perpendicular to the face of the work. Begin boring a series of overlapping holes, with the first hole just touching the end of the mortise and the last hole touching the opposite end.

With the work held securely in the vise, and using a small, sharp chisel, clean out the waste material by cutting out both sides of the mortise as the depth increases. Pare the walls of the mortise to the gauge line, keeping them perpendicular to the face of the work. The final step is to square the ends and remove waste material from the bottom by using a chisel a little narrower than the width of the mortise.

DOVETAIL JOINTS

Dovetail joints are used by skilled woodworkers in the construction of fine furniture, drawers for tables or desks, and projects where good appearance and strength are desired. A dovetail joint has considerable strength, due to the flare of the projections, called pins, on the ends of the boards, which fit exactly into similarly shaped dovetails. The spaces between the pins and between the dovetails are called sockets, or mortises. The pins are visible on the ends of the work, and the dovetails are visible on the face of the work.

The angle of the dovetail must not be made too acute; this would defeat the purpose of additional strength because an acute angle is weakened by the short grain at the corners of the angle.

The first step in determining the angle of the dovetail is to square a line from the edge of the board, measuring 5, 6, 7, 8, or 9 inches along the board from the edge. Measure from the line along the edge, and connect the points with a line. To mark the other angles make a template, that is, a pattern of cardboard or thin wood, of the angle selected, and use it as a guide.

While the strongest joints are those in which the pins and the dovetails are the same size, for the sake of appearance the dovetails are usually made larger than the pins, though not more than four times the width of the pins. The thickness of the pin and the width of the dovetails will vary in a great many instances, but it is considered good practice to make the pin or its corresponding socket about ¼ inch on the narrow side.

To make the common single dovetail joint with two half tongues and a whole dovetail, first locate the shoulder lines of the joint by measuring the thickness of each piece of wood. Mark the position of the shoulder line and square the line. On one piece, lay out the tongue with a template and cut to required size. Saw the sides of this piece with the backsaw and then remove the waste material to the shoulder line with a chisel. Hold this piece on the other board to mark the shape of the dovetail. Cut out with saw and chisel.

A multiple dovetail joint is merely a series of single dovetails extending along the entire length of the end of the board (Fig. 12-14).

MITER JOINTS

Miter joints are used often in making picture frames and screens. They are merely butt joints with the angle at the corner

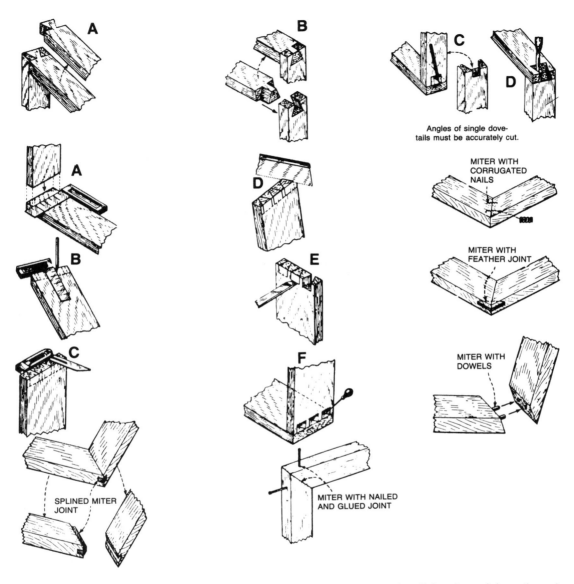

Fig. 12-14. The multiple dovetail (A-F) demands even greater accuracy in cutting so that all the pins and dovetails mesh.

halved between the two pieces that are to be joined. Miter joints are usually cut at an angle of 45 degrees. While it is a simple matter to mark out an angle of 45 degrees, miter joints are usually sawed in a miter box.

A miter box is an accurate tool for reproducing an angle of cut, from 30 to 90 degrees, in pieces that are to be fitted together.

The material is set in the miter box at the required angle and is cut with the backsaw. When a large number of miter joints are to be nailed or glued together, a special clamp or picture frame vise is used.

Dowels, tongues, or slip feathers are sometimes used instead of nails to strengthen the joint further. When tongued miter joints are made, each of the pieces is grooved, and a wooden tongue of required size is glued into the groove. This strengthens the miter joints, and also prevents warping. For more detailed instruction on miters and dovetails see next chapter.

TONGUE-AND-GROOVE JOINTS

It is impractical to make tongue-and-groove joints in the home workshop, as finished tongue-and-groove lumber, when specified, is supplied by the dealer.

Master Craftsmen's Joinery Methods

IN ROUGH CONSTRUCTION and in much carpentry you can put joints together with nails, but in furniture making the fastenings must be concealed. Doweling is an easy solution. Well made dowel joints are amply strong for most work. A typical use is in the corner of a frame, where the end of a rail butts against a stile edge, or where the rail combines with a cabinet leg or post, and again when two stretchers come together to form a T (Fig. 13-1).

USING DOWELS

In the simplest assembly, dowels pass through the stile into the rail, a satisfactory fastening where the frame edge will be covered by other wood or by opaque paint. To bore holes, clamp the well-fitting pair in a vise, making sure that the parts meet at right angles with the face sides in exact alignment. (See Fig. 13-2.) When one piece is thinner than the other, shim it. Mark meeting parts A-A for the first joint, B-B for the second, and so on.

Next, gauge a centered pencil line along the edge of the stile to be bored, and make cross marks to indicate dowel centers. As

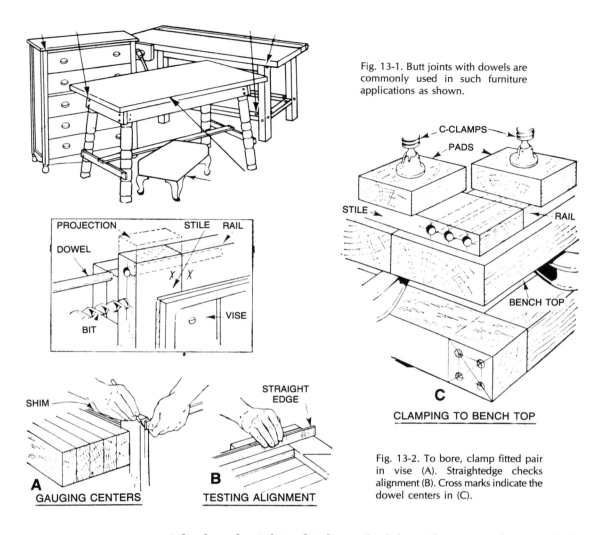

Fig. 13-1. Butt joints with dowels are commonly used in such furniture applications as shown.

PROJECTION STILE RAIL
DOWEL
VISE
BIT

C-CLAMPS
PADS
STILE
RAIL
BENCH TOP

C

CLAMPING TO BENCH TOP

SHIM
STRAIGHT EDGE

A
GAUGING CENTERS

B
TESTING ALIGNMENT

Fig. 13-2. To bore, clamp fitted pair in vise (A). Straightedge checks alignment (B). Cross marks indicate the dowel centers in (C).

a tight dowel might split the end of the stile, space the near hole down a little, say ⅝ inch, and the second hole ½ inch from the level of the inside edge of the rail. A third dowel would be centered between the others.

For ¾- to 1-inch stock, dowels ⅜ inch in diameter are commonly used. If the wood has alternating hard and soft grain, punch a starting hole for the auger bit with a small nail set. For boring, sight along the rail to parallel the bit with the work; if you're inexperienced, press a short straightedge against the face of the joint to check the bit direction. Continue boring until the hole in the rail is 1¼ inch deep. A bit gauge is valuable here.

Cut dowel pins slightly under-length, lightly chamfering one end of each. Apply glue to pins and holes and assemble frame, driving pins in. Clamp enough to close the joints, saw off projecting dowels, and clamp tightly. Pad blocks under the clamp jaws not only prevent marring of the edges but allow for dowels that might protrude as the points are tightened. Test for squareness.

If frame is twisted when taken from the clamps, sight along the sides to see if they are sprung. If not, joints are probably cut out of true, a condition shown by laying a straightedge across each. Correct by sawing along the joints, fitting them more accurately, and doweling again.

Dress the joints with light planing and scraping, drawing scraper diagonally across to prevent tearing the wood. Sand as far as possible lengthwise of the grain. Secure work to the bench top with C-clamps for boring through dowel holes. If stock is nearly square, or thick, a better spread of dowels is possible by centering them on a diagonal. For greater strength, use four dowels.

Through-doweling is featured in certain provincial furniture. The rail or apron is lapped over a leg and dowel holes are bored through. Square guidelines across the rails, or in "splayed" work—legs spreading toward the floor—use a bevel square. Bore rail separately and use as a template for marking the legs (Fig. 13-3).

Often dowels are featured in furniture decoration being cut long enough to project as a rounded button, or, cut a little short to leave the hole unfilled to the top, a commercial button plugging the cavity. Sometimes pieces are screwed together, the screwhead being countersunk so that a button, glued in, hides the screw.

In blind, or hidden doweling, you must match up holes in the edges of the stiles with those bored in the rail ends, a situation much like that of doweling boards edge-to-edge. First, join frame corners. After the squared rail end has been fitted to the stile edge, set a marking gauge for half the thickness of the wood, and working from the face side, scribe a line on the joint edge of the stile and on the rail end. Square lines across the rail end to locate centers, punch them, and bore, taking every precaution to keep them square with the end. A doweling jig is a useful accessory (see Fig. 13-4).

Mark dowel centers on the stile with the rail as a pattern; have the working faces of both to the same side and the working edges corresponding, usually the inside edges of the completed frame. Drill holes in a vertical position while pieces are held in the bench vise; in hardwood it is easier to drill end grain horizontally.

Cut dowels ⅛ inch short so they will not hold the joints open, and to allow for air and glue imprisoned in the holes. Chamfer the ends slightly to keep them from tearing the wood as they are forced in. Test frame assembly for alignment, but don't force the dowels too far in the holes if they are very tight, as it might be impossible to pull them out. Whether the joint is flat when clamped can be tested without the dowels. A frame that will not lie flat after assembly will eventually twist, even though it has been brought flat in the clamps and while drying.

In some period tables and cabinets, aprons and rails are set flush with the legs or posts, and the doweling layout is the same as above. When aprons or rails are set back ¼ to ⅜ inch from the faces of the legs, the marking gauge, after centerlining the rail ends, must be reset for the leg, allowing for the offset (Fig 13-5). That is, if T represents the thickness of the rail, set gauge for flush construction, as ½T, and use for marking legs and rails. For the offset, set gauge at 0—amount of offset plus ½T.

DUPLICATING JOINTS

Most pieces of furniture require duplication in joints. For instance, a rectangular table has eight joints between apron and legs, requiring eight separate layouts for dowel holes. Some time is saved by clamping the rails together with working edges down and facing sides all to right or left, so that four ends at once can be marked with dividers by sliding one point along the bench top. A marking template of sheet metal, plastic, or fiber, having a strip of wood nailed along the edge for a fence, and one at the end for a stop, locates dowel holes quickly and accurately.

One set of pricks can be made for use with a stile, where it is cut long to project some definite account, and another for the rail (which must be measured from the edge, and not from the stile projection). If stile is cut to net length, use the same set of pricks for both. Such a template is right- or left-handed, and will work only on one end of a piece (Fig. 13-6). To make it both right- and left-handed, add guides on the upper sides, aligning them with those beneath. For marking offset legs, make a second row of pricks.

Legs of upholstered furniture are often doweled to the lower edges of nailed or doweled frames. A triangular block glued into

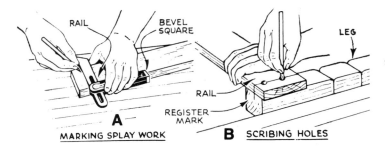

Fig. 13-3. In splayed work (A) bevel square is used; rail bored separately is a template (B).

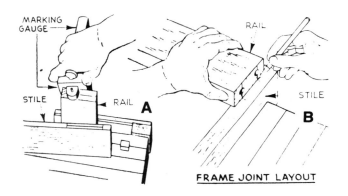

Fig. 13-4. Joining frame corners for blind doweling. A doweling jig is a helpful accessory.

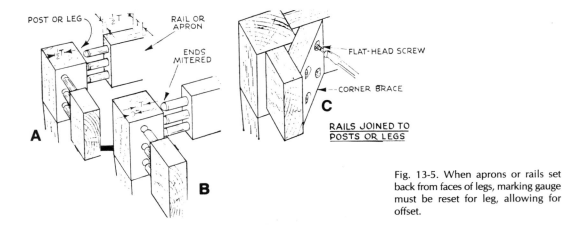

Fig. 13-5. When aprons or rails set back from faces of legs, marking gauge must be reset for leg, allowing for offset.

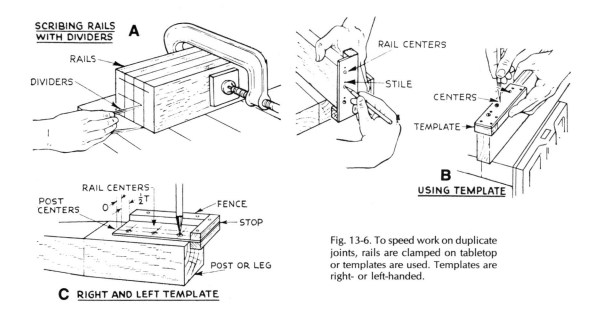

SCRIBING RAILS WITH DIVIDERS **A**

RAILS

DIVIDERS

RAIL CENTERS

STILE

CENTERS

TEMPLATE

B
USING TEMPLATE

RAIL CENTERS

POST CENTERS

O $\frac{1}{2}T$

FENCE

STOP

POST OR LEG

C RIGHT AND LEFT TEMPLATE

Fig. 13-6. To speed work on duplicate joints, rails are clamped on tabletop or templates are used. Templates are right- or left-handed.

each corner of a frame gives stock for boring ¾-inch dowel holes. The shaped legs are hard to gauge, but the dowel holes can be measured from the edges at the tops of the legs. Wrap the leg in a soft cloth and clamp lightly in a vise for boring. Incidentally, ready-shaped, carved and finished legs in many patterns can be purchased.

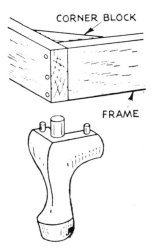

CORNER BLOCK

FRAME

Fig. 13-7. Legs of some furniture are doweled to frames. Holes can be bored into triangular corner block. Ready-shaped, finished legs are available in a variety of patterns. Wrap legs and lightly clamp the vise for drilling.

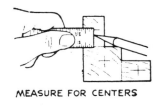

MEASURE FOR CENTERS

USING DRAWBOLTS

Tough joints for heavy jobs, such as workbenches are obtained by the use of drawbolts (Fig. 13-8). They can be tightened when shrinkage or work strains have loosened them, and are easily disassembled for knocking down or packing. In accompanying drawing, the top rails of a bench are bolted to the legs. Square the joining members to fit snugly. Bore two centered bolt holes through each leg at right angles to each other, one enough above the other to miss it and both square with the faces; in 4 x 4 inch or heavier timber bore half-way in from opposite faces. While holes can be made slightly larger than the bolts for fitting ease, it isn't necessary in careful work and lessens the rigidity of the joint. Next, bore a hole from the inside face of each mating rail to receive the nut and washer. It must be large enough to allow free turning of the nut, with the edge about 1¼ inch from the end of the rail. The joint is stronger if the hole doesn't pass through the rail, although this may at times be a convenience, as the nut can then be tightened from either side by driving a nail set against the corners. Chisel a flat on the rail-end side to seat the washer. Bore the bolt hole from the end into the nut hole. To assemble the joint, pass a carriage bolt through the leg and into the rail far enough

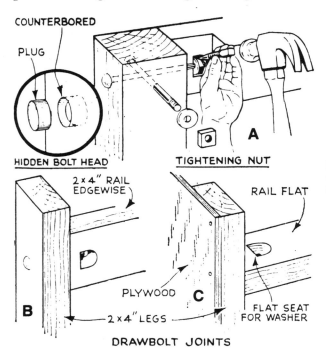

COUNTERBORED

PLUG

HIDDEN BOLT HEAD

TIGHTENING NUT

2 x 4" RAIL EDGEWISE

RAIL FLAT

PLYWOOD

2 x 4" LEGS

FLAT SEAT FOR WASHER

A

B

C

DRAWBOLT JOINTS

Fig. 13-8. Joints for heavy jobs like workbenches are obtained by use of drawbolts, shown.

to slip on a washer and nut, running up the nut with the fingers. Align the members before final tightening. Join posts and rails of rectangular section similarly by passing the bolt through the thickness of the leg and putting the rail in a vertical plane, or turning the rail to the horizontal, a better plan if drawers are to be built under the bench. For trim, closed-in appearance cover the ends with ¼-inch plywood, recessed to fit over the bolt heads.

Tabletops require special fastening to the understructure, but are often attached even in commercial furniture without much regard to requirements (Fig. 13-9). A plywood top, which neither shrinks nor swells, can be fixed solidly with screws. Bore the hole at an angle from the top edge of the apron, coming out inside about 1¼ inch from the edge. Gouge out a clearance cavity with a flat bottom and enter a flat-head screw that will go about ½ inch into the tabletop. Position the top by laying it face down upon a pad, and set the leg structure upside down on it, sliding it around to equalize projection. Run a pencil around the apron's outside for relocating in case the frame should be shifted. An inexpensive fastening is cleats screwed to tabletop and aprons. Rabbeted hardwood blocks locking into apron grooves or metal clips are also satisfactory.

To secure a tabletop made from solid lumber, provide sliding holders. Such a top may increase in width ¾ inch during damp weather, shrinking correspondingly when dry. If solidly attached during damp seasons, the glue joints will break open or checks will appear when it shrinks during dry spells, unless the outer fasteners tear loose. If screwed tight in dry weather, swelling will buckle it.

Fig. 13-9. Tabletops require special fastenings, several of which are seen here. Metal clips are common today.

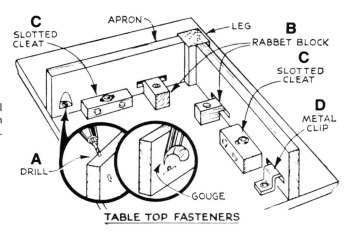

Fasteners allow movement when used as shown, being set away from the side aprons in dry-weather assembly and tight against them in wet times; clips are used in the same way. Slotted cleats with screws through washers into the tabletop, are satisfactory. Use a solid fastening at the middle of each end, which will overcome any tendency of the top to creep toward one edge or the other.

RABBETS, GROOVES AND DADOES

Even if you bungle with hand tools, you can make good furniture joints with your table saw. The rigid guidance from the fence and miter gauge demand only that you follow a few rules on setup and handling.

A practical way to rabbet the edge of a board, is to saw both sides. The table saw is unexcelled for edging rabbeted plywood cupboard doors. Remove the splitter and the guard, if it is mounted on the splitter. The operation is quite safe, for the saw is buried in the wood.

As in ripping, the rip fence guides the cuts (Fig. 13-10). To cut into the edge, set the fence at the required distance from the blade, measuring from a tooth set toward the fence, if the thickness of the flange is critical, or from a tooth set away from it, if the rabbeted face is to slide against the fence. This puts the kerf in the waste wood. Set the blade projection above the table accurately, for if it is too high it will score a crease in the corner of the rabbet, and if it is too low, the waste strip will have to be split out. Verify the setting with a test cut in a scrap piece.

Make the cut by feeding forward against the saw while pressing the board against the fence. Obviously, any rocking of the board against the fence would result in an irregular cut. If the piece is wide, face the fence with a high board, preferably made of plywood to prevent warping, attaching it with bolts or screws. If no holes are present in the fence, screw wooden clips to the back to clasp the fence.

To saw the face cut, reset the fence and the saw projection, and run the edge against the fence. As always, observe safety rules, and use a push stick on short or narrow work. The sawed rabbet is usually smooth enough for ordinary joints, with a ripsaw making the roughest cut, a combination blade a little smoother, and the hollow-ground blade producing a rabbet ready for fine sanding. A rough rabbet can be dressed with a rabbet plane or with a cabinet scraper. When more than one rabbet is being sawed, save time

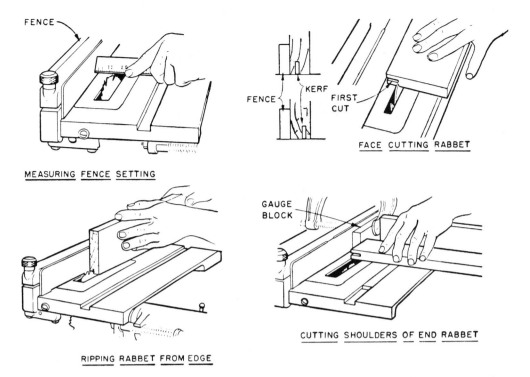

FENCE

MEASURING FENCE SETTING

FENCE KERF FIRST CUT

FACE CUTTING RABBET

RIPPING RABBET FROM EDGE

GAUGE BLOCK

CUTTING SHOULDERS OF END RABBET

Fig. 13-10. The rip fence guides your cuts. Verify blade setting with test cut in scrap. Note block in shoulder cut.

by ripping all pieces with the first setup, then changing over for the second cut.

When ripping an end rabbet, as shown in Fig. 13-10, a high auxiliary fence is necessary to ensure a vertical position for the piece. The shoulder of the rabbet is crosscut, the distance from the end of the cut being gauged with a block clamped to the rip fence where it will engage the end before the start of the cut. The rod gauge can also be used. For a single rabbet it is usually sufficient to make a pencil mark on the forward edge of the piece.

With a dado head the rabbet is cut in one pass; if it is wide, two or more passes may be needed (Fig. 13-11). When cutting a wide rabbet more than ½ inch deep, make more than one stroke. Most home workshop heads can be built up to a width of ¾ inch or ¹³⁄₁₆ inch. Arrange the cutters as illustrated, with the swaged, or spread edges of the inside cutters (chippers) evenly spread and those next to the blades set in the openings between groups of teeth.

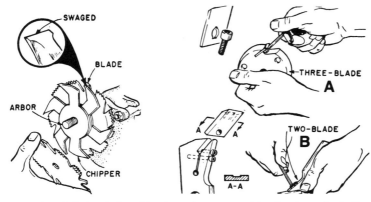

Fig. 13-11. With a dado head, the rabbet is cut in one pass. Most heads can be built up to ¾ inch width. Arrange cutters as shown at near right. Molding head is also a good tool for rabbeting. Two types: the 3-blade type (A) far right, 2-blader (B) below it.

The dado head is filed in a set, with the chippers cutting a little shallower than the blades, and the rabbets cut are a little uneven. This roughness is easily smoothed.

When using the dado head, the regular saw insert is replaced with another having a wider slot. To cut an edge rabbet the dado head must work to the edge of the board, or a little beyond. For this reason, an auxiliary fence is used, the projecting side of the dado head cutting into it. If the rabbet is too wide to make in one pass, cut the shoulder first and then shift to cut the remainder. In ordinary narrow rabbets the cut is made from the face or edge, depending on which is more convenient. If made from the edge, the flange can run between the fence and the dado head, and no auxiliary fence will be needed.

A molding head is another fine tool for rabbeting. Two popular styles are available—a 3-bladed kind and a 2-bladed. The blades are locked in position with socket set-screws. To ensure alignment, be sure that blades and seats are free from dirt.

As with the dado head, the ordinary rabbet is cut in one pass when the molding head is used. Handling of the work is almost the same for both. The cutters plane the rabbet smooth, leaving sharp corners. When rabbeting the end of a board, it is best to saw the shoulder to avoid tearing as the blades cross the grain. A backing strip between the edge of the board and the miter gauge is advisable to prevent splintering of the edge. As in crosscutting wide boards, the miter gauge can be turned end-for-end in the slot to seat better when working wide boards.

Grooving can be done with an ordinary saw blade. Set the fence for ripping one side, and then the other. Practically all the waste is removed by making several cuts between. This is done on the *Shopsmith* by setting the saw by quill movement, moving the hand lever to advance the blade for successive cuts. Lock the quill for each cut.

A setup for grooving by the wobble saw method is shown in Fig. 13-12. The blade is mounted on the arbor in a tilted position and, upon turning, cuts a swath in the board as wide as the throw of the saw. The depth is controlled by elevating or depressing the arbor or table. The only accessory needed is a pair of wooden washers equally tapered in thickness. Place one behind the blade and the other in front, with tapers in opposite direction. When the nut is tightened, the setup is complete. Since centrifugal force

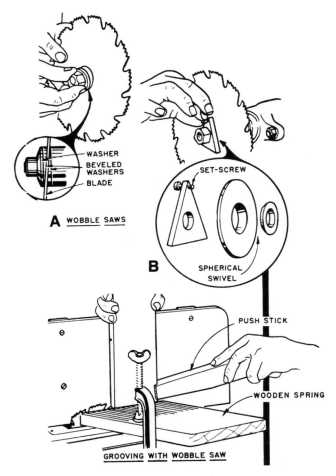

Fig. 13-12. Grooving with ordinary blade. Swath is as wide as throw of saw and depth is controlled by elevating or depressing table.

springs the blade slightly to a more vertical position, it grooves a little narrower than is indicated by the tilt, and for this reason the machine should not be stopped or started while the blade is in the cut.

Commercial devices make a wobble setup easy. The one shown has a washer swiveling on a spherical hub, to be placed behind the blade, where it adapts itself to any lean. A triangular plate located in front has a set-screw in one corner which, bearing against the blade, makes of the triangle a tapered washer giving the arbor nut full bearing.

To set up, adjust the device to make a normal cut. With this as a centerline, set the fence half the groove width away, lean the top of the blade against it, and run out the set-screw to touch it. Tighten the arbor nut and turn by hand to see that it clears the insert slot. If a test cut proves the setting inaccurate, loosen the arbor nut and adjust the screw.

Edge and face grooving is largely a duplication of rabbeting, except that the fence is set back at the required amount to space the groove from the face or edge of the board.

The grooving of the end of a piece with a wobble saw is illustrated in Fig. 13-12. The setup with a wooden spring bearing against the lower end and a push stick propelling the piece is excellent for duplication, not only for grooving but for all end sawing. The wooden spring is made by sawing kerfs $\frac{3}{16}$ inch apart for a distance of 4 inches in a piece of hardwood having ends mitered 45 degrees across the face. Set it close enough to the fence so that the work, in passing between, will spring the fingers out.

The dado head is a standard grooving tool. Using one blade, a $\frac{1}{8}$-inch-wide slot is made; two blades, $\frac{1}{4}$ inch. Other widths, in jumps of $\frac{1}{16}$ inch or $\frac{1}{8}$ inch are obtainable by inserting chippers between the cutters, and fine adjustments are made by using paper or thin cardboard washers between. Set for depth of cut and adjust the fence for locating the groove on the edge or face of the work.

By substituting the dado head with knives of proper width, smooth grooves can be cut rapidly. If more than one groove is to be made, move the fence to a new position. When several pieces are to be milled with two grooves, save time by inserting a wooden strip of proper width between the fence and work to space for one groove, removing it for cutting the second. This completes the grooving in a piece so that it can be piled back out of the way.

It often happens that a rabbet or groove must be "stopped" (discontinued a distance from one or both ends of the piece). If one end is to be open, advance the piece over the cutter until the end of the rabbet or groove, indicated by a pencil mark on the piece, is reached; or a stop block can be clamped to the table or fence where it will stop forward motion at the right time (Fig. 13-13). Should both edges be rabbeted and stopped at the same end, forming a pair, work from one side of the fence and then the other.

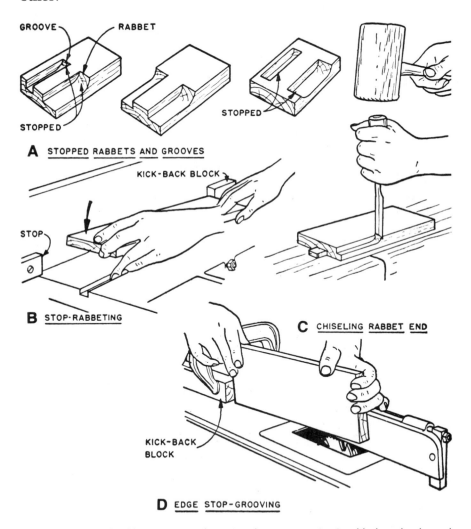

A STOPPED RABBETS AND GROOVES

B STOP-RABBETING

C CHISELING RABBET END

D EDGE STOP-GROOVING

Fig. 13-13. "Stopped" rabbets or grooves discontinued at a pre-set point. Stop block can be clamped to table as in (B). When both ends of rabbet are closed, clamp block to near end of table to prevent kickback (B and D). Chisel is used to trim groove or the rabbet square.

When both ends of the rabbet are closed, clamp a block to the near end of the table or fence to prevent kickback. With the end of the piece bearing against this, slowly lower the forward end over the revolving cutter until full depth is reached, when it is fed forward. Stop at a pencil mark, or upon contacting a stopblock forward.

Grooves and rabbets can be trimmed square with a chisel. Stop grooving of an edge is illustrated.

Tapered rabbets or grooves run bias with the length of the board, are handled in a tapering operation, using either the notched stick or adjustable tapering jig (Fig. 13-14). To avoid splintering the arris of the side cut against the grain when using a molding head, feed slowly. With some work the use of the dado head is best, the saws cutting clean shoulders.

A *dado*, also called a *gain*, is a groove cut across the board. Support the edge of the piece against the miter gauge, as in crosscutting, locating the spacing of the dadoes by means of pencil marks or by using the rod gauge. On long pieces use a miter gauge extension or auxiliary head, to which blocks can be clamped or screwed to determine dado positions. Multiple cutting with an ordinary blade, a wobble saw, or a dado head are effective for dadoing.

To cut small notches in the corner of a board, hold it upright against a deep miter-gauge auxiliary head to tip the side, then rest it on edge to cut the shoulder.

A hand accessory you can make yourself is a snap-on auxiliary fence. Saw the notched cleats from a single piece of 2- × -4 inch stock, notching the ends as shown in Fig. 13-15 and sawing the pieces apart with the tapered cut. Attach to the board with flat-head wood screws countersunk flush. Protect with a couple of coats of shellac.

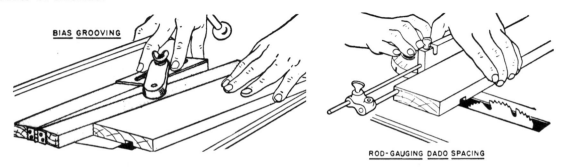

Fig. 13-14. For tapered rabbets or grooves, dado head (below) is used for clean shoulders. Pencil marks or rod gauge (right) can be employed to locate spacing of dadoes.

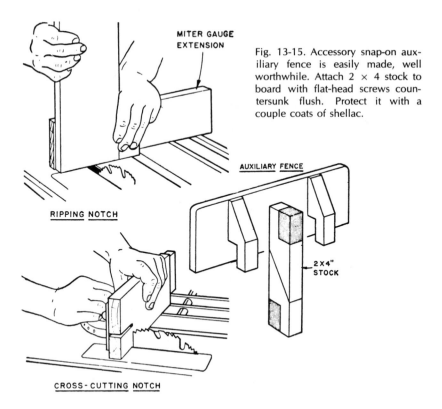

MITER GAUGE EXTENSION

Fig. 13-15. Accessory snap-on auxiliary fence is easily made, well worthwhile. Attach 2 × 4 stock to board with flat-head screws countersunk flush. Protect it with a couple coats of shellac.

AUXILIARY FENCE

2 X 4" STOCK

RIPPING NOTCH

CROSS-CUTTING NOTCH

MITER AND HOPPER JOINTS

Probably the simplest miter joint is the face miter in which the ends of two boards are cut at an angle of 45 degrees to make a square corner, such as in cabinet doors. If the joint is used in "rustic work," where the roughness of undressed lumber is displayed for textured effects, the ordinary combination blade will cut a satisfactory joint.

The setup for such a rough job is very simple. Elevate the saw blade above the table sufficiently for the teeth to project above the board, shift the rip fence out of the way, and set the miter-gauge to an angle of 45 degrees. Hold one edge against the head of the gauge with one hand, or both if the piece is wide, with enough end projection beyond the blade for a full-width cut (Fig. 13-16). Push the piece forward, holding it securely. On some saws this can be done from either side, whichever is more convenient. If a four-sided frame is being made, cut one end of all pieces first so there won't be any variation.

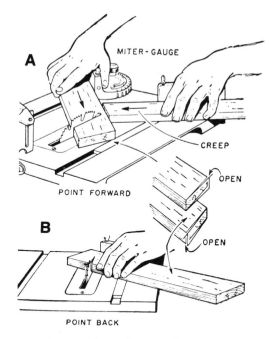

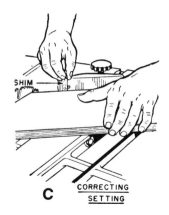

Fig. 13-16. Setup for "rustic" job. Hold one edge with one hand, or both if piece is wide (A). To cut other ends, place the longer, outer edge against miter gauge head as in (B), cutting in opposite direction. Shim corrects setting of gauge in (C). Details in text.

To cut the other ends, measure the length on one, turn it end-for-end with the other face up, and cut. Since the outer edge is longer than the inner, it is advantageous to place that edge against the miter-gauge head, cutting the end in the opposite direction. Use the cut piece as a length pattern for the others.

Use a smooth-cutting saw, such as a hollow-ground blade or a fine-toothed crosscut for fine cabinet work. If you haven't such a blade, dress cut ends with a plane to reduce roughness. Check the true angle of the miter-gauge with a test cut, for it may have been knocked out of true by a fall. Tightening the pivot pin corrects some miter-gauges, while others with round pins, engaging holes, or wedges entering notches may be true at some settings and slightly out at others. A shim of paper or a piece of tape stuck to the gauge head at the appropriate point may bring the angle back to a true 45 degrees.

Settings made by eye according to the scale are most likely to require test cuts. Place a test pair of corner pieces together in a square or form to check the fit. Once the setting is correct, cut the pieces. Aside from neat appearance, the fitting of a joint has much to do with its rigidity and durability, for if it is open at the center or a corner, only a small area of the jointing ends makes contact, and may crush under strain.

As the cut proceeds, the piece tends to creep toward the blade in an amount equal to the set of the teeth or hollowness of a planer blade at that side. It is hard to hold the work against the miter-gauge head solidly enough to prevent this. This causes the miter to be cut sharp if sawed from the outer corner, or blunt if it is cut from the inner corner. This peculiarity of the saw action can be overcome in various ways. One method is to clamp the piece to the miter-gauge. Two or three brads driven into the gauge extension and sharpened, or phonograph needles set in, will do the same thing (Fig. 13-17).

To gauge the length automatically, clamp or screw a block to the extension for the mitered end to stop against; and, since there's danger of crushing the sharp point and thereby altering the measurement, it is best to miter the gauge block to fit the mitered end of the piece.

In most doors the upper rail and stiles are of equal width while the lower rail is wider. This means that the lower stile ends must be cut to acute angles while the lower rail ends are correspondingly

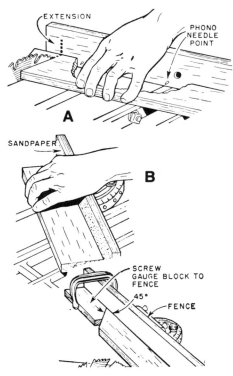

Fig. 13-17. Beat "creep" with brads or phono needles from toy (A), with sandpaper on extension (B) or with clamp on fence (C). Refer to the text for fuller explanation.

obtuse. On the rail measure back from a squared end equal to the width of the stile, and draw the diagonal (Fig. 13-18). On the stile set off the width of the rail, and draw the diagonal.

Occasionally a door panel is built up of four mitered pieces and assembled to run the grain around it. In the reverse of this assembly the grain radiates from the center. The cutting of the pieces is no different from that of making rails and stiles, except that usually the stock is wider and the pieces are triangular.

Moldings are mitered the same as flat pieces if they are within the capacity of the saw, as most solid moldings are. Sprung moldings, which are wide and made on the face of thin stock having the back chamfered at top and bottom to give bearing surfaces, must be cut with special care. One chamfer slides on the table, and the lower chamfer lies against the gauge extension. If the mold slips down ever so little, the joint will not be accurate. A sprung mold being mitered for coping is shown in Fig. 13-19. The profile outlined by the cut is a guide for cutting the mold to fit against another piece in an inside corner.

Moldings fitted around complicated geometrical forms such as stars are more numerous but not much more difficult to fit. The angle to cut is half the assembled angle. A convenient way to test the joints is to draw the figure full-size on a piece of plywood, laying the pieces in place against strips tacked to the plywood, as shown.

Box and chest corners are often mitered. The end-beveling operation requires an accurate right-angle setting of the miter-gauge. Tilt the table or arbor, the angle depending on the number of sides. When using a tilt table, support the work on the low side, a position best served if the lower end butts against a stop block

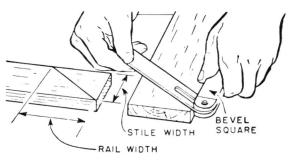

SETTING BEVEL SQUARE

Fig. 13-18. Drawing diagonal on stile for door. In most doors, upper rail and stiles are of equal width with lower rail wider.

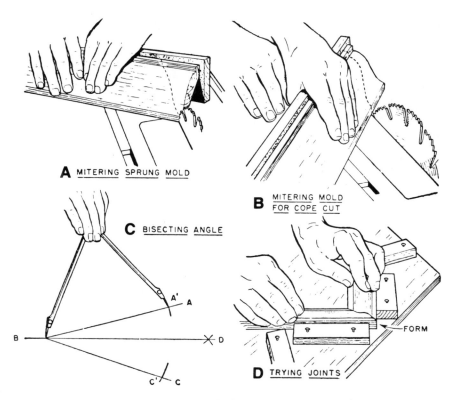

A MITERING SPRUNG MOLD

B MITERING MOLD FOR COPE CUT

C BISECTING ANGLE

D TRYING JOINTS

Fig. 13-19. Mitering moldings. Lower chamfer lies against the gauge extension in (A). Sprung molding is mitered for coping (B). Angle cut is half assembled angle in complicated geometrical forms (C). Test joints as in (D) on plywood, laying pieces against tacked-down strips. Fitting such angles is not difficult.

on the gauge extension. Miter one end of each piece; then turn end-for-end, if edges are parallel (Fig. 13-20). Set the stop block for gauging the length, and cut the other end. If edges aren't parallel turn the gauge end-for-end to keep the head against the same edge.

A miter-gauge clamp prevents slipping. The two clamp screws are positioned in a yoke held by means of a thumb nut at the head and a post screwed into the guide rod. Note use of rod gauge for determining the length.

In end mitering, try to flatten a warped board, If this isn't done, and the center bulges up, the end will curve outward slightly at the center, requiring correction by hand.If the hollow side is up, rock the board on the bulge, contacting the table with the part being sawed.

Column work requires that the staves be rip-mitered, a beveling job. This again calls for tilting of the arbor or table with

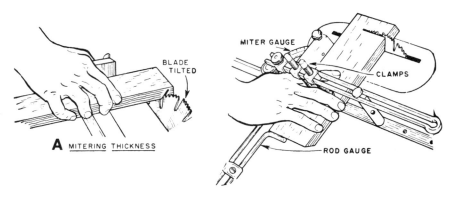

Fig. 13-20. For accurate miters, accurate miter gauge setting is needed. Miter an end of each piece (A), then turn end for end, if edges are parallel. Clamp (B) stops slippage.

the angle half that of the assembled joint. A planer blade will cut smoothly enough for gluing. A piece for a 3-sided column, being cut at 30 degrees, is out of range of the saw tilt and must be held against the fence or an auxiliary fence for ripping from the edge. The guard is in the way for this operation.

When the sides of a box or column slope, the angle of cut, taken at right angles to the edge, is no longer 45 degrees in the square assembly nor half of the normal corner for other numbers of sides (Fig. 13-21). This introduces the hopper joint, which by regular methods involves rather difficult calculations. To find the miter gauge setting for cutting the end of a side piece follow the procedure shown. The same principle works in the layout of tapered column joints. On the end of a side measure back for amount of lean and draw a line to the measured length of the stave, establishing the taper. Set a tapering jig to this slope.

To cut the other end, swivel the gauge in the opposite direction, setting it by degrees read from the other setting, or with a bevel square. By turning the gauge end-for-end the head will bear against the same edge. A similar method applies to column mitering. Draw the common miter on the beveled end and align with the blade as the side bears against a tapering jig.

Mitered corners can be joined by any of several methods. However, since the table saw is an excellent grooving tool, a slip tongue or spline glued into grooves is an easy-to-make reinforcement. A suitable spline for ¾-inch stock is a strip cut from ¼-inch plywood or a piece cut across the grain from hardwood. Set up a blade to cut slightly deeper than half the width of the strip. Make the groove by repeated cuts, by using a wobble saw, a couple of dado blades,

146

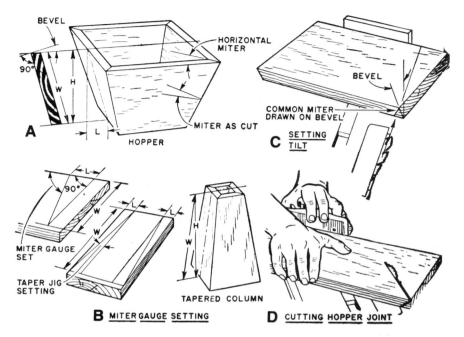

Fig. 13-21. When sides of box slope, find gauge settings for side ends as in (A). See (B) for table tilt for hopper joints. Tilt saw until blade aligns with mark as in (D).

or a molding head. In the first instance the waste is cleared by taking inside cuts, shifting the fence as necessary.

The setup for grooving a face miter is illustrated in Fig. 13-22. The auxiliary fence supports the piece while the face side is slid against it. The miter cut must rest fully on the table, or the depth of groove will taper, causing interference when the joint is being assembled. It is evident that one cut must be made against the grain if the same face side is held against the fence.

Feel the bite of the saw, and gauge the feed accordingly. If the lumber is uniform in thickness the opposite face can be placed against the fence, *providing the groove is exactly centered.* Failure in this makes assemblies like those shown, which require much surfacing of the joint and reduction of thickness.

Splines must enter mitered ends and edges at right angles. The closer the groove to the heel of the cut, the deeper it can be, as there's more stock. To cut the groove in an end miter on a tilt table, place the edge against the miter gauge, end miter down, on the upper side of the table, and use the rip fence for positioning. The position is similar if the arbor tilts. As the saw blades are

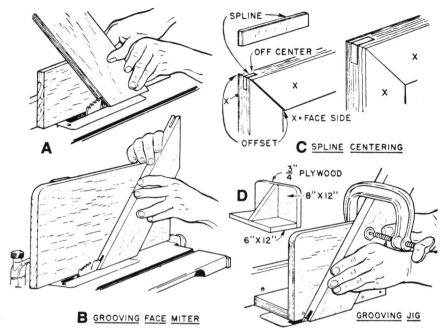

A

SPLINE

OFF CENTER

X = FACE SIDE

OFFSET **C** SPLINE CENTERING

¾" PLYWOOD

D 8"X12"

6"X12"

B GROOVING FACE MITER

GROOVING JIG

Fig. 13-22. Setup for grooving face miter is seen in (A) at left. Miter cut must rest fully on table. One cut will be against grain if same face side is held against fence (B). Sliding jig (D) contributes convenience and safety. Note triangular plywood brace between vertical, upright of the jig.

buried under wood the operation is safe, and the guard may be dispensed with.

In the thin wood used for small boxes a single saw kerf is wide enough to receive the thin spline needed. Clamp nails are excellent in such work (Fig. 13-23). They are flat, finned nails that are driven into a No. 22-gauge saw cut, drawing the joint together and holding it without glue. Where possible, drive a short nail in the top and bottom, rather than using one long nail.

DOVETAIL JOINTS

Dovetail joints are a badge of fine drawer construction, but drawer making is only one use of dovetailing. Old Spanish cabinetmakers joined the corners of their *varguenos*, or chest-on-trestle writing desks, with common dovetails, and mounted the slab tops of their tables on dovetailed rails, which permitted shrinking and swelling of the wide boards without warping. Early American furniture makers dovetailed tray corners of their tea stands.

The one outstanding advantage of a dovetail joint is that it holds by itself, without glue, in the direction of greatest strain.

Fig. 13-23. In thin wood of small boxes, clamp nails, right, are dandy, drawing joint together without glue. A short one, top and bottom, is suggested instead of long one.

Joints that are dovetailed remain strong even after the adhesive deteriorates. In its simple form a single common dovetail joint is made by cutting a flaring tenon on the end of one piece and sinking it into a socket made in the other. The spread of this tenon, or pin, prevents its withdrawal.

Figure 13-24 shows the steps in making a single, common dovetail useful for joining rails and stiles. Always begin with a squared board and lay out the pin and socket with a sharp pencil, as scored lines across the pin bases mar the surface. There is no objection to using a knife point to mark the pin and socket sides. Square a line around the pin piece at a distance from the end equal to the thickness of the socket piece, or slightly more if you plan on dressing the pin end flush after assembly.

Lay out the pin width at the narrow base about one-third the width of the piece (for a single pin), and slope the sides 1 inch: 6 inches for hardwood, 1 inch: 5 inches for more flare in softwood. To set a bevel square to the slope of the pin and socket sides, draw an inclined line on a board, aligning the inside 12 on the blade and 2 on the tongue with the near edge, marking along the tongue. Holding the handle of the bevel square against the edge, align the blade with the mark and lock it and use it to lay out the sides. On narrow pieces holding the handle against an edge gives a better bearing. Square lines for the pin across the end of the work.

Clamp the piece upright in a vise and saw through the pin sides, running the blade in the waste wood outside, just grazing the line. If you find you're cutting into the pin, back up and twist the saw back into alignment. Cut the shoulders last. If you cut

149

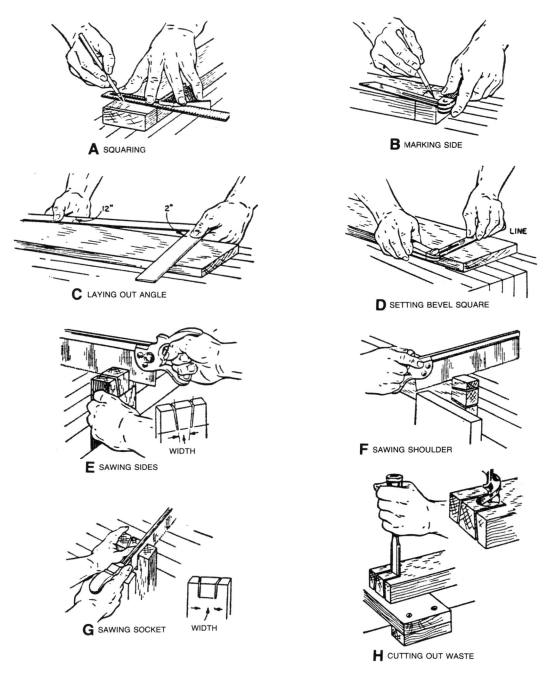

A SQUARING

B MARKING SIDE

C LAYING OUT ANGLE

12" 2"

D SETTING BEVEL SQUARE

LINE

E SAWING SIDES

WIDTH

F SAWING SHOULDER

G SAWING SOCKET WIDTH

H CUTTING OUT WASTE

Fig. 13-24. Steps in making a single common dovetail: (a) begin with a squared board, (b) mark pin and socket sides with square, (c) pin angle is layed out at 1:6 ratio, (d) set bevel square to slope of pin and socket sides, (e) hold in vise and cut pin sides, (f) cut pin shoulders, (g) saw out socket with saw inside cut lines, (h) chisel half way into each face; boring lessens tear.

them first, lack of support may cause the waste blocks to split out as the pin is sawed.

While you can lay out the socket in the same way, drawing the sloping sides on the end of the piece, instead of the face, it is customary to scribe the socket-piece end by holding the pin at right angles and run a pencil along the sides. If the pin is a little inaccurate, the socket layout will then correspond. Saw out the socket, this time with the saw inside the lines to cut in the waste wood. Since the pencil, in scribing, draws a line slightly outside the pin, a cut along the line will ensure a tight fit between the members.

Remove the waste block from the socket by chiseling halfway in from each face. Remember that the flat side of the chisel crushes back somewhat, so start the cut just inside the line. Do not undercut, but chisel straight in from the faces. Try the joint dry before assembling with glue. In heavy work, you can save yourself some heavy chiseling by boring a hole at the bottom of the socket. Boring out part of the waste also lessens tearing of the wood when chiseling soft lumber.

Hardwood can be driven together in assembly with a mallet (Fig. 13-25), but you should protect softwood from scarring by using a block over the joint. When dressing a dovetail joint, push the plane at an angle for a skew cut and work toward the center to avoid splintering the edges.

Frame corners made square with the edges are dovetailed through the width, rather than the thickness, and the pins are correspondingly thinner, with less flare. A face dovetail (Fig. 13-26) is an effective method of splicing two pieces of lumber together.

While the common dovetail is strong and neat, sometimes in fine furniture building, you'll want to hide the end of the pin, concealing the joint from that side. A half-blind joint as in Fig. 13-26 can be made by shortening the pin and cutting the socket into its piece from one face only, the remaining web hiding the end grain of the pin. Obviously, you can't saw the sides as in a plain joint, but you can saw out the important edges by cutting diagonally to the bottom of the open face side and end. Chisel or bore the bottom and trim as in Fig. 13-27, applying rocking pressure with the right hand and guiding the blade with the left. In heavy going use a mallet.

To make a common dovetail joint between a drawer guide and a cabinet rail edge (Fig. 13-28), scribe the pin on the edge,

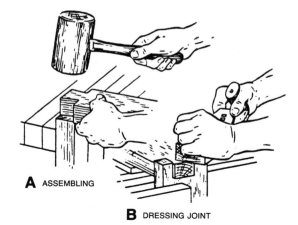

A ASSEMBLING

B DRESSING JOINT

Fig. 13-25. A hardwood dovetail can be assembled with hammer mallet.

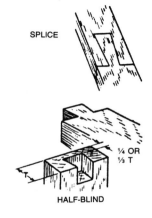

SPLICE

¼ OR ⅓ T

HALF-BLIND

Fig. 13-26. Face-dovetail splices two pieces of lumber together. Half-blind dovetail provides better appearance.

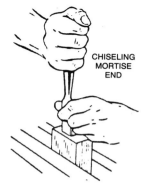

CHISELING MORTISE END

Fig. 13-27. Half-blind mortise is made by rocking chisel back and forth, carefully guiding blade.

152

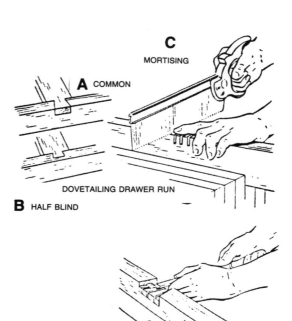

Fig. 13-28. Drawer guide and cabinet rail edge can be jointed with single dovetail.

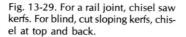

Fig. 13-29. For a rail joint, chisel saw kerfs. For blind, cut sloping kerfs, chisel at top and back.

CHISELING BOTTOM

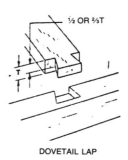

DOVETAIL LAP

gauge the depth and saw the socket sides. Make other kerfs to depth to break the chips and chisel out as in dadoing, inclining the bottom upward from both faces until made flat with final paring cuts (Fig. 13-29). If the socket is blind, make the sloping saw cuts and chisel from top and back.

The pin at the end of a drawer guide may be thinner than the thickness of the rail, forming a lap dovetail. The shoulders of the lap increase resistance against compression loads. The dovetail may be common or half-blind, according to the character of your work. Lap dovetails are especially effective when the rail lies flat, so that the pin enters the face, instead of the edge.

The baldface or half dovetail (Fig. 13-30A) is an easier version. For the unskilled person the keyed version (Fig. 13-30B) is good, as the socket is made a little wide and a slightly tapering wooden strip or key is driven in. The tapering key ensures a tight joint, even if the socket isn't cut to specified width. You can glue these keyed joints and saw off the ends of the key flush afterward, or you can leave the joint dry for disassembling by driving out the pin. This keyed half dovetail joint is useful in fastening a rail to a heavy member. The socket must be wide enough to admit the full tail, as the pin takes up the slack. You can also make blind joints with the pin driven in from behind.

A "multiple" dovetail joint includes two or more pins (Fig. 13-31). In most work the piece carrying the pins has a shoulder at each edge, and the spaces between the pins are much narrower than the pins themselves. Make the edge shoulders somewhat wider than half spaces, and to space the pins evenly, gauge edge lines, inclining a scale to include the necessary number divisions. Gauge pencil lines from these points to the end and lay out the pins. Usually at least two pieces must be cut, and a little time is saved by sawing a pair at a time, the two being held in a vise and squared across the ends. Scribe the pins on the ends of the mating pieces for the sockets as you did with the single dovetail. The half-blind version is used for drawers, as well as in other places where common dovetails detract from appearance.

If you must lay out many similar dovetail joints, make a template of sheet metal or plastic nailing it to a guide strip and stop block to locate it on the work. Figure 13-32 shows a dovetailed drawer with a front inclined, an example seen in some traditional furniture as well as modern. Lay out pins with center lines parallel to the drawer side edges. Mark one side of all pins with one setting of the bevel square, and then reset it for marking the other sides.

A single dovetail teams up with a tongue on end of upper dresser rail (Fig. 13-33). The dovetail enters a socket in the corner post, and the tongue fits into a dado in the end-panel rail, so that the rail tenon couldn't be withdrawn from its mortise even if the glue weakened. Such a combination allows as much space as possible between the tongue and groove and the shoulder of the panel rail, to strengthen the cross-grained wood against stripping.

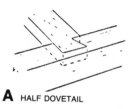

A HALF DOVETAIL

Fig. 13-30. The half dovetail (A) is one of the easiest versions of the dovetail joint. In the keyed half dovetail (B), the socket is made a little wide and a slightly tapering wooden strip is driven in.

B KEYED HALF DOVETAIL

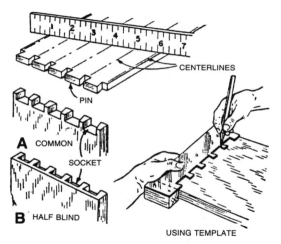

Fig. 13-31. Multiple dovetails can be layed out with a template. Basically, multiples are made the same as singles.

CENTERLINES

PIN

A COMMON

SOCKET

B HALF BLIND

USING TEMPLATE

In the blind square lap dovetail, sockets are cut two-thirds or three-quarters into the thickness of one piece, and corresponding tails are sunk into the face of the other, with a flange projecting at the end (Fig. 13-34). When assembled, this flange covers the solid edge of the other piece and the completed joint resembles a plain rabbeted corner.

In the blind mitered lap both ends are worked into combination rabbets and miters, the thin flanges being mitered. Cut the pins in from the face of one side, and the sockets into the end of the other. Finally, miter the upper pins. When assembled, this appears as a simple mitered joint. Since such blind dovetail joints cannot be inspected for fit they require a good deal of labor.

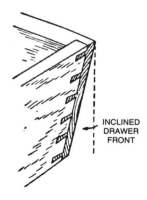

INCLINED DRAWER FRONT

Fig. 13-32. Dovetail drawer with front inclined: Lay out pins with center lines parallel to the drawer side edges. Mark one side of all pins with one setting of bevel square, and reset to mark the other sides.

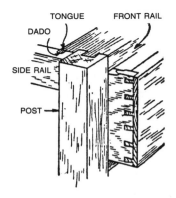

TONGUE   FRONT RAIL

DADO

SIDE RAIL

POST

Fig. 13-33. Dovetail and tongue team up on dresser rail. Post has socket, side rail has dado.

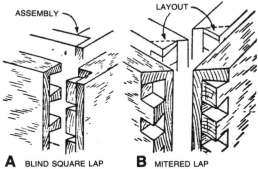

ASSEMBLY   LAYOUT

A BLIND SQUARE LAP   **B** MITERED LAP

Fig. 13-34. Blind square lap: Sockets are cut two-thirds into thickness of one piece, and tails cut into face of the other with a flange projecting at the end.

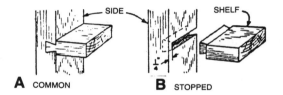

SIDE   SHELF

A COMMON   **B** STOPPED

Fig. 13-35. A housed dovetail joint is one with the pin on the end of a shelf or partition and socket in the case side or shelf. This kind of joint is self locking.

156

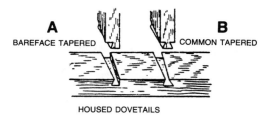

Fig. 13-36. A tapered housed dovetail is an especially good joint because it doesn't tighten until the very last. Bare-faced or common are both easy to make.

A housed dovetail joint is one with the pin on the end of a shelf or partition and the socket in the case side or shelf (Fig. 13-35). Such a joint is self-locking, making some assemblies easier because you can hold them together without clamps. It is nearly impossible to cut accurate pins on warped shelves, so housed dovetail joints are limited to comparatively narrow work. The joint is made blind from the front by stopping the socket about ¼ inch behind the front edge and cutting back the pin an equal distance. Such a joint can be made barefaced by dovetailing only one side.

Almost as easy to cut is the tapered dovetail (Fig. 13-36). Such a joint assembles easily because it doesn't tighten until the very last. It is made bareface or common, and can be made blind by stopping the socket behind the edge and cutting the pin back.

The Art of
Bending Wood

PROJECTS THAT REQUIRE the bending of wood may be the ones most often avoided by the do-it-yourselfer. But wood bending isn't as difficult as it seems, if you know a few simple tricks. And if the results can be so impressive that it makes the little added effort worthwhile. With this knowledge, you can make a variety of objects such as skis, a toboggan, a chair with curved back and arm rests, or you can jazz up practically any furniture project you have in mind with stylish curved surfaces.

Wood can be bent in three different ways: 1) by use of steam or boiling water; 2) kerf sawing; and 3) lamination.

STEAM

The use of steam actually plasticizes the wood to impart an unnatural, temporary flexibility and softness so that the wood fibers can be compressed to form the inside of the desired curve while simultaneously being stretched to form the outside of the curve. Wood can be made pliable by prolonged (2 to 4 hours) immersion in boiling water or, preferably, by subjecting it to steam (to prevent excessive water from soaking into the wood).

The boiling-water method requires only that you find a container, large enough to hold the piece of wood (weighted down to keep it from floating), and keep the pot filled with boiling water for several hours. Add boiling water to the container from time to time if putting the container atop a stove is impractical.

For long pieces of wood that require overall or mid-section bending, fashion a chimney for a large pot by fastening a length of old stovepipe to a pot lid made from scrap plywood. Hang the wood inside the vertical stovepipe and close the top to keep in most of the steam while allowing enough venting to prevent pressure buildup. Boil water in the pot for several hours (a barbecue grill is handy) until the wood is pliable enough for shaping. If only the ends of long pieces require bending, just stick them into a pot of water, leaving most of the lumber sticking out through whatever type of cover or plug you can devise to help hold in the heat and steam. Be sure to have heavy work gloves ready.

Bending requires the use of a jig that holds the softened wood in the desired shape for several days, until it dries sufficiently to hold its new form (Fig. 14-1). The actual drying time depends

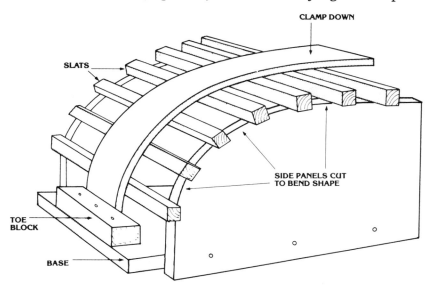

Fig. 14.1. You may want to construct a jig on which you can form your wood after it has been softened in boiling water or steam. If you have a number of pieces that must be bent to the same curve, a jig such as this one will ensure that all of the curves are uniform. Let the wood set in the jig until it is completely dry. Drying time depends on wood thickness.

upon the thickness of the wood being worked. To shape something like a curved chairback, you can use a very simple jig consisting of a board with two blocks of wood nailed on top, about the chairwidth apart. Place the steamed wood on the blocks, then pull the center of the steamed board downward and hold it there with a clamp until the wood dries.

For other bends, you may need to build more elaborate jigs from scrap wood. For example, saw two scrap boards to the desired shape and nail them vertically along the two edges of a third board. Then nail wood blocks crosswise, from one curved board to the other, to form a sort of curved "step-ladder" form against which to bend the work after one end has been clamped down. Use other clamps to hold the formed wood in place until it is dry.

This relatively time-costly steam-bending technique is best when you want a curved piece that shows no saw kerfs or laminations.

KERF SAWING

If only the main surface of the bent wood will be visible, and if some sacrifice of strength is acceptable, a saw kerf method is much faster and easier. This involves sawing evenly-spaced, sawblade-width parallel slots (kerfs) partway through the back side of the work.

How deep and far apart the cuts should be made depends upon the thickness of the wood, how sharp a bend is desired, and the width of the kerf made by the saw blade. To find the right combination, make a more or less arbitrary series of cuts, say three-quarters of the way through the wood and uniformly spaced from one-fourth to one inch apart. Bend the wood until all kerfs close fully, and see if the curve is anywhere nearly right. Vary the number of cuts to change the curvature—more for a sharper curve and fewer for a lesser curve. Be sure to use scrap wood of the same kind and thickness as will be selected for the final project. If the wood does not bend easily, without cracking, make somewhat deeper kerfs.

It is important to space the kerfs accurately to obtain a truly uniform bend. Either carefully mark the kerf locations on the work, or use a brad tacked to the radial arm saw fence that can engage one kerf after the next to provide equal shifts for succeeding cuts. A bench saw or radial arm saw is very convenient for kerf cutting, partly because it is easy to get cuts of uniform depth.

Once the kerfs have been cut correctly, fill them with glue and bend the wood to the planned shape. Use clamps or rope to keep the bent wood in position until the glue dries, then smooth and finish in whatever way is appropriate.

You can also experiment with the following method of figuring in advance the appropriate number of kerfs. Determine the radius of the bend you want, and mark this distance along the length of a test board, measuring from the end of the board. Make a single kerf cut at the mark. Hold the board firmly against a flat benchtop and lift the end of the board until the kerf closes fully. Measure the distance from the benchtop to the bottom of the raised end of the board. Divide the bend radius by this measured distance to get a pretty accurate approximation of the number of equally-spaced kerfs (of the width and depth made on the test board) needed to obtain a 90 degree bend (Refer to Fig. 14-2).

LAMINATION

You have undoubtedly often noticed those very thin and flexible strips of waste wood that fall on the floor when a board is slightly narrowed with a bench or radial arm saw. The very thinnest can almost be wrapped around a finger without breaking. Therein lies the non-secret trick of making bends by lamination.

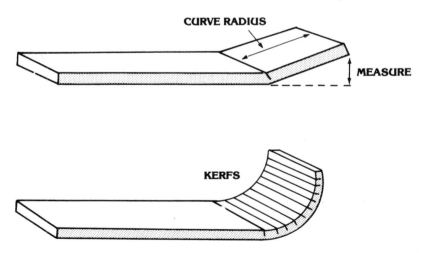

Fig. 14.2 Top drawing shows how to calculate the number of kerfs you will have to cut in order to achieve a certain degree of curvature. Determine the radius of the bend, mark this distance along the length of the board, make a single kerf cut at the mark, hold board flat on benchtop, measure distance from benchtop to bottom of raise board end, divide bend radius by measured distance to get number of equally-spaced kerfs needed.

Simply cut a number of very thin strips of wood, bend and clamp one of them around a form that determines the shape of the final product, and glue additional strips to that first one to build up adequate thickness.

Usually, the grain of each strip is made to run parallel to the bend. But there may be occasions when maximum strength (perhaps for a chair seat or back) requires orienting alternate layers of wood at right angles to each other.

The lamination method is especially good for making sharp bends that are difficult or impossible to achieve by either the steam or kerf method. To make very sharp bends you can steam the thin strips of wood first and form them to approximately their intended shapes before lamination.

Making Decorative Cuts with Common Shop Tools

REPETITIVE PATTERNS easily cut with many conventional shop tools can make conversation pieces out of simple woodworking projects.

What appears to be intricate carving is the work of a fly-cutter (Fig. 15-1). With this and other common tools, you can emboss, scallop, pierce or striate wood and hardboard to create more attractive panels, cabinets, cases, moldings, picture frames, and trim of all kinds (Fig. 15-2).

Raised Cones

One particular fly-cutter differs from the usual type in that it has a cutting bit that projects from the shaft at a slight angle. Called an *Adjust-A-Drill*, it leaves a raised cone when depth of cut is limited. To increase the deep-carving effect, overlap circles, which will provide faceted areas and cut into the basic cone.

Since this and other type fly-cutters have a pilot drill, a center hole becomes part of your design. You can dress it up with a countersink, or eliminate it altogether by grinding down the drill

Fig. 15-1. A fly-cutter can be adjusted to cut circles of varying diameters. This particular one has an angled cutting bit that produces sloped inner walls when depth of cut is limited.

point so that the only thing cutting is the bit. If you do this, be sure to clamp work securely for each cut. Either way, use a slow drill press speed and feed the cutter steadily into the work.

Inverted Cones

A single countersink doesn't resemble much, but a series of them produces an intriguing decoration. You can obtain good contrast for the finished job by staining the entire surface, including countersinks, then sanding the surface thoroughly so only the dimples retain the stain. If drill press capacity is too limiting for the work you want to handle, use countersink in a portable electric drill.

Sloped Scallops

A multispur bit producing a flat-bottomed hole doesn't create very interesting designs on a flat surface, but if you slope the work a bit, the overlapping circles will end up as multileveled scallops. As you move the work back, be sure to adjust depth of cut of the bit.

Fig. 15-2. Intricate concentric patterns can be created easily with ordinary drill attachments.

Strip-cut Moldings

With the multispur bit, you can also cut a section of a hole by drilling close to the edge of stock. By drilling a series of holes and then strip-cutting the work on a table saw, you can produce interesting moldings which need little finishing if you use a hollow-ground saw blade. Work with short or long pieces of stock, depending on ultimate use of the decorated pieces. For more intricate designs, form half-holes on each edge of the stock or change the centerline of alternate holes.

Embossed Moldings

Picture frames call for use of the angled-bit fly-cutter, but work only on the stock edges. This requires a fence and a stop that can be set to space the cuts. Select a long, straight board and joint one edge. Then drill a series of holes in that edge spaced about one inch apart. You can suit the spacing to your own requirements after you've had a chance to experiment for different effects.

Clamp the fence to the drill press table so the center pilot of the fly-cutter won't hit the work. Then it's a matter of setting depth of cut and using a nail in the guide holes to set the spacing between cuts.

Striated Surfaces

Even an ordinary saw blade can be utilized to do more than just cut through wood. It's just a question of running the blade back and forth as you move the stock. A blade with set teeth does this job best, with depth of cut very, very light (Fig. 15-3). You can do this faster on a radial arm saw but a table saw will be satisfactory.

To vary the texture, change depth of cut a little as you work; also change distance between cuts.

Pierced Paneling

If you set a saw blade (or a dado assembly, for that matter) to a height little more than half the thickness of the stock, and then make passes on both sides of the work, you will pierce the work where cuts cross and form square holes that combine with

Fig. 15-3. A striated pattern can be made with a saw when the blade is set for a very shallow cut. Changing depth of cut and distance between cuts produces different designs and textures.

Fig. 15-4. Pierced paneling patterns are made by cutting both sides of the panel with a saw blade or dado head set slightly higher than half the thickness of the stock. Frame is added later.

the grooves to form a pattern (Fig. 15-4). The airy effect achieved is especially good for breaking up a large expanse of panel in a divider or in a sliding door.

Lined with a translucent material such as fiberglass, small panels treated like this can be used as fixtures for atmosphere lighting—indoors or out.

Incised Scallops

These cuts can be formed with a sawblade. Set the rip fence so the distance between fence and outside surface of the blade equals thickness of the stock. Butt the work against the screw-clamp stop block, then slowly lower it over the turning blade. For the smoothest cut, use a hollow-ground blade, but lower the work slowly if you want to avoid burning either the blade or the work (Fig. 15-5).

Inlays

Perfect inlays are easy to prepare if you form the circular grooves with a conventional type fly-cutter. Be sure to set the bit

Fig. 15-5. Incised scallops are formed by setting the fence so that the cut is only the thickness of the saw blade. Lower work onto blade, allowing it to cut slowly, to avoid burning the wood.

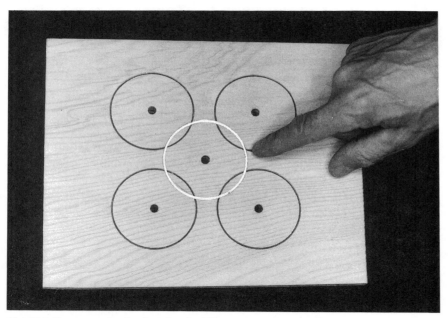

Fig. 15-6. You can make circular inlays by filling grooves cut with a fly-cutter with a contrasting wood filler, or else a soft metal like copper or aluminum. Use a router for irregular cuts.

so it will contact the work before the center pilot. If you clamp the work and keep the drill press speed slow, the grooves formed will be uniform and smooth.

Fill grooves with a contrasting plastic wood, let this dry hard and then sand the surface for a perfect inlay (Fig. 15-6). You might also fill grooves with copper wire. Form a shallow groove so you can force the wire in place; then sand off the surplus.

168

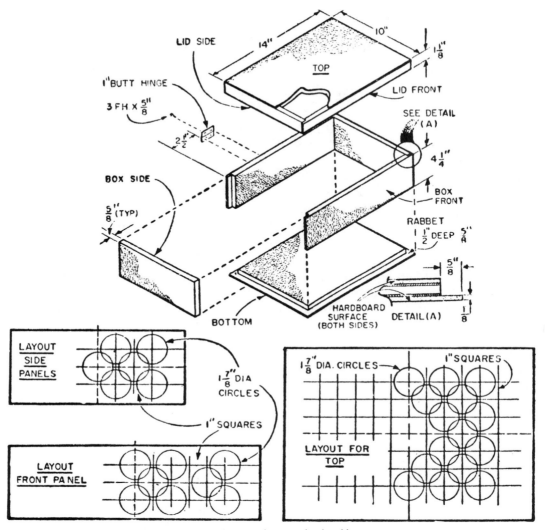

Fig. 15-7. Dimensional diagram showing top, bottom, front, and side of box.

Table 15-1. Bill of Materials

Quantity		Size and Description	Purpose
2	⅝″	10″ × 14″ hardboard	top and bottom
2	⅝″	4¼″ × 14″ hardboard	box front and back
2	⅝″	1⅛″ × 14″ hardboard	lid front and back
2	⅝″	4¼″ × 9¾″ hardboard	box sides
2	⅝″	1⅛″ × 9¾″ hardboard	lid sides
as needed	⅝″	#3 flat-head wood screws	

Note: Also need butt hinges, finishing nails and glue

169

If you want an irregular line instead of a perfect circle, substitute a router for the fly-cutter.

Building A Decorative Box

Make the box out of ⅝-inch hardboard-surfaced plywood, which is available from many building supply and plywood dealers. It comprises ⅜-inch plywood sandwiched between ⅛-inch plies of hardboard. Plain hardboards are also satisfactory. If you use wood, it should be free of grain as in sugar pine or as dense as maple so that the grain will not spoil the fine cutting.

You can cut all the box parts specified in Table 15-1 from one 2- × -3-foot panel, after studying the drawing in Fig. 15-7, top and bottom, also front and back pieces of box and lid. Rule off top, front and side pieces in 1-inch squares to establish pilot hole locations for the fly-cutter and make the decorative cuts.

The back of the box can be left plain or you can duplicate the front pattern. Assemble box with glue and 6d finishing nails. Set nail heads and fill holes with wood putty colored to the shade of the wood.

Making Decorative Inlays

A S GENERALLY UNDERSTOOD, inlaying is the art of decorating the surface of a panel with designs in contrasting colors of wood or other materials, like metal, ivory, bone, tortoise shell, mother-of-pearl, or plastics (Fig. 16-1). Strictly speaking, it relates only to the mortising of one material into a ground or base piece of another material of contrasting color, a craft of great antiquity. The ornamental effect is that of a painting. Its successful application depends as much on the artistry of the design as it does on the skill of workmanship or beauty of materials.

INLAYING WITH BANDS

The simplest method of inlaying is the use of strips, or bands, of wood set into the ground piece. These bands may be plain wood or elaborate strips of ornamentation built up in several colors and sold in 36-inch lengths of veneer thickness. They may be inlaid as simple lines paralleling the edges of a surface, or as elaborately interlacing bands. Guitars and similar musical instruments often carry inlaid borders called *purfling*.

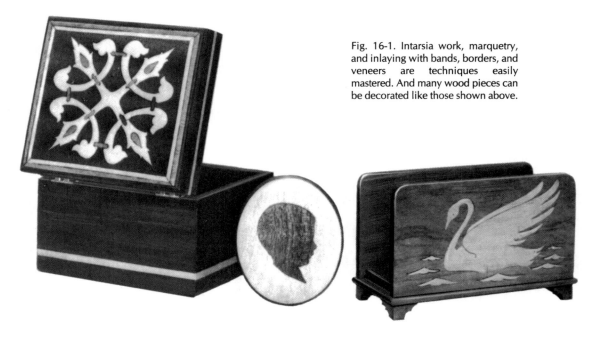

Fig. 16-1. Intarsia work, marquetry, and inlaying with bands, borders, and veneers are techniques easily mastered. And many wood pieces can be decorated like those shown above.

Plain inlay strips can be purchased so inexpensively that it hardly pays to make them. For special uses, however, the strips can be cut from veneer, using a framing square for a straightedge and a veneering saw or a knife with teeth filed in it for cutting. Clamp between boards and joint by sliding the plane on its side.

The simplest method of making a groove for veneer is to use a drill press or portable power router, cutting the groove to exact width and slightly less in depth than the thickness of the band. Square the groove corners with a chisel, miter the ends of the strips and run glue into the grooves with a stick. After pressing in the bands, weight or clamp them and lay aside to dry. Then sand them down flush with the panel.

If the ground is to be stained, ''stop'' out the bands with thin shellac accurately applied with a fine brush to keep the stain from smearing the inlay. Guide the brush by sliding your little finger along the edge of the work. The shellac will later be removed in the normal process of finishing.

Interlacing Bands

In designs with crossovers, interest is added by interlacing the bands. To make pieces for length, lay them in place in the groove, the crossing member lapping over the other, and scribe

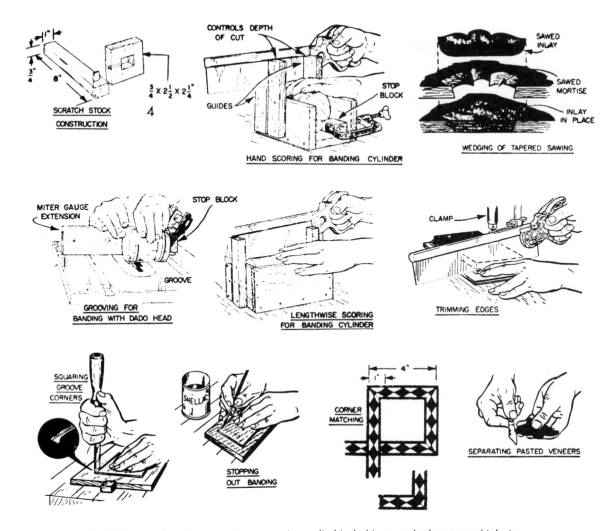

Fig. 16-2. Scratch stack construction, grooving, cylindrical objects, and other steps of inlaying.

the edge on the length to be cut. Unless the design is engineered to be divisible by the units in the built-up bandings, miters of the border cannot be smoothly joined.

If power equipment is not available, make grooves with a scratch stock built as shown in Fig. 16-2. Using a piece of hacksaw blade for a cutter. Advance it like a marking gauge, with the grain leading away from the edge of the panel to draw the shoulder of the scratch stock against the edge. Clean out the waste between the scores with a narrow chisel, which can be ground on the tang of a file.

Grooving Cylindrical Objects

Cylindrical objects, such as turned boxes, can be grooved for banding on the lathe or with a dado head mounted on a circular saw. Rotate the box against the miter gauge extension and regulate groove distance from the end of the box with a clamped-on stop block. Wrap strip of paper around the groove to find the length of the inlay strip needed.

Since a joint cannot be avoided, capitalize on it by dividing the band with V-grooves elsewhere, making segments of equal length, alternating long with short, etc. If you do not have a dado saw, make a miter box cutting the vertical guides to such a length that the depth of cut is reached when the bar of the back saw contacts them. Chisel out the waste. A miter box built to saw lengthwise grooves for vertical banding of cylinders is also shown. Mark the divisions on the box before sawing.

PREMADE INLAYS

Craftsmen's supply houses offer a wide variety of factory-made inlays for centerpieces and corners, featuring vases of flower, shell and fan designs, lodge emblems, and others in colored woods. These are about $\frac{1}{20}$ inch thick and are applied both as overlays and inlays.

If linen-backed, the face side of the inlay is exposed, but if paperbacked, the reverse is true. Hold the inlay in place on the ground and trace around it with a sharp, hard pencil to outline the mortise. Rout to a depth slightly less than the thickness of the inlay, glue in place, and cover with a board for clamping or weighting. When dry, sand flush and stop out with shellac if stain is to be used.

CUTTING YOUR OWN INLAYS

A complete inlaying job involves the cutting out of the inlay itself. A good example is the silhouette of a child's head set into a light ground. Trace the profile from a snapshot and paste on a piece of veneer or thin dark wood. Saw out with a blade about .02 inch thick and 0.70 inch wide, cutting the line with the blade in the waste wood and the jigsaw table tilted 3 degrees for slight undercutting (Fig. 16-3).

Now trace the inlay on the ground, set up a drill press with a routing bit adjusted to cut slightly less than the depth of the inlay thickness, and work a groove about $\frac{1}{32}$ inch inside the line.

Fig. 16-3. The inlay should be cut on a jigsaw with a blade about .02 inch thick and .70 inch wide, cutting the line with the blade in the waste wood and the saw table tilted at 3 degrees for slight undercutting.

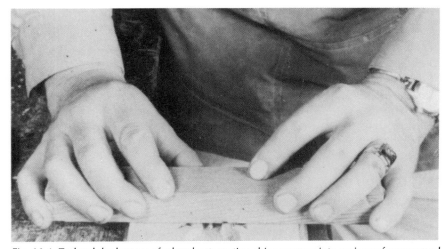

Fig. 16-4. To level the bottom of a hand-cut mortise, drive a screw into a piece of scrap wood to the correct depth, turn upside down and use the sharp edge of the screw's head to plane away any high spots in the mortise.

Next, excavate the mortise inside, and moving the work against the rotation of the router bit, trim the outside to the line. Trim skips by the router with a knife point, applying finger pressure over the point. If the mortise is chiseled by hand, the bottom can be leveled with the head of flat-head screw projecting from the underside of a wooden bar slid on the piece being mortised (Fig. 16-4).

Fig. 16-5. Whatever the method used to produce the inlay its fit must be checked against the mortise. The tapered edges should be carefully pared so the inlay will wedge tightly all around when glued in place.

Place the inlay in the mortise and give it a light squeeze with a clamp. This will leave an imprint of the inlay on any remaining stock to be trimmed from the edges of the mortise. With careful paring of these impressions, the tapered edges of the inlay will wedge tightly all around upon being glued in place, making a perfect fit (Fig. 16-5). Clamp and let dry. Light scraping and sanding prepares the work for finishing. Such inlaying can be repeated with other colors of wood by treating the inlaid panel as a ground.

INTARSIA

Intarsia offers a simpler method of inlaying by stacking two veneers and sawing them at one time, producing the mortise and inlay at one cutting. By tilting the saw table, the pieces are tapered in thickness with the inlay large enough to wedge tightly into the hole cut in the under veneer. Since the veneers are thin and limber, they are stiffened by being tacked with brads to a backing of ⅛ inch basswood, three-ply, or other material (see Fig. 16-6). Cut the pieces ½ inch oversize all around, drill for brads, and nail from the bottom. Bend the points over the top.

Brads can be eliminated if the veneers are glued together with paper between them; use mucilage or library paste. Apply in spots close enough to hold all small parts. The resulting "pad" is flat, with any buckles in the veneers eliminated, thus permitting the best condition for sawing.

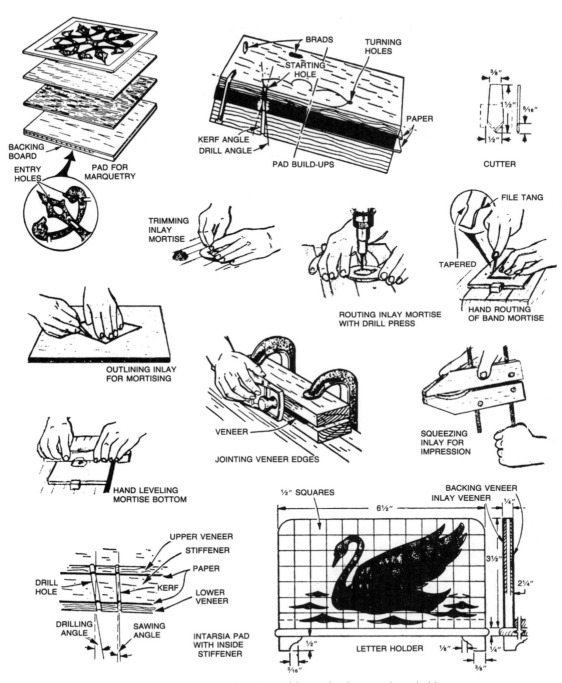

BACKING BOARD

ENTRY HOLES

PAD FOR MARQUETRY

BRADS

TURNING HOLES

STARTING HOLE

PAPER

KERF ANGLE

DRILL ANGLE

PAD BUILD-UPS

CUTTER

3/8"

1 1/2"

5/16"

1/2"

TRIMMING INLAY MORTISE

ROUTING INLAY MORTISE WITH DRILL PRESS

FILE TANG

TAPERED

HAND ROUTING OF BAND MORTISE

OUTLINING INLAY FOR MORTISING

VENEER

JOINTING VENEER EDGES

SQUEEZING INLAY FOR IMPRESSION

HAND LEVELING MORTISE BOTTOM

UPPER VENEER

STIFFENER

PAPER

KERF

LOWER VENEER

DRILL HOLE

DRILLING ANGLE

SAWING ANGLE

INTARSIA PAD WITH INSIDE STIFFENER

1/2" SQUARES

BACKING VENEER

INLAY VEENER

6 1/2"

3 1/2"

1/4"

2 1/4"

1/2"

3/16"

LETTER HOLDER

1/8"

3/8"

1/4"

Fig. 16-6. Marquetry, intarsia, and layout for the swan letter holder.

177

It is evident that with veneers 1/20 inch or less in thickness there must be considerable tilt to the table to wedge out the saw kerf, even if the blade is only .01 inch thick. The tilt is greatly reduced by padding the veneers at top and bottom with the stiffening sheet sandwiched between. A prime material for this purpose is 1/8-inch sheet balsa, obtainable at hobby stores. Clamp lightly to avoid compressing the balsa.

The amount of tilt must be determined by trial and error, as it depends both on blade thickness and thickness of the pad. Table 16-1 gives theoretical tilts for blades when veneers are of standard 1/28 inch thickness. With this as a starting point, the precise table tilt can be found by trial cutting of a sample pad.

Holes drilled to admit blades must be at least equal to their width and entered with more slope than the sawing angle, piercing outside the line in top veneer and inside in the lower. Thus, the holes in both veneers lie in parts to be discarded. Drill the holes at inside angles. If the drill press chuck will not hold fine drills, secure the drill in a pin vise cut to suitable length, or in a chuck from an inexpensive hand drill held in the drill press chuck.

A good blade for sawing this pad is .012 inch thick and .023 inch wide. Chuck it to move in a straight line with the back guide barely touching, and the hold-down above, but not touching, the work. Release the upper end of the saw blade from its chuck and thread through a starting hole, chucking it again with enough tension on the blade to hold it taut.

Since the hole angle varies from the cutting angle, the blade must cut into the starting position. This can be conveniently done by turning the machine by hand for two or three strokes. Because the kerf is fine, you can make the cut directly on the line.

—————————— **Table 16-1. Theoretical Tilts for Blades** ——————————

| | Table tilt | | |
Blade thickness	veneers together	veneers 1/8 in. apart	Drill size per blade width
.010	15⅔°	3½°	.021,No.75
.012	18½°	4⅓°	.023,No.73
.016	24°	5¾°	.035,No.65
.017	25½°	6 + °	.043,No.57

NOTE: Blades for use on inside cutting, to be threaded through holes, must be of uniform width. Wide-end blades must be cut back to teeth. In emergency a sewing needle may be used as a drill, but tends to drift.

An abrupt change of direction, as at the tip of a pointed leaf, can sometimes be negotiated by drawing the work forward until the back of the blade contacts the wood while the turn is started. If this is not successful, drill holes at these points, at the same angle as starting holes. The drill can be a little smaller than for starting. Direct the hole along the axis of the angle to be sawed. As the separate pieces are cut, stop the jigsaw to remove them.

If the design is elaborate, fasten the pieces on a master plan with a drop of shellac or paste, right-side up. If the designs are simple, lay them in a shallow box.

With the cutting done, pull out the tacks or pry the pasted pieces apart with a knife blade. Inlay cutouts from the upper veneer are saved, while the corresponding pieces below are discarded. Assemble the parts on a flat surface, and fasten to a sheet of kraft paper or cardboard with rubber cement. Paste or other water glue is likely to warp the pieces out of assembly. At this stage, if bands for a border are to be put around the design, clamp the sheet between boards, aligning one end of the upper board with a border edge to guide in trimming the edges. Reclamp for each edge cut.

Coat the panel backing with glue and allow it to stand a few seconds, then press down the assembled inlay, paper-side up. To drive out excess glue, clamp the center first. A pad of newspapers between the inlay and its board will make up for variations in veneer thickness, distributing the pressure.

After drying, remove clamps and boards, peel off the paper, and scrub off remaining shreds of paper with gasoline. Sand smooth and apply any needed shellac for stopping stain.

If the inlay is applied to solid wood, there is a likelihood that the drying veneer will warp the piece of wood. A veneer glued to the underside of the wood at the same time that the inlay is attached guards against this.

MARQUETRY

Inlaying in the form of marquetry consists of sawing square through a stack of veneers, usually producing several complete patterns at one cutting. Since there is no beveling, an outline equal in width to the kerf surrounds each piece. This is not necessarily a defect, as the decorative effect may be strengthened by the outline. Since like parts are interchangeable, inlays for several panels can be cut at once, or the outside of a door can have a design with light parts on a dark ground, while the remaining pieces are assembled for the inside as dark on light.

Illustrated is a pad of three colors to be tacked or glued to the backing board (Fig. 16-6). From these three cuttings, six color arrangements are possible, and three can be assembled, making use of all the pieces. More sets could be added, either as groups of the same woods or of other colors.

In the design shown drilled holes give sawing access to all parts. If it is difficult to hold many veneers with only a lower backing board, use a top cover also.

When assembling the marquetry panel, space the pieces evenly, showing uniform edge spacing all around. Rubber cement the paper topping, turn the assembly over, and fill the joints with plastic wood or a mixture of sanding dust and glue, working it in with putty knife.

To economize with expensive veneers as well as to facilitate grain direction, small parts are sometimes roughly cut out and set into cheap veneers or cardboard cut out to receive them, and entered into the pad like solid veneers. This can result in thinning the pad for easier sawing, or in allowing more copies to be made at one time. For production work, the parts may be cut out in separate pads for fitting together.

SWAN LETTER HOLDER

Details for making a letter holder decorated with an intarsia swan are shown in Fig. 16-6. After cutting the inlay, glue it to a backing of mahogany. Rabbet the base all around and shape to the half-round fillet. Glue the sides into the side rabbets and fasten with brads from below. To make the feet, miter ¼-inch stock and jigsaw the molded profiles, gluing them in pairs joined at the miters to the bottom. The original was made of inlaid pear wood in cherry. For more contrast, use holly for the inlay.

Section III

Restoration, Finishing Processes and Final Details

Stocking Your Refinisher's Cabinet

FURNITURE REFINISHING IS neither as difficult nor as involved as some experts would have you think. A minimum investment can let you do it at home where you can save money. Refinishing can even become a pleasant pastime. It's easy enough if you know the tricks, and the tricks are in the materials you buy for your refinisher's cabinet.

You don't need a vast array of equipment but you will need special solutions to remove old finishes, bleaches to lighten stains and water marks, materials such as shellac and varnish, and perhaps a few stains. None of the items is expensive or difficult to find, and a professional refinishing cabinet can be assembled at a reasonable cost (Fig. 17-1).

REMOVERS AND BLEACHES

The first step in any refinishing is the removal of the old finish. Wood alcohol is a basic ingredient here. If you're refinishing antique furniture, it's a must. It is used to remove old

Fig. 17-1. A small number of inexpensive items are all that is needed to meet your refinishing requirements.

shellac and for thinning new shellac that you'll apply as either a primer or a finish coat.

Varnish finishes are relatively new and chances are that furniture more than 30 or 40 years old is finished with shellac. The old shellac is easily removed with wood alcohol; a quart will handle an average chair.

Pour about a cup of alcohol into a shallow bowl. Dip a small pad of medium-grade steel wool into the bowl and liberally soak a small area. Let the alcohol penetrate for a few seconds, then rub the area with the steel wool pad. Alcohol evaporates quickly and, if you wait too long between dousing and rubbing, the shellac can become gummy instead of soft. If this happens, don't try to rub the gum from the wood; add more alcohol and wait less time.

If you work small areas, rubbing fast with light, gentle strokes, the old finish will strip off easily. If some areas seem stubborn or the alcohol evaporates too quickly, try adding a small amount of lacquer thinner to the alcohol.

Paint removers are designed to remove hardened paint and work nicely on both painted and varnished surfaces, if the coats are not too thick. A quality paint remover is essential on varnished wood, since neither alcohol nor turpentine will soften the hardened finish. Nothing but paint remover will work with complete safety on painted areas.

When using any remover, be sure to follow the manufacturer's directions. Use the remover in light coatings. Thick layers of paint are best removed in two or three passes.

You'll find that most paint removers leave wax in the wood pores. This should be removed before repainting or shellacking, and the job can be done by scrubbing the wood with steel wool dipped in turpentine.

A paint scraper is a handy refinishing tool. It helps peel stubborn paints and lifts loosened surfaces off the wood. Generally you can use a scraper without danger to the surface, but once in a while paint is stubborn enough to require real scraping. Unless you're careful, the scraper will leave indentations and the only answer is resanding. When you resand you'll have to start the refinishing with a primer coat. If you plan to varnish, be sure to prime with two or three coats of thinned shellac.

If small traces of the old finish seem to stand in the wood pores, scrub the surface with a medium steel wool pad dipped in bleach. The scrubbing will help lift the trapped finish and the bleach will do an even job. It isn't necessary to rinse a chlorine bleach. When it dries, all traces are gone.

Oxalic acid is a mildly acid solution that's handy for bleaching water marks—the black spots so often found on tabletops. Mix two ounces of oxalic crystals in a quart of water. Apply nearly boiling with a brush.

These bleaches will handle most of the jobs you'll run into. Just remember this rule: oxalic acid for the darker water marks, chlorine for all other stains.

In a few instances, you may want to lighten the natural color of woods such as walnut and mahogany. Neither oxalic nor chlorine bleach will work, and you'll need the rougher professional hydrochloric acid bleaches. These are dangerous solutions, so buy only enough for one job. Don't store the acid in your shop.

Hydrochloric acids are available under several trade names and generally come in two-bottle solutions. One bottle contains the bleach, the other the neutralizer. Follow the manufacturer's recommendations to the letter.

ABRASIVES AND EQUIPMENT

Furniture refinishing requires few tools and a small investment will buy everything you need. Steel wood is a must. It's used in both the removal and refinishing stages. Use it in medium and medium-fine grades to remove old paint and in finer grades to rub out and polish new finishes.

You'll get your best value when you buy a full package. Separate a small ball of wool from the pack and shape it into a pad. Don't try to economize by carrying partly used pads from one step to another. You'll get better results by using a fresh pad for each step.

Sandpaper is another must. Again, don't try to economize. Cheaper papers are coated with flint abrasives. Flint is excellent for roughing-in jobs, but it's not suited for fine furniture. Use the orange-colored garnet papers. These are well-worth the difference in price. They cut faster than flint and leave a smoother surface, the only secret of a professional-looking final finish.

Paint scrapers are also important. They're handy for removing old paints and varnishes and can be used to smooth slightly roughened surfaces.

A cabinet scraper is a small hand-held blade designed for one job: smoothing roughened and uneven areas before sanding. Although experts sometimes make do with a paint scraper, a cabinet blade is the ideal tool for a smooth job. Never try to sand uneven surfaces level and smooth with abrasive paper. A scraper is the solution and a few minutes with one can make sanding faster and easier.

PAINT, VARNISH AND SHELLAC

When the old finish is off and the surface smoothed, the next step is the application of a new finish. The kind of new finish you carry in your shop depends, obviously, on the kind of new finish you prefer. If you like paint, then a selection of paints, toning colors and brushes is all you need, but since we are dealing with furniture, the beauty of natural wood grains is generally more important and more desirable than the color accents of paint.

Shellac is a must. It is used as the final finish on many pieces of furniture and as a primer coat when you varnish. While it is available in both clear and orange tone, you'll find the clear is the best choice. The orange shellac is just too heavily toned for most woods, although you may find you like the warmer tone that's possible by mixing a small amount of orange shellac with the clear.

Mix the shellac with the wood alcohol before applying. If you like antique-looking, hand-rubbed surfaces, try mixing shellac with 4 or 5 parts alcohol and rubbing the preparation into the wood. If you prefer to apply shellac with a brush, mix it with 2 or 3 parts alcohol. Either way, apply several coats.

Tables and counters need a heavier, more protective surface, such as a varnish. Be sure to use a clear synthetic; it dries faster, has a harder surface, and has less effect on wood grains.

For a hand-rubbed appearance, try adding a final coat of dull varnish over one or two coats of clear. Let the varnish dry thoroughly, then rub lightly with 00000 steel wool and wax.

Turpentine is another refinishing staple. It is used as a thinner for varnish and for some cleanup work. Most experts prefer the less expensive turpentine substitutes: these mix as well with real turpentine and cost about half the price.

When thinning varnish, use turpentine sparingly. A good trick is to warm the varnish to make it flow. You'll find warmed varnish brushes better and dries faster than most thinned versions.

Stains are seldom needed in refinishing, but when you need to change the appearance of the wood, nothing else does the trick. Most wood workers overdo staining, and the result is an unattractive blob in place of what could have been beautiful grain. Avoid the commercial stains that contain pigments. These hide, rather than uncover, grain patterns. Instead, try penetrating oil stains. Simply spread them on the wood, let stand for a few minutes, then wipe off.

Brushes are a must, and while most workers spend startling sums buying the best available, you'll find cheaper brushes are actually better. You can use them once, then throw them away. The result will be a better job.

INCIDENTAL SUPPLIES

Boiled linseed oil is often used as a final finish in place of either shellac or varnish, but you'll find that a true linseed oil finish collects dirt, becomes grimy and dull and is generally uninteresting long before the job is done.

It is better to apply linseed over 2 or 3 coats of thinned shellac. The result is a warm, soft glow which looks like the real thing and never collects dirt.

Purists insist that the final rubdown be done with pumice and rottenstone. There's nothing wrong with these techniques. They work and the result is a soft, glowing patina that has the life and look of real furniture. The only trouble is that pumice and rottenstone take time. They must be mixed with water to form a paste, then rubbed until your arms nearly fall off.Most experts have found that a final rubbing with a super-fine steel wool—00000 or 000000—gives the same finish with less effort. Few, if any, experts can tell the difference.

Wood fillers are handy for any refinishing kit. There are may types available and most work nicely. The wood plastics are easy to use, although they will not take a stain once they have dried. A few firms offer precolored wood plastics (although the colors seldom exactly match the piece you are working on), but most must be colored at home. The plastics can be stained before they are applied by adding commercial stains a drop at a time until the dough is tinted to match the wood. When the plastic dries, it can then be smoothed for final finish.

These are the only items you'll need to do professional refinishing at home. The materials are neither costly nor bulky, and the best part is you can start your refinishing cabinet with little more than wood alcohol, paint remover, and steel wool. It's easy enough to add the other items when you need them. Chances are once you try furniture refinishing, you'll have a full refinisher's cabinet before a month is over—refinishing is that easy and the results are that pleasing.

All about Abrasives

WHETHER YOU CALL it sandpaper or coated abrasive, it's the same thing and it does the same jobs. The readily available abrasive types are five in number. The one you use depends on the job to be done and the material involved.

TYPES OF ABRASIVES

There's a technique in using any of these abrasives to get the best result. To see the overall picture, let's look at the abrasives first, then the methods of using them.

Flint, a natural abrasive, is the oldest of the common woodworking types still widely used. It has a short working life and relatively poor cutting power. But, being the lowest in price, it's very popular for work that clogs the abrasive quickly and requires frequent replacement, as in heavy paint removal. It is grayish white, but acquires a yellowish tinge from the adhesive that holds it to the paper.

Garnet is another natural abrasive. It has much sharper cutting edges (when crushed) than flint, and is much harder. So it cuts faster, lasts longer, and is a good low-cost woodworking abrasive. It is easy to recognize by its red color—the same red color that makes large pieces attractive when faceted and polished for jewelry use.

Emery, also a natural abrasive, was once the major metal-finishing type. It is black, slow-cutting, and short lived. But its rounded, slow-cutting crystals have very good polishing qualities that give it a lasting place in the workshop. It is also used by tradition-minded craftsmen and by those unfamiliar with the more efficient artificial abrasives now available for cutting rather than polishing action.

Aluminum oxide, a reddish-brown artificial abrasive, is perhaps the most versatile and widely used of the synthesized types. Being extremely tough and sharp, it is excellent for wood, metal, and the majority of other materials usually handled in the home workshop. It far outlasts any of the natural abrasives, and cuts much faster.

Silicon carbide, a blue-black artificial abrasive, is almost as hard as the diamond, and is the sharpest of all five common abrasive types. But its crystals are too brittle for general use on metals like iron and steel. It is a good choice, however, for softer metals like aluminum and bronze, because it cuts very fast without excessive speed or pressure. It also has ample strength for use on glass, and is widely used in glass work. It is the ideal abrasive, too, for many soft materials like leather. It is, in fact, one of the leading abrasives in shoemaking and shoe repair.

Pumice and rottenstone are natural abrasives not commonly available retail in coated-abrasive form. They are obtainable, however, in fine powdered form through paint stores, and are widely used in producing the desired sheen in fine furniture work. The powder is mixed with No. 10 motor oil, or similar light oil, to make a creamy paste. (Water mixtures and others are sometimes used.) The application is described later.

COARSENESS GRADES

The coarseness of coated abrasives is measured in several ways, according to the type of the abrasive, its application, and to some extent, the market to which it is sold.

Industrial users, for example, prefer to specify coarseness by grit size—the minimum size sieve openings through which the abrasive grains will pass. (The extra-fine and super-fine sizes are graded by air flotation and water sedimentation processes.) An extra-coarse abrasive might have a grit size of 16, extra-fine might be as high as 600 (each representing the number of sieve openings in a given area).

Some users, on the other hand, still think in terms of the old symbol system, using 0, 2/0, 3/0, etc. And many home shop workers like the simplified terminology of extra-fine, fine, medium, and so on.

A coarseness grading term from at least one of these systems will be found printed on the back of your sandpaper (coated abrasive). The grit size is also printed on screen-backed abrasive. The nonwoven pad types, however, usually have to be identified as to coarseness by color. Check on this where you buy unless you find the coarseness grade printed on the package.

The backing of coated abrasives is usually paper or cloth, though combinations are also used for special purposes. For most workshop applications a paper backing is the choice, with cloth backing reserved for heavy-duty jobs, as in some forms of metal work. In general, lighter-weight backings of either type are used with fine grit sizes for flexibility. Heavier backings go with coarser grits that are likely to be used under conditions of greater stress.

Open-coat abrasive paper is made with abrasive grains separated by preset distances so that the abrasive covers only about 50 to 70 percent of the surface. The gap between abrasive particles greatly reduces clogging with sanded material. This type can be used for most sanding work with a saving in time and expense, and is available from the usual sandpaper sources.

Wet-or-dry coated abrasives can be used with water or other liquids to wash away abraded material. Use it on car body work and other jobs requiring a very fine abrasive that would be subject to frequent clogging.

SANDING METHODS

Sanding methods depend on the job, and whether the work is done by hand or power. The number of different grades of coarseness the job requires depends on the initial roughness of the surface to be smoothed. If you are starting with rough wood, for example, as it might be after cutting to size on a workshop table saw, you would start sanding with a 50- or 60-grit size, sand with the grain, and continue until the entire surface has the same sanded texture. Then switch to a grit size of about 100. Work in stages to a finishing grit size around 220 or 240, never skipping more than one grit size when switching from one stage to the next.

If the wood is smooth-surfaced (as dressed lumber from the lumberyard), you can start with a grit size around 120. All this, assuming you want an extremely fine finish. After sanding, it is extremely important that all dust be removed from the work. Otherwise, dust specks will appear in whatever finish is applied.

Using powdered abrasive, like pumice, is a simple matter. The purpose is the reduction of a high gloss to a softer sheen— desirable on many furniture projects. Mix the pumice (available from paint stores) with inexpensive No. 10 motor oil to form a creamy paste. Rub this paste over the work with a soft cloth and light pressure. Wipe off the paste frequently. (See Fig. 18-1.)

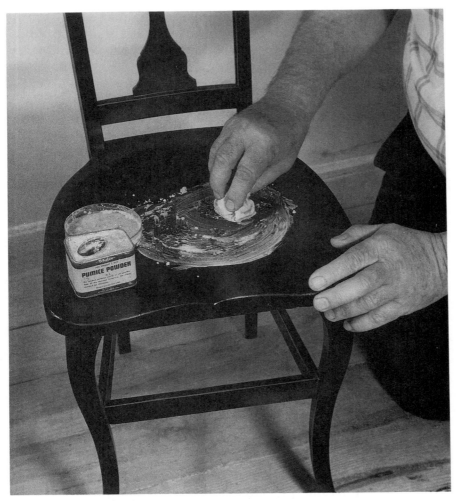

Fig. 18-1. To use powdered pumice, simply mix with No. 10 motor oil and rub over the piece. Be sure to wipe off excess frequently.

Abrasive pads can do much the same job without the need for cleanup (Fig. 18-2). Your best bet is to try the grades on a concealed area of the piece to be rubbed, starting with the finest. A minute of rubbing will usually tell the grade best suited to the job. Steel wool can be used for this purpose, too, but usually requires more work to produce equivalent results.

POWER SANDERS

Power sanders are made in various basic types that should be matched, where possible, to the type of work. Some of the more versatile types can be used for a wide variety of jobs.

Reciprocal sanders operate with a back-and-forth motion, much like with-the-grain hand sanding. They do the same job as

Fig. 18-2. Experiment with different grades of abrasive pads to determine the one best suited to the job at hand.

Fig. 18-3. Be sure to use the proper sander for each specific job. Shown in the photo (clockwise, from top left) are the belt sander, orbital sander, and disc sander with rigid disc attachment.

hand sanding, but do it faster. And they should be used with the same grit-size stages as in hand sanding.

Orbital sanders (sometimes combined in dual types for selective reciprocal or orbital motion) move the sandpaper in a small rotary orbit. Instead of moving back and forth, the sandpaper combines a side motion, producing an "orbit" about ⅜-inch in diameter. The orbital motion is very useful where the wood grain meets from several directions, as at a miter. Instead of sanding with the grain on one piece and crosswise on the other, as a reciprocal sander would, the orbital type sands with the same rotary motion on both pieces. Both this and the reciprocal type are good finishing sanders for most work.

The belt sander provides a unidirectional motion by means of an abrasive-coated belt that operates much as the treads of a bulldozer. Hence, it is essential to keep a good grip on the sander to keep it from "running away" across the work. The motors in these sanders are usually much more powerful than those in other types, and they are fast cutting when used with coarse grit belts. For the fastest cutting they are often used at a 45-degree angle across the wood grain, first in one direction, then the other. Final smoothing is with the grain.

Disc sanders are made in three basic types. The flexible-disc sander, probably the most common and inexpensive, is simply a rubber disc with a center shaft for mounting in a power drill chuck, and a centered screw flange gripping the abrasive disc. This type cuts fast and is suited to rough work.

The rigid disc sander is often mounted in place of the blade of a table saw. The sandpaper is stuck to the disc with a special "peelable" adhesive that permits abrasive removal and replacement quickly and easily. This type can be used for smoothing and for wood trimming, much as a planing machine might be used.

The ball joint disc is also a rigid form. But the sandpaper disc is attached in the same manner as on the flexible disc, by a screw-flange at the center. The ball joint permits this disc to be used flat on the surface of the work, driven by a power drill. The centered screw flange is recessed so it does not contact the work surface, and the ball joint prevents the disc from digging in if the power drill is tilted during the operation. This is also a good finishing type of sander in the low price range.

All power sanders should be used with progressively finer grit sizes in finishing work, and must be kept moving over the work. If allowed to stand still while running, they will cut a recess in the work surface. The technique of use, however, is quickly acquired. The best bet, practice on scrap material before tackling your first project.

Preparing Raw Wood for Finishing

PREPARATION OF RAW WOOD is more than half the battle when it comes to giving raw wood a solid finish. Taking care at this stage of the project can make the project much easier at the end.

PRELIMINARIES

There are a number of things to be sure of. First, the wood must be absolutely clean. If you have removed finish, make sure that every trace of the remover is gone. Any bits of remover will bleed through, as will dirt, wax, and other foreign materials. Even supposedly clean bare wood can be soiled, so it is best to clean it thoroughly with paint thinner or a liquid sander, such as UGL D-Gloss Liquid Sander. If you raise the grain on the wood after doing this, be sure that sanding removes the whiskers.

Whether you finish wood that has been stripped, or material which is brand new, it is likely that some areas will have to be patched: gouges and the like filled in. Various patching materials are now available, including ones which are mixed with water.

The ready-mixed works best. It comes in various colors as well as a natural which can be colored with universal colorants.

The material is simple to use. You just press it in place with a flexible putty knife or scraper and draw off excess. The material dries hard and can be sanded just like wood.

FILLING

One aspect of finishing raw wood which is sometimes forgotten by wood finishers is filling—applying a material to fill the wood press of particular woods.

Woods can be classified as open grained or close grained. Open grain means that the wood cells are more open; in fact, they can be visible to the eye, such as with oak. In close-grained woods, such as maple, the wood cells are dense (See Figs. 19-1, 19-2.) If you don't fill an open-grained wood and you apply stain, it can lead to spotty results. The stain will soak in more heavily in some areas than others.

Filling can be done in a variety of ways, and instructions will be on the container of the filler you buy. Basically, though, it's

Fig. 19-1. This is an open-grain wood. When finish is applied it will soak into pores creating a spotty finish. Seal it.

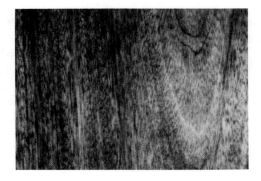

Fig. 19-2. Close-grain wood. This has a very nonporous surface and will not absorb finish. Sealing is not required on this.

just a matter of wiping the paste-like filler—in an appropriate color—onto the wood, working it in, then wiping off excess.

SANDING

Sanding is the final and most important part of finishing raw wood. Yet although sanding and preparation are the secrets of a professional, perfect finish, most of us like to take advantage of shortcuts when we can. Quick machine sanding and easy touch-ups by hand can deliver an acceptable finish for most projects, but when perfection is important, forget the shortcut.

Perhaps you've already learned that a fine finish is the result of meticulous care. If you haven't, then try this system when a project really counts. You'll be pleasantly surprised at the way it unlocks a new range of tones and patina in the wood.

Preparing the wood for staining or varnishing takes time. It takes hard work and requires hand work. Belt sanders—so handy for most jobs—are out. Orbital and straight-line sanders can be used for part of the job, but the preliminary and final stages must be done slowly by hand.

Preparing for sanding

No wood, not even the most expensive milled stock, is ready for sanding as it comes from the lumber yard. The rougher the stock, the more preparation needed before you can sand. When wood is extremely rough, as many hardwoods are, you'll have to plane the surfaces first.

If the stock is narrow, or if your machinery is big enough, the preliminary smoothing can be done on a jointer or planer. But if you lack these refinements, the work can be done with a hand plane. Work the surface end to end until it is level and smooth. In most cases, you'll do this before you begin building your project.

Most woods must still be smoothed before they are ready for sanding. The job can be done before the piece is assembled, or after the project is built. The choice depends on the job. If the material will be difficult to work after the job is put together, smooth the surfaces beforehand. The smoothing should be done with a cabinet scraper, the proper tool for the job and a more important tool than many people realize.

Don't underestimate the importance of a scraper (Fig. 19-3.) The amount of care spent scraping a piece of wood has a lot to do with the results you get from sanding.

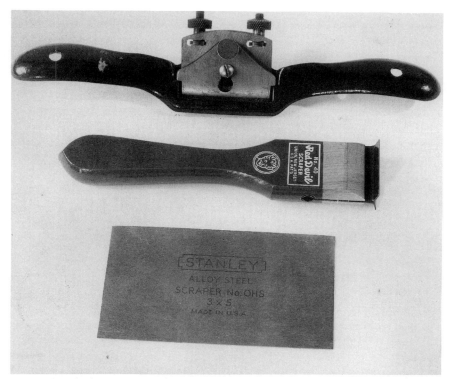

Fig. 19-3. Types of scrapers: Top, blade mounted in holder like a miniature plane, used for rough work. Center, blade in handle for removing surface coatings. Bottom, blade alone for fine work.

Some people feel a scraper should remove only fine dust. In fact, it should do much more. If you've sharpened the blade properly—instructions come with the blades—the scraper works like a very fine plane, cutting off fine shavings as it surfaces and smoothes the wood.

You can work the blade on either a push or pull stroke, but it's best to work only one way. When the blade is pushed, hold it firmly with both hands, fingers on one side, thumbs on the other. Tilt the blade away from your body to avoid blade chatter as you work. If you work on the pull stroke, tilt the blade toward you.

Some scrapers are designed to work in holders, like miniature planes (Fig. 19-4.) Others are simply metal blades, hand-held. The mounted blades are excellent for preliminary work on rougher surfaces; you'll get better finish results with the hand-held blade (Fig.19-5.) The blades come in several sizes, from 2 × 3 to 6 × 7 inches. Choose the size best suited to your work.

Fig. 19-4. A mounted scraper blade works similar to a plane. Both blade depth and angle of cut can be regulated by knurled screws. This kind of scraper is handy for the early surfacing stages.

Scrape with the grain, never across, and work over the entire surface, covering small areas at a time. Repeat several times until the wood has a smooth, even glassy feel.

Starting to Sand

When you are through scraping, the wood is ready for sanding. Begin with a fairly fine grit (100 to 120 grit should be course enough), since a rough grit would scratch the surface. Do the preliminary sanding by hand. Wrap the abrasive around either a commercial rubber pad (Fig. 19-6) or a flat piece of wood.

If you use a wood block, place a pad of soft paper between the block and the wood, to give a little flexibility to the cutting surface of the abrasive (Fig. 19-7.) The softness, slight as it is, will work better over the few high spots which still exist. A small piece of paper toweling folded two or three times will give you just the pad required.

Sand with the grain, covering small areas on each pass, working the full surface evenly each time. Repeat two or three times, then change to a finer grit. When you move up to a finer grit, discard the towel padding. If you use a flat block on these final stages, you'll get a flatter surface.

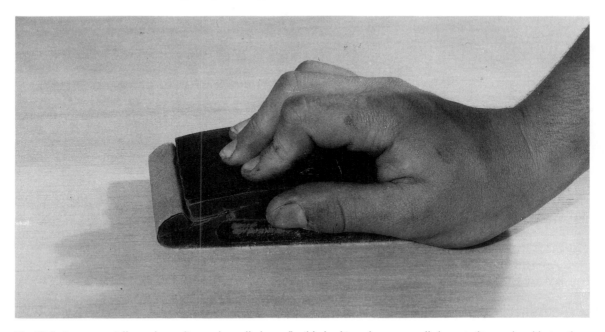

Fig. 19-6. A commercially made sanding pad usually has a flexible backing plus an overall shape to fit your hand better than a wood block; a feature you'll appreciate when sanding a large area.

Fig. 19-7. When using a wooden sanding block, add a flexible material, like a folded paper towel, as a backing for the sand paper. This produces better surface contact and speeds the sanding.

Move progressively to finer grits. Don't jump from the relatively rough 100 grit to a very fine one. Make the transition slowly. If you started with 100 grit, for example, move to 120, then to 150. If you prefer, you can use an orbital or straight-line sander. These early stages can be done by hand or power, and it's impossible to tell the results apart.

Be sure to remove the wood dust often and thoroughly. Either blow it off the surface or remove it with a brush. Don't use cloth; most cloths leave a lint that's nearly as troublesome as the dust (Fig. 19-8.) Check the abrasive paper often. The dust will collect in the open areas between the abrasive and when the paper is clogged, either clean it by hitting the paper against your clothing or replace the paper.

As you move to the finer grits—about 180 on—start raising the softer grains of the wood (Fig. 19-9.) This is best done by wiping the wood with a sponge *dipped* (not saturated) in water. A little moisture goes a long way; the idea is to bring the softer grains upward, raising or swelling the fibers above the surface of the harder grains. Here, they can be cut down by the abrasive.

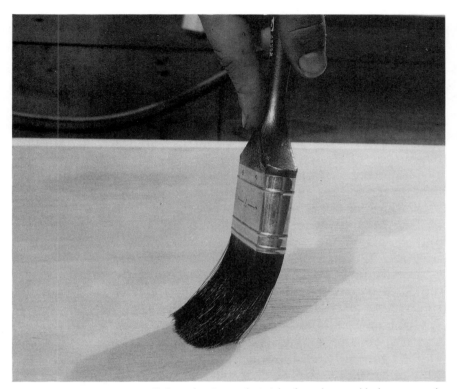

Fig. 19-8. Be sure to remove all dust, abrasive, and particles from the wood before you apply the finish. Use a brush or compressed air, but avoid fabrics, which may leave troublesome lint.

Fig. 19-9. As you move toward finer sanding, start raising the softer grains of the wood. This is best done by wiping surface with a sponge dipped (not soaked) in water. This raises the fibers.

The result is a surface smoother than you imagined possible by any other system.

On most woods the softer fibers are tough enough to stand erect like whiskers after they've been raised with water. But on some woods—mahogany is one—the fibers may bend under the force of the abrasive. You can keep them erect during sanding by adding a little household glue to the water. When the glue hardens, it will keep the fibers upright while you sand, and if you don't overdo the glue, it will not interfere with the grain pattern.

Raise the grain several times, each time sanding the fibers back to the harder areas. Repeat this as you move to even finer grits. Continue until the soft fibers no longer raise above the sanded surface. On most woods it will take four to six passes with water and abrasive; a few woods may require as many as ten or twelve wettings. But be patient. This is an important step.

Continue to work your way through the grits until you get the finest available—generally a 320 grit available most frequently in a wet or dry paper. Use this dry.

The end grain is as important as the top and side surfaces, and it should be sanded with the same care. But since the end grain is generally harder, it rarely needs to have the grain raised. You can usually work this dry all the way through.

There is a very real danger of splitting when you sand the end grain. The job will be easier and safer if you clamp two straight-edged boards top and bottom across the end grain, and add two smaller blocks on the edges. This four-sided protection will prevent splitting and will give you a guide to keep the ends from being rounded as you sand.

The sanding is relatively easy since most surfaces are flat, but here are a few tips for those hard-to-reach areas.

Crevices and routed areas can be sanded best with unbacked paper bent to fit the depression. The paper will bend more easily if you'll pull it, abrasive up, across the edge of a table two or three times. Pre-bending will prevent cracking.

Try wrapping the paper around a sharpened stick when you must sand a groove or a rounded corner. Fold the paper over the end of the stick and use the finer point to reach into the smaller grooves.

Don't try to sand a large area down to smooth a small dent. It's generally easier to raise the fibers in the dent by carefully dropping water into the depression. An eye dropper is excellent for small areas, but be exact. If you drop water on the surrounding high areas as well as into the low spot, you are not altering the relative depths at all. Stubborn dents which refuse to raise with repeated soakings can often be raised by heat and moisture. Place a damp cloth over the dent and heat it gently. A hand iron works well on larger areas; a soldering gun is perfect for small spots.

FINAL PREPARATIONS

Once you've finished sanding with abrasives, polish or rub down the wood with two or three grades of steel wool before you apply a stain or a finish. Start with a fine (000) wool and finish with at least a 00000. The gentle polishing will further smooth the surface and will unlock the subtle tonal variations in the grains you'd miss otherwise.

Be sure to remove all dust, abrasive and steel wool from the wood before you apply stain or shellac. You can remove most of the dust with a brush or paper towel, but if you use toweling be careful of lint. Some paper products can leave nearly as much lint as sandpaper leaves wood dust. Continue to clean the surface until it's completely clean. Do not use water—water at this point would still raise the grain just enough to require another round of sanding.

The wood should be completely clean, free of oil, dirt, and dust before you finish with stain, varnish or shellac. And when you finish, be sure to use materials which enhance the grains you've uncovered. Not all finishes do this, so pick the right kind. At this point you've brought out all the beauty the wood can offer. Don't waste it.

Surfacing a Board

NOWADAYS IT'S FAIRLY EASY TO obtain boards which are straight and true, so why should you want to bother surfacing a board? Well, for one thing, that straight and true lumber is going to cost you an arm and both legs, especially if you want something harder than pine. For this reason, it pays to reclaim used boards. Used lumber is generally available from wrecker storage yards and is usually much cheaper than the same lumber new.

And maybe you've discovered that the straight and true stock you purchased a short time back isn't as even as it first appeared. Perhaps the boards lost moisture through the end grain which wasn't sealed, or maybe they were stacked improperly, or were exposed to weather, or somehow marred. The lumber now has to be resurfaced or else discarded. Probably the best argument of all is that the sure-handed ability to work a piece of timber into true is one of the criteria which separates the craftsman from the novice.

The first step in evening up a board is to work the surface, or face, which must be flat, not only to be serviceable and to look good, but also because it is a working base for other steps in fabrication.

NECESSARY TOOLS

You'll need three tools for surfacing—a solid bench to hold the work, a plane to dress the piece, and sandpaper to smooth it. Having nothing better, use a stout table for a bench, tacking a strip of wood across one end as a stop to plane against (Fig. 20-1A). At small expense a couple of good planks can be set up on a frame and equipped with a similar ledge. Add to this an inexpensive iron vise (obtainable with a continuous screw or a quick-acting screw that slides the jaws to contact and locks the work with a twist of the handle), and you have a means of clamping the edges of the board to prevent it from swiveling (Fig. 20-1B). Such clamping is useful only on stiff board, for thin stock is bowed at the center by the pressure. Best of all is a cabinetmaker's bench equipped with a tail vise (Fig. 20-1C,D), which locks the ends of the board while fully supporting it from beneath.

Spare your edged tools by dusting or scraping clean the board you are to plane. If it is cupped or *in wind* (that is, if wood is twisted), a condition you can discover by sighting over a couple of sticks having parallel edges, lay it bowed-side up to reduce the

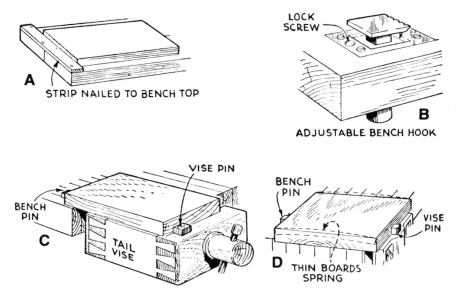

Fig. 20-1. Bench holding devices.

207

tendency to rock (Fig. 20-2A,B). If you only want one good side and the cupped side is the choice, lay it up and shim the high corners with chips. Also, place the board to plane with the grain (Fig. 20-2C). One stroke of the plane, by cutting smoothly or chipping the wood, will show whether the piece has the right end forward. When wood is cross-grained, there isn't much choice.

The modern plane (Fig. 20-3) is an engineered tool that evolved from a simple iron blade set into a block of wood. The cutting blade, or plane iron, is reinforced with a cap iron, which breaks the shaving and curls it forward. The closer the edge of the cap is to that of the blade, the sooner the shaving is broken after it parts from the board, reducing chipping into the board if it is cross-grained. Locked together, the irons are called the *double iron*. They are clamped to a frog having a lateral adjustment lever which retracts a projecting edge corner by swinging the top of the double iron from side to side.

Turning the adjustment nut regulates depth of cut. By loosening the base screws the frog is moved forward to narrow the mouth as a further method of preventing chipping, because of nose pressure close to the cutting edge.

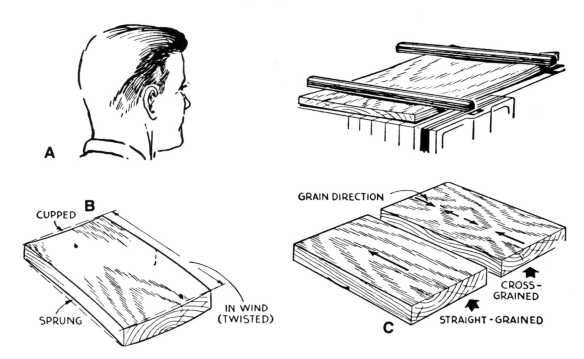

Fig. 20-2. (A) Sighting over windsticks. (B) Two warping faults. (C) Grain character.

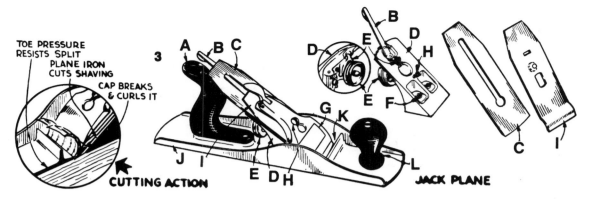

Fig. 20-3. Parts of a jack plane: (A) plane handle, (B) lateral adjusting lever, (C) single plane iron, (D) frog complete, (E) adj. nut, (E1) "Y" adj. lever, (F) frog screw, (G) lever cap, (H) lever cap screw, (I) plane iron cap, (J) plane bottom, (K) plane mouth, (L) plane knob, (C&I) double plane iron.

If you buy only one plane, let it be a *jack*. It is long enough to span most hollow spots in a board, guiding and straightening it, yet it's short enough to follow gradual curves that can be taken out in nailing or otherwise assembling the piece with joining members. Make a straight cutting edge in this case. If you also have a smooth plane, sharpen the jack with a crowned edge and reserve the straight edge for the smooth plane (Fig. 20-4).

PLANING A BOARD

To plane a board, take an easy standing position with the left foot advanced, and begin a stroke at the left edge. Press toe of the plane down firmly to prevent the heel from dropping, which dubs off the wood at the start. Toward the end of the stroke shift your weight to the left foot, and, when finishing, lift the plane clear, preventing it from nosing down. Carry it back instead of dragging the edge back over the wood. Overlap the strokes as you work toward the right edge.

Shaving Thickness

The shaving thickness depends on the amount of stock necessary to smooth the board. Don't take fine cuts when a roughing cut is needed. Test the edge projection by inverting the plane and sighting along the bottom or, feeling lightly with the

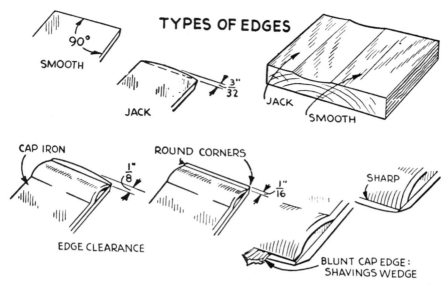

Fig. 20-4. If you have both a jack and a smooth plane, sharpen the jack with a crowned edge and reserve straight edge for a smooth plane. Wedged shavings mean dull cap edge.

finger, shifting the lateral adjustment level toward the side of a projecting corner.

A second going-over with a finer cut further smooths the piece. Check the flatness with the corner of the plane laid crosswise of the board. To plane the bowed side of a warped board, reduce the center first. If cupped side is up, plane the edges first; and if there is *wind* (twist), rough off high corners, plane diagonally across the piece, and finish lengthwise. Sometimes it's best to plane along both diagonals.

SHARPENING YOUR PLANE

It takes a sharp plane to do good work. Even a slightly dull edge balks on flat-grained fir, digs into the soft wood, and skids over the hard parts. Nicks in the edge leave ridges on the planed surface. Time lost in sharpening is more than made up in improved action of the tool and the pleasure in using it.

Whetstones are made in a variety of sizes and materials. A high-quality combination oilstone having coarse grit on one side and medium on the other is best for general shop work, and should be mounted in a fitted box with an oiled pad in the bottom. Soak the stone with light oil and, when using, drop on a little kerosene to float away metal particles. Stroke the length of the stone parallel to the edges (Fig. 20-5).

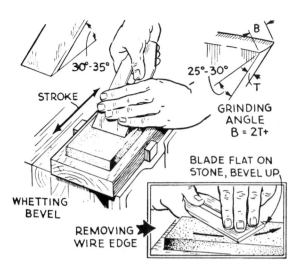

Fig. 20-5. To get a sharp edge, hold plane iron as in diagram, right, and stroke the length of the stone parallel to the edges. Continue until fine wire edge is formed.

The sure way to sharpen is to continue bevel whetting until a fine wire edge can be felt. Remove this laying the flat side on the stone to avoid any possible beveling. Wipe the coarse side before turning the stone over, and whet again, this time eliminating the wire edge by alternate strokes on the flat side and the bevel.

A nicked edge, or one rounded by much whetting, must be ground. If you use a power wheel, take care not to burn iron. Avoid heavy pressure, and cool the iron in a dish of water after each pass from side to side. A hand wheel is good, if you can handle the iron with one hand.

A wet grinder is an easy machine to use and will not burn the plane iron. To remove nicks and square the edge, point the plane iron toward the center of the wheel, and after truing, grind the bevel. An angle of 25 or 30 degrees is about right—indicated by a bevel a little wider than twice the thickness of the iron. After grinding, whet.

Keep edge of cap iron smooth and sharp, with enough bevel underneath to ensure tight contact with the plane iron; otherwise, shavings will wedge between and choke the plane. Assemble double iron by engaging cap screw in the plane iron slot and closing the two like scissors to prevent contact of edge with arch of cap (Fig. 20-6). Tighten screw when cap edge has been slid up

SHARPENING PLANE IRON

ASSEMBLING IRONS

Fig. 20-6. Use care when assembling the cap iron and plane iron, left, to prevent nicking the edges.

to position near the cutting edge, which, with very close-grained wood, is as close as possible.

Take care to seat the double iron properly on the frog, engaging all projections in the openings provided for them, and clamp by placing lever cap and pushing down the lever. Clamping pressure must be enough to keep the plane iron regulated by turning in or out the screw passing through center of double iron and lever cap.

REMOVING PLANING MARKS

Sometimes planing leaves the wood in condition for sanding. More often plane marks remain because it tends to follow the curve of large irregularities. In all but very soft woods the scraper is the tool to use after planing. It is essentially a plate of steel with sharp, burred corners (Fig. 20-7). Incline it until the edge bites, flexing the center a little, and pushing it forward. With some grains it's best to slide the blade a trifle edgewise, as well. You can also draw the tool toward you; and to protect your fingers from the edges and the heat generated, a slitted block can be slipped over for a holder.

HAND SCRAPING

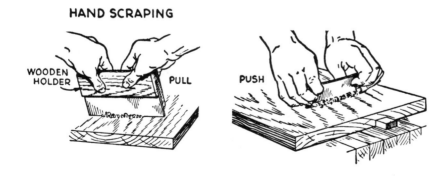

WOODEN HOLDER   PULL   PUSH

Fig. 20-7. A hand scraper is the tool to use after planing. It is a steel plate with sharp, burred corners and is inclined when scraping.

Sharpening Your Scraper

There is a certain knack in sharpening a scraper, but the operation is really simple. Clamp the blade in a vise and drawfile the edge with a mill file by stroking lengthwise of the edge (Fig. 20-8). Continue until corners or *arrises* of 4 edges are all sharp; then rub off burrs on an oilstone. Next whet edges by holding the scraper upright on the stone, and work off all burrs. Be sure all arrises are as sharp as possible.

Now lay blade on the bench and using pressure, rub sides with a burnisher or a nail set resting flat. Next stroke, the edge 2 or 3 times, beginning with the burnisher held nearly vertical and gradually inclining it toward the blade. Some woodworkers stroke from corner to corner; others from center toward the corners. A drop of oil, or wax rubbed on the burnisher, improves the action. If this is properly done a keen, fine burr is raised on the arris that will cut down cross-grained wood to a smoothness that few planes can equal.

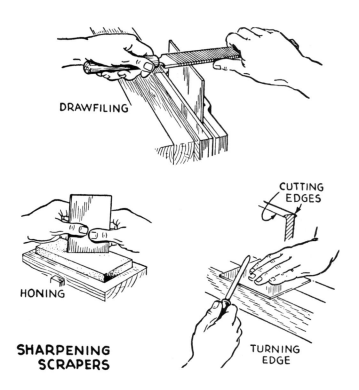

DRAWFILING

CUTTING EDGES

HONING

TURNING EDGE

SHARPENING SCRAPERS

Fig. 20-8. Sharpen with draw file and whetstone. Remove burrs from edge and, using pressure, burnish sides with nail or burnisher.

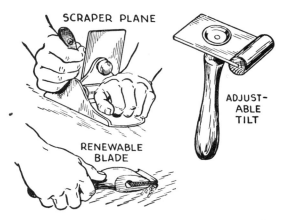

Fig. 20-9. Scraper holders come in several forms. A scraper plane is not that common, but the square-edge hand scraper is the best all purpose tool.

Turn all 8 arrises in this way. When the tool dulls, lay it on the bench and rub flat on the sides to straighten the burr; then turn it again by stroking the edge. Edges can be dressed in this way 3 or 4 times before blade needs to be filed and whetted again.

Scraper Holders

Scraper holders are made in several forms (Fig. 20-9). A popular type has renewable blades which are discarded when dull. The crowned, chisel edge cuts fast, but is not the equal of the square-edge hand scraper for fine work. Various holders of the plane type usually employ a chisel edge which is turned toward the flat edge of the blade, since the bottom of the holder limits depth of cut.

Sanding provides final smoothing. Sanding blocks are good, but don't use a padded one on such woods as fir, because it will take out the soft grain and leave the hard grain. On hardwoods 4/0 paper is good for final sanding.

How to
Enamel, Stain
and Finish Wood

UNFINISHED FURNITURE MAY BE stained or enameled, but the beginner is better off tackling enameling first—preferably a bookcase or other small section. Also, this furniture is not particularly suited for staining or "clear" finishing with shellac or unpigmented lacquer. The reason is that the furniture is built of solid lumber consisting of glued-up board widths, and when clear lacquer of shellac is applied, the variation in the color of the boards is accentuated—especially where they are joined.

ENAMELING PREPARATION

Before starting the enameling project, decide on the color shade and also on whether you want a high-gloss or satin finish. Enamel is available in a wide variety of colors, or you can buy white enamel and color it with pigment from tubes to suit yourself. Any quality enamel of a reputable brand can be used. The undercoating or "primer" should be of the same brand as the finish enamel.

Start by removing all drawers and hardware, these are finished separately.

Then "clean" the wood. Unfinished furniture comes presanded, but it is essential that you go over it again to remove surface fibers and smooth rough spots (Fig. 21-1). Use a fairly coarse sandpaper at first, such as 2/0 garnet cabinet paper, held across a block of wood or fitted in one of the commercial sandpaper holders. An electric sander isn't necessary—and by no means use a disc sander; this will just gouge and score the wood.

Apply the sandpaper firmly, working only with the grain. Follow up by smooth-sanding with finer 4/0 paper, then dust the furniture carefully with a soft, dry brush. Finally, wipe all surfaces with a clean cloth.

Fig. 21-1. Most unfinished furniture is sanded before sold, but not so smooth that you can go right ahead and enamel it. Sections should be carefully hand-sanded to smooth out rough spots. Use sanding block or commercially made holder.

APPLYING UNDERCOAT

Now you are ready to apply the enamel undercoat. This should be tinted approximately the same color as the surface coat by adding pigment from a tube (Fig. 21-2).

Use a quality-bristle brush 3 or 4 inches wide for applying the enamel when the undercoat has dried. Dip the brush in the can to a depth of about an inch, then apply the enamel to the surface, brushing out the paint in straight lines along the grain. Stay in one line at a time, working in the enamel thoroughly until it is spread evenly and the brush seems almost dry.

It is important to develop the right stroke with the brush. Move it in a single stroke from near one edge clear across the work until the brush leaves the other end; then repeat the stroke from the other side. The final strokes should be done with the tips of the bristles, holding the almost-dry brush at a right angle to the work and applying very little pressure.

Fig. 21-2. The primer, or undercoat layer goes on first; this should be tinted approximately the same color as the final coat. When applying the enamel to the surface, work the brush in a straight line with the grain.

When this stage of the work is completed, leave the furniture to dry overnight. Keep all windows closed so that no dust will blow on the wet paint. Wash out brushes in turpentine or solvent, then rinse them in sudsy water. Wrap the brushes in heavy Kraft paper until they are ready to be used again.

Before the final cost is applied, the undercoating (or first enamel coat) must be thoroughly sanded. Use 2/0 sandpaper to remove brush marks, following up with fine 4/0 sandpaper until the surface is perfectly smooth. Then dust carefully.

APPLYING THE FINAL COAT

The final coat is applied in the same manner as the first. Take particular care that the finishing strokes of the brush are very light and straight (Fig. 21-3).

Drawers, drawer hardware and other removable parts are painted separately and replaced only after the entire unit has dried completely (Fig. 21-4).

A clear paste wax may be applied after waiting at least a week for the enamel to dry thoroughly and harden.

STAINING FINE WOOD

Too often, and in too many places, beautiful pieces of rare woods have lost their exciting identity, with grains suppressed

Fig. 21-3. When enameling, brush strokes should be very light and straight.

Fig. 21-4. Hardware such as drawer pulls can be enameled, then set upright to dry in holes drilled in a piece of scrap stock.

by sullen, opaque stains. It's an easy way to finish wood, but it's not the right way.

Properly finished, the grain of wood becomes an integral part of the furniture, and not every length of wood is worth the time and effort. If the wood you are working with is not worth the trouble, paint it or hide it with cheap stain. But if the wood is rare and the grain exciting, do the job right—let the grain shine through.

There are more ways to hide grain than to bring it out. You can find plenty of pigmented stains, colored varnishes and tinted shellacs. None of these has any important place in furniture finishing. All hide or obscure the grain.

Pigmented stains are the worst offenders. They're compounded with opaque materials which work harder to kill the luster and depth of wood than they do to beautify it. They're helpful in only one case: when it is necessary to fake a grain.

If you want to use these stains, try this idea. Avoid mixing the colorless liquid which rises to the top of the can with the heavier pigments which sink to the bottom. Instead, lift the liquid from the top without mixing. The color is fairly weak, but it works nicely when a light effect is needed.

Oil Stains

Stains can deliver excellent results if you'll take the time to find the clear-oil types. In many stores you'll find them under the name "penetrating oil stain." These can be used to tone wood to any shade or color without affecting the grain patterns.

Wipe on a liberal amount of the stain, let it penetrate into the wood for a few seconds, then wipe it off (Fig. 21-5). The longer the stain is left on, the less you remove; the more coats applied, the darker the effect. For light tones, dilute the stain with turpentine or a substitute (it doesn't matter which). Be sure to put a good primer coat over the stain. Shellac is a good material, but if you prefer a commercial sealer use a clear one. The primer-sealer serves one function: It gives a surface on which you can build up final, smooth finish coats.

Clear and penetrating oil stains are available in many tones and shades, but if you buy three—walnut, maple, and mahogany—you have enough to mix any tone you may need (Fig. 21-6).

Certain of the better "prepared stains" are worth trying on some woods. One is a nearly clear stain with added plastic compounds which build up a smooth, tough surface (Fig. 21-7). The oil colors the wood only slightly; it is clear enough to let the beauty of the grain come through. On lighter woods, the stain has a slightly yellow coloring—something you may or may not like. On darker woods it's hard to beat.

Aniline dyes darken the wood without affecting the grain. They are available as water-soluble or alcohol-soluble materials. You buy them as a dry powder, mixing a small amount with the proper liquid. Anilines are strong and one or two ounces will handle several large pieces of furniture.

Water-soluble anilines are applied directly to the unprimed wood. Most woods have distinct areas of "dense" grain and "porous" grain—layers grown in the spring and summer and in the fall and winter. The faster-growing spring and summer layers are the most porous. They absorb more color and the fibers can lift. The water-soluble dyes raise these fibers and you'll have to resand the wood after the stain dries even if you've raised the grain several times during sanding.

220

Fig. 21-5. Oil stain should be allowed to penetrate pores, then wiped off evenly with a clean rag.

Fig. 21-6. Clear oil stains, which are available in many tones and shades, will give good tonal qualities without obscuring the fine grain of the wood.

Resanding is safe and easy if you'll apply a thin coat of shellac after the stain has dried. The shellac will hold the fibers erect. You can smooth the surface without working into the stain—if you sand lightly with a very fine abrasive paper or with steel wool. A 000 or 00000 steel wool is preferred.

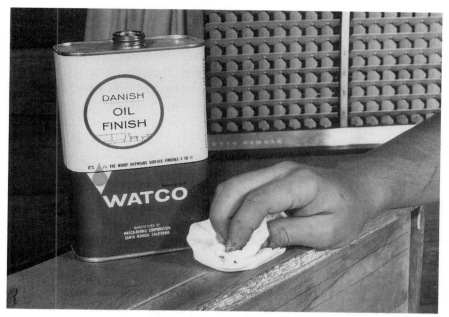

Fig. 21-7. Some stains contain plastic compounds and are worth trying on some woods. They require no other surface care. One nearly clear stain builds up a smooth, tough surface. Oil colors wood only slightly, letting the beauty of the grain come through.

Chances are you will have to resand even when you prime-coat wood without staining. A brush drawn over wood pulls up tiny fibrils. The primer holds these erect as it dries. The result is a rough surface which can be smoothed by a few light rubs with steel wool. Be sure to thoroughly clean the surface before adding another coat.

Alcohol-soluble stains seldom raise the grain and, if they do, have less effect than a water stain. They can be used over raw wood or mixed with shellac or varnish.

Although anilines are available in a host of colors, you will need only a few. Buy three: walnut, mahogany, and maple. From these you can mix any color for any wood.

An example: If you want a mahogany brown, add a small amount of walnut to the maple stain. The result is a rich mahogany stain you can't buy ready-mixed. Want a dark cherry stain? Add a little maple to a mahogany base. For a lighter cherry, add a little mahogany to a maple-walnut base.

Faking Wood Grains

Some woods are nearly uninteresting in their own grains but become much more interesting when they are stained to look like another wood. The New England whitewood or tulip poplar is one example. It is much more exciting when it has been stained to simulate cherry, mahogany, or even birch or cedar.

Here, pigmented stains are helpful. A clear stain can change the grain coloring, but it does not obscure the grain pattern—the one thing necessary in this case. Pigmented stains not only color the wood, but help hide the grain.

In some cases even the opaque pigments may not alter the grain enough. A thinned wood filler might be just what you need.

Mix a standard wood filler–white is best—with turpentine to make a smooth, not-too-thin paste. Tint the paste with stains to the color you want and spread the filler over the wood surface. Wipe off the filler. The amount you leave on the wood will control the amount of grain showing through. A little experimentation will let you simulate both the color and the grain of many woods this way.

FINISHING THE SURFACE

The type and the amount of stain are dictated by the wood, its coloring, and its grain. In some cases no stain at all is dictated. What is required is a simple, protective finish that gives good depth and luster. Early cabinetmakers found the answer in the French polishing method, which can be used on either raw wood or stained wood (Fig. 21-8). It is not often used today, but works well and can be worth the time required.

Use white or clear shellac, about 3- or 4-pound cut (which means that 3 or 4 pounds of shellac gum have been dissolved in one gallon of alcohol). Thin the shellac with wood alcohol and

Fig. 21-8. In the French method, thinned shellac is brushed into the surface. Not used often today, it works well and can be worth time required.

brush it onto the wood, rubbing the wet shellac into the wood after brushing.

Use a rubbing pad made by placing a wadding of cotton inside a soft cotton cloth. Pick up a little linseed oil on the bottom of the pad (the oil is used only as a lubricant during rubbing). Rub the shellac uniformly before it dries.

Repeat the brushing and rubbing process 6 to 12 times, making each pass with more shellac and less thinner. Some finishers prefer to make the first coats with a one pound cut, increasing the mix by moving to increased shellac-cut percentages, finishing the final coats with 3- or 4-pound cut shellac. After the first two coats are on and dry, you should sand between each additional coat with a fine grit paper or with fine steel wool.

A plain shellac finish has many uses. It's easier than the French system and gives comparable results. Again, use clear shellac, thinning it with three or more parts wood alcohol. Brush on each coat of shellac, sanding with abrasive or steel wool after the coat has dried. Cover with three to five light coats, then polish.

Be sure each coat has dried thoroughly before you sand. It may be an overnight procedure. When the finishes are on and rubbed, polish with a good wax.

On warm days you may find the shellac is dry enough to sand in 3 or 4 hours. On humid days, the alcohol in the shellac may draw moisture from the air, creating a white film on the surface. The only solution is to remove the shellac with wood alcohol and start again when there's less humidity.

Varnish is absolutely essential if the wood is to be used around hot places or moisture or if it is to get tabletop treatment. It's best to prime the wood with two or three coats of thinned shellac, although a commercial sealer will work as well. Let the primer or sealer coat dry, then rub it lightly with 000 steel wool. Clean the surface with a brush and cover with a layer of quality synthetic varnish. The synthetic varnishes dry faster and give a better surface.

Use a new brush for each varnish job. You'll get best results if you varnish with cheap brushes, better than if you've used a good brush which has been cleaned several times. Don't try to save varnish—it is seldom as good the second time around.

When you varnish, try thinning with equal amounts of turpentine or turpentine substitute if it seems hard-flowing (Fig. 21-9). A thinner varnish is less apt to show brush marks. Anoth-

Fig. 21-9. Varnish is a tough, durable finish coat. You should use turpentine or a good substitute to thin—a thinner varnish is less likely to show brush marks.

er trick, often better than thinning is to heat the varnish. Heated varnish will flow easily and dry faster.

Linseed oil finishes are becoming popular again, after a hiatus of many years. Avoid the true linseed oil finish as you would pigmented stains. Such a finish collects dirt as it is applied, and from then on. The result is a grimy finish that is both without luster and without grain. A far better answer is the *fake linseed oil* finish several wood finishers use.

Coat the raw wood with a mixture of varnish thinned with 2 or 3 parts turpentine. Rub the mix into the wood with your hand, working vigorously for 3 to 5 minutes, until you feel your hand become hot and the varnish become tacky. Wipe off the excess with a clean dry cloth. Let the coat dry, then sand lightly with 00000 or 000000 steel wool. Apply two or three additional coats of varnish, sanding between each coat.

Let the final coat dry thoroughly then sand again lightly. Brush linseed oil over the varnished surface, covering areas not varnished for extra protection. Let the oil soak into the surface for 12 to 15 minutes, then rub clean with a dry cloth. The result is a finish that is clean and durable and that looks like a real linseed oil finish but lacks its obvious drawbacks.

Conditioning Finishes

All finishes except the "fake linseed oil" finish can be protected with wax. The linseed oil should not be waxed, but it can be brought back to life from time to time by removing the oil surface and resurfacing with another round of oil.

The other finishes should be well sanded with super-fine steel wool (0000 or finer), then covered with a good furniture polish or wax. The final result is a finish that has more luster, more depth, more patina than any finish you can get through short-cut methods. And beneath the finish you can see the beautiful, rich, natural grain of the wood. That's the right way to finish wood. It's well worth the effort.

The Fine Art of Furniture Refinishing

THE FIRST STEP in furniture refinishing is deciding how much refinishing is actually necessary. It is not always essential to take the finish down to the wood, and often it is definitely not advisable. If the finish shows the grain of the natural wood, and if the piece is old, you may destroy much, if not all, of the mellow patina of age by removing the finish entirely. In so doing you will remove the surface layer of wood that has been toned to mellowness by age.

Even if you do the job with paint remover rather than by sanding you will remove elements that contribute to authentic antique appearance. Once they are gone, as experts acknowledge, it is extremely difficult to simulate them.

Before planning your refinishing, determine the type of finish originally used. Shellac is the most likely. To test for it, saturate a wad of cloth with shellac-solvent alcohol (not antifreeze types) and rub it over a small area on the back or underside of the piece in a location that does not show.

228

Aged shellac is commonly many tones darker than when it was originally applied, and will lighten as alcohol rubbing progresses. This tells you the method to follow from that point on. And, if the piece is shellac-finished, your job will not be too lengthy or troublesome. Further alcohol treatment, as described shortly, will do the trick, and will give you control of the tone as you lighten it in preparation for refinishing.

NEW LIFE FOR OLD SHELLAC

Many a drab, dark-toned piece with no evidence of grain pattern can be restored to its original warmth and mellowness (with a bonus produced by aging) simply by repeated wash-downs with alcohol. Do the job outdoors, wear rubber gloves (as shellac alcohol is a bit hard on the hands in lengthy doses) and avoid breathing the fumes as much as possible. The first wash-down is the least effective, but it softens the aged coating and makes the next application relatively fast working.

Work so the surface being treated is toward the sunlight, and watch closely for a lightening in tone—especially for the appearance of a grain pattern through the previously opaque finish. Once you reach this stage, proceed with caution lest you lighten the tone more than you want to.

Look also at the condition of the surface. Often it is possible to retain the original smoothness simply by wiping carefully so as not to leave ridges of softened shellac. If you do exceed the lightness of tone you want to achieve, you can darken slightly with a thin coat of dye-toned shellac, but you'll miss the full benefit of the original natural toning.

When you have reached the desired tone, wipe the surface smooth with the alcohol-soaked cloth and let it dry thoroughly (about 4 hours). Then sand it lightly with fine cabinet paper and apply a coat of fresh 2-lb. cut white shellac. You're not likely to find an excessively darkened finish on pieces of recent manufacture. Most often, it will be on furniture a half century or more old. Originally the piece was stained to make the most of the grain pattern and color of the wood used, often producing a tone considerably darker than natural, but still revealing the wood pattern. Age dimmed and spoiled the effect (since shellac as well as many other finishes) darkens over long periods of time.

On old pieces, especially of the early American type, it might be better to apply the shellac with a cloth pad rather than a brush. Wear rubber gloves to avoid sticky hands, and simply dip the cloth pad in a shallow saucer or bowel of the shellac. Then slide it along the surface. It deposits a smooth, thin coat without brush marks or sags. And you can discard the pad when you're through.

If the luster is too dull, use a second and possibly a third coat to add sparkle. And if you end up with too much gloss, let the finish harden thoroughly (a day or two) and then rub it down with rottenstone mixed to a paste with No. 10 auto engine oil (Fig. 22-1). (Pumice powder is faster cutting but might cut through a new finish.)

To avoid rub-through in any rubbing, wipe the surface clean with a fresh cloth at frequent intervals to examine the finish. To simulate the effect you will have at completion, use a cloth moistened with a little diluted household detergent to clear away the oil film. If you over-dull, a little furniture polish will usually save the day. Best bet for beginners; practice on a concealed part, a section at a time. Then be guided by the portion that looks the way you want it.

OTHER FINISHES

Varnish or lacquer that has deteriorated must be removed with abrasive or paint remover. If the piece is modern and is to be completely refinished, either one may be used. If it is an old item, especially one with extensive carving or fluting, your best bet is paint remover (Fig. 22-2). It eliminates the risk of sanding off minute decorative details and of producing irregularities in narrow surfaces.

Fig. 22-1. Polyurethane coating is being used to produce a high gloss finish. Rottenstone or pumice can be used to soften the luster afterwards. Remember that after repairs are made or parts replaced, match original finish by using one that can be toned with pigments to match almost any wood.

Fig. 22-2. If major finish damage requires complete refinishing, paint remover may be used. Raised lip around this table prevents power sanding. Paint removers work fast; wrinkled, blistery surface tells when finish can be removed. Wipe with wadded cloth, rinse.

On ornate cabinetwork apply the remover liberally, let it work for ample time, then use steel wool to slide off the finish on mildly convex and concave surfaces. Use a small stiff brush on fluting and carving. A toothbrush is ideal in fine detail work (Fig. 22-3). On lathe-turned portions you can use any coarse cloth in "shoe shine" fashion to slip away the softened finish.

Intricate carving presents the greatest problem in finish removal as deeper tone is retained in crevices. However, as the new finish will darken the overall tone (unless you plan a distinct change of style), this darkening simply tends to emphasize the pattern. *Caution:* when using paint remover, particularly with a bristle brush, wear protective glasses. Many removers are extremely dangerous to the eyes, and brushes can spatter them for a considerable distance.

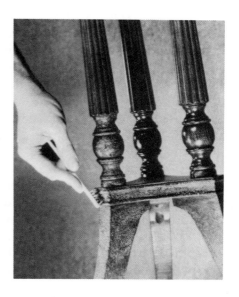

Fig. 22-3. An ordinary toothbrush is a very handy tool to use in order to remove finish from fluting, molding, and carving after paint remover has lifted and softened it.

FILLING DENTS AND SCRATCHES

If a tabletop or other flat furniture surface has been dented or deeply scratched, there are several remedies. To minimize the refinishing required, you can use a plastic type wood compound such as *Plastic Wood* or *Wood Patch* in a tone to match the surface. Most brands are available in a variety of wood tones.

Apply the compound to the marred area with a flexible putty knife and immediately remove any excess from the adjacent finished surface so the solvent in it won't lift the finish. Allow it to dry thoroughly according to directions on the can, then sand the immediate area with fine cabinet paper on a block. The sanding levels any raised area of the wood plastic. If the plastic shrinks and produces slight hollows, apply another layer to bring it up slightly above flush. After drying, sand it even.

Use the same fine grit cabinet paper to sand the entire panel or tabletop lightly with finger pressure (not a block). This removes the gloss to provide a "bite" for the overall finish coat.

A single coat of finish (same as originally used) should then be applied over the entire area. This assures that the repaired area will blend perfectly with the rest of the panel. On very small repairs you can skip the extra overall coat by very carefully blending out a coat of finish over the local area, then rubbing with rottenstone after the finish dries so the luster of the repaired area will not be higher than the rest.

WHEN TO "START OVER"

Where the surface has widespread damage, such as dents and numerous cigarette burns, spot patching, as above, becomes tedious. Your best bet is complete sanding down to re-level the surface. (This may not be possible on veneered surfaces. Another method for this is described later.) A belt sander is best suited to furniture work. To remove thick layers of old finish, it may be used at an angle of 45 degrees across the grain top to speed cutting. This clears away finish and wood surface fibers quickly with medium grit on the belt. It must then be followed by use parallel to the grain with the same grit, followed by successively finer ones.

If you lack a belt sander, you may use a reciprocal type (back and forth motion), orbital (back and forth plus sidewise motion), or a universal-joining disk type. Do not use an ordinary flexible (rubber) disk sander unless you are an expert at handling it. Mishandling this type results in fast cutting on one side of the disk, producing deep circular digs in the surface.

Fig. 22-4. Where a surface has widespread damage, the best thing is complete sanding with a power sander. After this, finish the job by block sanding with the grain.

Whatever sander you use, keep it moving constantly, overlapping each pass along the grain about an inch with the next pass, so no "digs" or levels are produced. And finish the job by block sanding with the grain by hand with very fine grit cabinet paper (Fig. 22-4).

SMOOTHING AND PRE-STAINING

For the best final surface, use a wash coat of 3-lb. cut shellac thinned 1 part shellac to 5 parts alcohol. *Use only a single coat.* Allow it to dry thoroughly—preferably about 4 hours. Then sand with very fine cabinet paper.

The wash coat does two things. It stiffens minute hair-like fibers on the wood surface so the final sanding can scuff them off. And it is absorbed by the most porous areas of the wood. This is especially useful on soft pine and pine plywood, as the shellac wash absorption by the porous wood prevents it from absorbing an excess of stain later, causing unpleasant "blotching" of the wood. The result of the shellac wash treatment is an automatic overall evening out of tone when the stain is applied.

STAINING

Staining is usually a matter of brushing on the stain, allowing it to remain until the tone is as deep as desired, then wiping it off (Fig. 22-5.) This requires an overnight wait (for thorough drying) before the first coat of finish can be applied. If you want to speed things you can use the stain differently. Pour some in a shallow saucer and dip a cloth pad in it. Then, using rubber gloves to avoid stained hands, wring out some of the stain from the pad. Apply the stain to the wood by rubbing the pad lightly over it—with just enough pressure to provide an even tone. There should not be so much stain on the pad that it "soaks" into the wood.

Fig. 22-5. Staining is usually a matter of brushing on the stain and allowing it to remain until the tone is as deep as you desire. Alternative way is to make use of a saucer and cloth.

Properly done, this method gives a surface stain that dries sufficiently in an hour or so to permit finishing to proceed. It has another advantage, too: if the tone of the overall job varies, it is a simple matter to rub on a little extra stain where needed. Some stains are made with this type of application in mind. Ask your paint dealer for the type he handles.

PAINTING

Painting over an old finish requires less preparation than natural wood finishing, as you need only a smooth, well-bonded old finish surface to start. There is one important precaution, however, particularly with some deep-tone stains that may be in or under the original finish: be sure the surface is sealed so the old stain will not "bleed" through the paint. A coat of shellac is often used first for this purpose. Any other good sealer coat can do the trick.

In general, a brush is the handiest furniture painting tool, as it adapts easily to varied contours. One of the most common brush painting troubles is paint "sag" caused by overloading the brush and applying too much paint at a time. Load the brush lightly, apply the paint or enamel evenly, and watch for the sags that warn you of overly heavy application.

Several thin coats are better (in most finishes) than a single heavy one. If you spot a sag after the pint has begun to dry, *do not* try to wipe or scrape it off, and *do not* try to brush it out. Tampering with tacky paint can only make a far worse blemish. Let the sag dry thoroughly, then sand it off with care. It takes only a minute or two of sanding, and the next coat conceals the sanded area completely.

In any stain-finishing job there is a consoling remedy if your final tone is too light. Shellac finishes can be given a deeper tone simply by a few extra coats of orange shellac, or of shellac colored with alcohol-solvable shellac dyes. These are available in most wood tones from larger paint dealers. Similar products are available for many varnishes and lacquers.

In applying any of these toned finishes, the trick is to avoid unevenness of color. This can result from applying the finish thicker in one are than in another. To lick the problem use two brushes. One applies the toned finish, the other is kept in a small container of the proper thinner for the finish. If you spot an area too deeply toned as you work (and they show up readily), simply pick up the thinner brush and use it to even the tone. Try the system on a scrap of wood first. The knack comes quickly.

A soft luster is best. Don't aim for extremely high gloss in your furniture finishing. Look at the finish on high priced furniture of the same general type and you'll find that its sheen is moderate. There are practical reasons for this, one being that too much gloss tends to emphasize even a small amount of dust that may settle. And for the nonprofessional there's another more important reason: a super gloss betrays every flaw in the finish. (Even plastic laminate counter-tops are made in both glossy and satin finish—the latter to to conceal the results of wear, scratches, etc.) But apply your finish to produce its full gloss. Then use rottenstone or pumice to soften the luster as desired.

SANDING BETWEEN FINISH COATS

The reason for sanding between coats of finish is often misunderstood. Its purpose is to remove embedded specks of dust and level off any minor unevenness in the finish *while removing as little of the finish as possible.* It should be done only with fine cabinet paper and with light fingertip pressure. Do not count on inter-coat sanding to do major leveling. That should be done before the first coat of finish is applied.

To save time plan your furniture painting so an entire coat can be applied in one step whenever possible, leaving no portion of the piece unpainted. Basically, this calls for leaving "handling" areas free of paint temporarily so the piece can be turned or shifted as required to complete the job. On a chair, for example, you can start by resting it upside down with the seat on a paper-protected table. Paint the outside of the back, the legs, and so on, but leave several rungs unpainted so you can turn it right side up for completion. Then paint the unpainted rungs.

IMPORTANT FINISHING TIP

On chairs, benches, and other furniture where the finish will be subjected to considerable contact pressure, allow more than enough time for complete drying. If you're in a hurry to get the piece back in use, apply a finish that dries quickly. This is especially important in humid weather. During a muggy spell a varnish that normally dries hard overnight may require several days. Yet to the casual touch it seems ready for use. But let someone sit on a chair varnished under such conditions, and he'll leave a fabric imprint on the finish of the seat—and perhaps require a dry cleaning job on his clothes as well. For hurried jobs use lacquer such as a quick-drying acetate type. If the weather is humid, you can add a "retarder" fluid to prevent "bloom" or moisture whitening. Hard, fast-drying floor finishes like *Fabulon* are also handy for this type of rush job.

VENEER DAMAGE

Although major veneer work calls for equipment and knowhow not all homeowners possess, the average do-it-yourselfer can make minor repairs very successfully by exercising care and a few simple tricks. Such veneer repairs are necessitated when deep dents or cigarette burns are found on veneered tabletops. You can't sand down to level deep dents or mars, as you would remove the veneer entirely.

The simplest way to solve this problem is by buying a small sheet of the same type of veneer from a cabinetmaker's supplier like Albert Constantine & Son, 2050 Eastchester Rd., New York, N.Y. 10461. Then use a small square or rectangular piece of cardboard as a template to mark off an area of the tabletop enclosing the damage. Use a sharp single-edge razor blade or a trimming knife to cut along this line deep enough to penetrate the veneer. Then use an ordinary flatiron, set at moderate temperature, to heat the enclosed damaged area. The heat softens the glue (usually animal or polyvinyl) so that the damaged veneer section can be lifted out by slipping a thin spatula under its edge.

Work carefully. Once the damaged veneer is removed, scrape the surface beneath to remove glue and smooth it. If the dent or burn goes still deeper, fill it in with a wood putty and allow it to harden thoroughly. Then smooth it off, using a very small sanding block or a strip of aluminum oxide paper bent around the square tip of a small wood strip.

Next, use the same cardboard template that outlined the veneer cut to outline it again on the new sheet of veneer, with grain direction matching. Cut the patching piece of veneer very slightly oversized. Set one corner down in the cut-out recess and note any variations from fit. Then trim the opposite edges carefully with razor or trimming knife.

Glue the patch in place with hide glue or polyvinyl, wipe off any squeeze-out and cover the area with several layers of tissue paper. Then place a flat-bottomed weight on the patch, after first placing the cardboard template on top of the patch, matching edge for edge.

Leave it overnight, then remove the weight and sand off any tissue paper that may have stuck to the surface. Use wood putty to fill any gaps that show up around the patch edge. (We can't all get a perfect fit, but it doesn't matter if it's fairly close.) The wood putty in matching tone will conceal small errors. After this, treat the tabletop as described for regular refinishing after small repairs. Sand lightly and apply a finish.

How to Buy
and Restore
Used Furniture

USED FURNITURE can be a boon or a bust. A few tips on what to look for can be of great help to the novice at this type of venture. What may appear to be a complete wreck at first glance may very well be a wise investment.

Take a night table, for instance. The drawer is completely disengaged from its guides, the shelf is unhitched, the back is loose. Sounds pretty miserable, doesn't it? But this very looseness—even the gluing blocks are askew—is a hidden benefit. Reassembling the little piece is a cinch, much like a kit! Regluing and refinishing are easy, as parts may be sanded, refinished, or waxed (except where glue is to be used), without the bother of sanding in tight corners; the drawer can be cleaned, and a new pull added to blend the piece with other furnishings where it will be used.

After removal of old glue and refinishing of all parts, reglue the piece. Wipe off any squeeze-out as soon as possible, and your "kit" is ready to take its place as a night table, lamp stand or handy stand for a record-player. The stretcher-shelf is useful for stacking record albums or books. Cost? This one sold for a few dollars.

METAL FURNITURE

Metal furniture, if no parts have rusted badly or been distorted out of shape; is almost always a good buy (Fig. 23-1). Look for baked-on enamel.

If cushion springs and padding are in good condition, use ready-made covers. Most sizes are available with zippers that allow easy removal when time comes to clean or replace them. One thing to look for when purchasing cushioned goods of any kind: the tag that states the object has been sterilized as required by law in most states. This assures you of a sanitary ready-to-use piece (Fig. 23-2). If your state does not have such a requirement, exterminators and bedding manufacturers have facilities to take care of this at a minimal cost. It is good health insurance.

Aside from the condition of the finish, a good quality note is the use of self-leveling glides on all legs. A little work with paint remover and a can of spray lacquer can restore the finish, but legs

Fig. 23-1. The frame is obviously sturdy and cushions can easily be recovered.

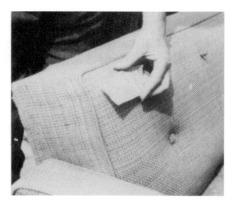

Fig. 23-2. This tag on used upholstery shows that the piece has been sterilized.

that cut into rugs and carpets and mar your wood or composition flooring may prove a costly item in the long run. Skip any furniture with loose rivets or cracked welds.

MISSING OR BROKEN PARTS

Many a time while exploring a second-hand furniture mart or a housewrecker's yard for a certain type of table or chair, you may find just what you had been searching for but, alas, a leg may be broken off right at the seat. (Refer to Table 23-1 for complete troubleshooting checklist.) Matching the leg would in most instances be impossible, but all is not lost. By the use of a glue such as resorcinol resin on dark wood, or epoxy on light wood, to join the wood parts of the leg, with a hardened spiral flooring nail driven into the mended leg from the top of the seat, the leg will support for years (Fig. 23-3).

Many antiques are embellished with beautiful and elaborate carvings that add to the charm and grace of the piece, be it a table, chair, chest or headboard for a bed. If you are lucky enough to find such an antique, and discover that one or more parts of the carving are missing, look around you before you turn it down. Often you will discover a real mess that has been relegated to the

-------------- Table 23-1. General Tips on Used Furniture --------------

GENERAL TIPS ON USED FURNITURE

Fastenings: Screws and dowels are more substantial than nails. Dovetail and "finger" joints are better than simple nail-and-glue types. Joints held by glue only, though separated by dampness in old pieces, may be made waterproof by regluing with modern resin glues like the acrylics, polyesters and resorcinols. Strength of joint will be greater than original.

Upholstery: Unless you are experienced at upholstering, leave tufted work to professionals. Smooth surfaced forms are within range of most do-it-yourselfers. Complex spring-and-padding systems are best replaced with foam cushioning. Many upholsterers will cut the foam to your pattern, if you buy it from them.

To buy or not to buy: If you can do the work required or have it done and still have a bargain, buy the piece you want. Used furniture savings often run to hundreds of dollars on a single piece.

Fig. 23-3. The loose gluing block makes it that much easier to reglue leg.

back room for similar reasons, but has carvings or, say, period knobs suitable for the reclamation of your dream piece. It may be just a lone drawer with a pair of pulls to answer your purpose, and very cheap in the bargain. Another time it may be just an old-fashioned frame for a picture or mirror, but the molding may fit the style and period of your decor.

If a piece originally had two carved parts, and one has been lost over the years, search around for a discard (most secondhand places have such a section where real finds are to be had). You need not locate an exact match; perhaps a new pair of carvings will blend with the original work.

Don't worry about removing the carvings. Leave the whole thing out in the weather, or soak it for a while in water, and the carved portion will slide right off, as most of this type of work was assembled with hide glue which is readily softened with water.

If you have no luck in this department, molded wood carvings in traditional designs are available from cabinetmaker's supply houses. When they are finished to match the wood in your purchase, or gilded for contrast, they can transform the lowliest piece into a replica of an authentic antique. Moldings are also made in a more modern style, if that is what is called for.

UPHOLSTERED FURNITURE

Do not be alarmed when an upholstered sofa or chair is popping at the seams (Fig. 23-4). Many times the padding can be shoved back into its original position and the torn covering handsewn to hold it in place. Then a reupholstery job can be done

Fig. 23-4. Don't be alarmed if the padding is popping. Recovering is simple.

at home or, for a really excellent job, by a professional at far less than the cost of a new item.

Also, where the padding is visible, you can test its resiliency—and at the same time determine if it has been waterlogged or otherwise damaged before you buy. Now is the time to look for moth damage, and springs that may have to be replaced or retied. On sofas and easy chairs, damage may very well be confined to the cushions. In this case, replacement units of spring construction are sold by mail-order houses, which also stock foam units in rubber and polyurethane.

When there is an odd or offbeat seat shape, your local upholstery shop can follow almost any pattern. Simply cut out a template in cardboard, and it can be duplicated in foam of either type. Foam is also handy for giving resiliency and form to a flat seat. Simply place the foam, cut to shape, on the wooden seat and pull the fabric covering so that it gently rounds out the pad. Luxurious comfort and elegant appearance are your reward.

Trim of all sorts is another item to be had at a reupholstery shop. This includes a wide assortment of fringes, welting, guimpe and upholstery nails. These, which are available in a variety of styles, can save the day when the redoing of a chair seat by wrap-around method is not practical. Simply draw the fabric down to the base of the rim, fold under the loose edge of the fabric, anchor with a few staples (they won't show in the finished job) and make a neat and decorative border with the nails. The ornamental nailheads will conceal the staples.

HELPFUL HINTS

Browse around. If this is your first venture into secondhand land, look before you leap. It will pay to spend some spare time

Table 23-2. Used Furniture Trouble-Shooting Checklist

Problem	Remedy
Chairs and Similar Pieces	
Missing piece of carving	Remove counterpart to balance appearance or replace with similar pair of carvings.
Upholstery, stuffing, springs	Remove completely, replace webbing and redo with foam cushioning. Reupholster.
Open dowel joint	Clean away loose glue, recoat with gap-filling glue and clamp joint until glue sets.
Cane seat broken	Replace with new caning sold in sheet form by cabinetmaker's supply houses. Or cover area with plywood, use foam cushion.
Short leg break near seat	Fit broken ends together carefully after coating both with gap-filling glue. Drive hardened spiral flooring nail down from top to reinforce.
Casters missing	Replace all or front or rear pair. If holes are undersized for new casters, redrill.
Short break in mid leg	Drill broken ends about 3 inches to take ¼- or ¾-inch steel rod reinforcement before gluing ends as for short break above. Rod is available at large hardware stores. Do not use polyvinyl glue.
Long split in leg	Glue parts together with polyester, acrylic or resorcinol glue.
Wide split that will not close	Place cellulose tape firmly under split and over end to form dam. Then fill split with acrylic glue. When glue sets, remove tape.
Cabinets	
Local veneer "blisters"	If small, cover with layer of heavy paper, press down with hot electric iron. Slide block of wood on blister as iron slides off. Hold till cool. Heat softens hide glue, so blister is reglued. On large areas, slit blister so it can be flattened, then repair as above.
Cracked marble top	Glue parts together with polyester glue made for purpose. If small pieces are missing or edges chipped, fill with the glue, matching marble color with mixed-in pigments.
Veneer edging separating	Iron back in place, as in blister treatment above. Or remove completely by wet rag soaking, and replace with new edging made for plywood. Buy it at lumberyards.
Missing period hardware	Try matching it at cabinetmaker's supply house. If it can't be matched, replace with nearest type.
Parts separating due to glue failure	Separate parts completely, clean away old lumpy glue from joints. Reglue with white (polyvinyl) glue on non-load-bearing joints. Use casein, aliphatic resin or other non-creeping glue on bearing joints.
Rot in cabinet feet or base due to damp storage	Drill into rotted part, restore hardness to rotted wood by permeating with liquid resin which soaks into rotted areas, hardens, and makes wood stronger than new.
Plywood de-laminating	If only small area is involved, run glue into inter-ply spaces, spread with spatula and clamp plies tightly to rebond. If area is large, it's best to replace entire panel.

Fig. 23-5. "Rabbit ears" reveal age of chair. Rush seat can be rewoven cheaply.

Fig. 23-6. Corner braces and the firm gluing blocks on this chair show quality.

in as many shops as you can. Compare prices, try to spot the little deviations in style and design that mark a piece as valuable, such as the "rabbit-ears" on the back posts of the chair in Fig. 23-5. These are prized by many collectors, and make the difference between a real find and an ordinary "kitchen" chair. Sometimes a little effort to remove layers of old paint will reveal a lovely Early American piece. (See Table 23-2.)

Don't be afraid to turn things upside down! Corner braces and substantial gluing blocks are clues to quality construction and materials (Fig. 23-6).

Rebuilding an Old Rocker

A BATTERED WRECK of an old rocking chair was initially purchased from a housewrecker for less than one dollar in change. The original seat had been replaced by a home-made job of rope; slats were missing from the back; rungs and cross-members were loose, as were the rockers themselves. It hardly seemed like a bargain even at that price. However, a little work and ingenuity transformed it into a charming and serviceable piece that would do justice to the decor of any room (Fig. 24-1).

The methods of restoring and reinforcing used on this chair would apply to any chair of similar structure, rocker or not, such as a dining chair or a ladder-back occasional.

WHERE TO START

The first chore was cutting away the old rope seat (Fig. 24-2). In the course of this, it was discovered that the rope was about all that held the seat rails together, which made it a simple task to remove them for regluing. Next, the new seat rails were cut from dowels and dry fitted, and the crossmembers of the back were taken out, as well as the remaining slats.

Fig. 24-1. Before and after comparison of the rockers. You can use the same methods to restore dining chairs or ladder-back occasionals.

When replacing rungs, you can almost always find dowels to match. The slats in this particular chair were thin and delicate, thinner than stock lumber. If stock lumber is too heavy, trellis can be planed down to fit. However, in this case, wood from a fruit crate proved to be the exact thickness required, and with a little sanding, provided enough material to make the two missing members.

Before reassembly, old flaking paint was scraped off, then the whole thing was washed thoroughly with soap and water and allowed to air dry (Fig. 24-3). Scrubbing down an old piece like this often reveals minute cracks in an apparently firm member, which if replaced at this time makes future repairs unnecessary.

Old glue was dug out of the sockets to prepare for new gluing. The glue chosen in this instance was a polyester resin type that is good in cases where fit is not too accurate, as it is not only a gap-filler, but actually hardens to a solid resin that will not powder out, and is completely waterproof. Available at boat supply stores,

Fig. 24-2. The first step is to remove the seat covering and check the strength of the slats, seat rails, braces and rungs.

it can be pigmented to match wood tones if a natural finish is desired, or, as here, it may be painted.

If your chair does not require disassembly, but merely additional stiffening at joints, glue injector will save a heap of work. A $\frac{1}{16}$-inch hole can be bored right into the heart of the joint. Then the glue can be forced under pressure into the loose parts. Check with the manufacturer to be sure the glue you use is suitable for this type of application.

REGLUING

First the sockets were coated with glue, then ends of rungs and slats. The rungs that form the side rails of the seat were set

Fig. 24-3. Before assembly old flaking paint is removed and then the whole thing is washed thoroughly with soap and water.

in place first. Then the slats were placed in the crosspieces of the back, and then came the tricky part. The back rungs, reglued, were very lightly put in place, leaving the long upright members free enough to allow the back to be inserted without popping out the rung. A little patient working of all the parts with a light touch, and the job was done.

Since proper clamps were not at hand, the assembled work was tied with rope with cloth pads protecting the wood; the rope was twisted gradually to put the right pressure on the newly glued joints. Excess glue was removed quickly, as unsightly squeeze-out glue may be difficult to get rid of after it has set.

MAKING A NEW SEAT

Using a sheet of cardboard, a pattern was made by cutting and trimming for a snug fit, and traced on ½-inch plywood. Blocks fore and aft on the underside prevent the seat from slipping.

Cellulose fiber padding was placed on top, and a remnant of upholstery fabric—in this case a gold brocade—was pulled neatly around the wood, allowing the padding to roll slightly over the top edge for appearance, and to protect the fabric from undue wear. The material was fastened to the underside with a staple gun. For a professional touch, guimpe to match the brocade was applied around the edge of the seat with regular guimpe tacks (Fig. 24-4).

Fig. 24-4. When making the new seat, staple the fabric to the wood to anchor the padding. Then tack the guimpe in place.

FINISHING

Since there was now a variety of woods—some old, some new, some from a crate—a natural finish was out of the question. To match the elegance of the new seat (which was made while waiting for the glue to harden), a black and gold scheme was used.

First, a coat of flat black enamel was applied and allowed to dry thoroughly. Then a small can of gold leaf enamel and a small artist's brush were used to paint a design of flowers and fruit across the top of the back and on the outside of the rockers. Tiny, even, curved strokes produced a dainty effect on the slats and lower crosspiece. Slight brushing of gold was used on the rims of the finals on the back uprights.

To keep the design from being smeared, as the flat black does have a slight tendency in that direction, a coat of clear shellac was used for a final finish. This also gave a soft satiny luster which is most attractive.

When all was dry, the new seat was popped into place, and the old wreck was restored to its original use, a comfortable rocker.

When parts do not have to be replaced but simply reglued and reinforced, a natural wood finish can recapture the style of the original period. Most old pieces were finished with shellac, an easy-to-use quick-drying product which does not pick up dust before setting.

If there are old layers of shellac on the work which have darkened over the years, an alcohol wash-down may be all that is needed to prepare for a new finish. If possible, do the job outdoors, and wear rubber gloves, as denatured alcohol is hard on the hands. Avoid breathing in the fumes as much as possible. The first wash may seem disappointing, as it merely softens the old shellac, but successive washes will gradually reveal the original tone of the wood. Use lint-free pads so that you work to a smooth surface.

When the old finish is removed to the point where you want to restore luster, thin, even coats of clear shellac will bring back the brilliance without darkening the tone. Sand with fine cabinet paper between coats to achieve a professional, "silky" finish. Buffing with paste wax can be used as a final touch, but in most cases is not needed.

Your battered old rocker will be unrecognizable after you have finished the restoration process, and will look like a brand-new piece of furniture.

How to Reupholster
a Chair

IF YOU RECOIL from the thought of reupholstering your own easy chairs because learning all the tricks of the trade seems like too much work, consider this: by using just *one* simple "trick" and by working patiently and methodically you can do at least as good a renovation as is shown in Fig. 25-1, on the first try.

TAKING NOTES

What's the magic trick? Simply this: *remember everything you see as you slowly take the chair apart*. To do that, you make copious notes to remind you how each section of upholstery had been sewn, tacked or stapled in place by the original maker (Fig. 25-2). Use simple sketches when words do not suffice. After the original upholstery has been removed, and you have used the old parts as patterns to cut replacement pieces from the new upholstery material, rebuild the chair by reading your notes *backward*. This way there's never any question about what piece goes on next and how it is fastened, provided your notes are complete. Leave

252

Fig. 25-1. Instead of buying a new chair, you can save a lot of money recovering the one you have.

nothing to memory. Put it all down on paper in orderly sequence, and you have it made.

REMOVING THE UPHOLSTERY

Resist any temptation to buy new fabric until after the old covering has been removed. Lay the old upholstery sections on the floor, between two parallel strings set 54-inches apart (the width of typical upholstery material), and move them about until you have the most compact arrangement. Be sure that each pattern is oriented in the proper direction so that any stripes or other patterns in the *new* material would run in the proper direction (Fig. 25-3). Also allow a little extra, when possible, so that the patterned material can be shifted sideways to match strips or other patterns on adjacent panels.

Fig. 25-2. Carefully examine worn chair to determine how it was built. Keep series of notes as chair is disassembled by sections.

When you have the most efficient arrangement possible, including allowance for welting if it is to be made from the same material, you will know exactly how many yards of material to buy. You are now sure, that you will neither run short, nor waste money on excess material.

If you are at all handy, this is all the information you need to tackle a reupholstery job. But to save you a little time and head-scratching, we'll add a few general tips.

NECESSARY TOOLS

The tools you need are few and quite inexpensive. The basics include curved and straight upholstery needles, long-nose pliers

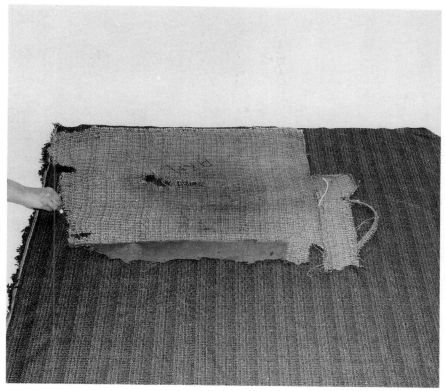

Fig. 25-3. Lay old fabric sections on new material, check most economical cutting method. Match designs on pieces joined at seam.

for pulling the needles through thick cloth, staple and ⁵⁄₁₆-inch staples, medium and large tacks (same sizes as those removed from the chair), large shears, Exacto or another sharp knife for trimming, marking chalk, an old chisel and hammer for removing tacks. If new webbing is needed, get a webbing stretcher (Fig. 25-4).

CUTTING NEW FABRIC

When you cut out the new fabric pieces using the old pieces as patterns, cut them *oversize* whenever this does not lead to material wastage. Also, do *not* slit or notch the fabric until you are actually fitting it onto the chair when it will be evident just how much you must cut into the fabric to part it so that it can be run around two sides of a frame member.

If you leave some extra material on a rough-cut piece of fabric, you can get a better grip on it to pull it tight when stapling

Fig. 25-4. Make sure webbing isn't frayed or shredded. If it must be replaced, buy and use an inexpensive webbing stretcher.

or tacking in place (Fig. 25-5). After the cloth has been fastened, trim off any excess material.

The original springs may still be good, but may need to be retied or renailed in place (Fig. 25-6). Before tearing out old string, study it carefully so that you can duplicate the original tie methods. Still safer: remove the old string while you are simultaneously adding the new string.

Reuse any padding material that is still good; replace padding that is lumpy or for other reasons has obviously seen its day. Shape any new padding carefully to provide the same bulk and shape as the original. If the insides of a seat cushion are in bad shape, the easiest solution may be to have a foam pad of proper dimensions made up by an upholstery supply shop, and just sew a cover to fit.

INSTALLING PRESEWN SECTIONS

Some sections—like the arm pieces on this chair—should be presewn before installation (Fig. 25-7). Take plenty of time doing

Fig. 25-5. Stable cloth to the wooden frame unless there are too many layers of material for staple to secure. Use tacks instead.

Fig. 25-6. Knock out old tacks with chisel, check springs, padding. Replace if necessary, then refasten springs, tie cords in place.

Fig. 25-7. Carefully and accurately fit presewn sections like arm pieces. Take the time also to smooth the padding underneath.

this so that both arm pieces have the same *shape* as well as size when viewed from the front. Fit both arm pieces onto the chair, snug in place, but do *not* staple or tack down.

Stand back and compare the two arms critically. You might find that one arm has "squarer" corners than the other because you sewed some corners into fairly tight and square right angles and others into more curved corners. If you goofed, take an arm piece apart and do it again. If the fault is a minor one, you may get by with a little hand stitching to pull things into proper shape.

Watch the padding underneath, especially the vertical sections which might have dropped off wholly or in part while you were working on other sections of the chair. Poke in fresh bits of padding if you find empty spots under the fabric; pull out any lumpy padding.

WELTING

You can buy ready-made welting that will harmonize with the fabric you choose. Or you can buy welting cord and make your

Fig. 25-8. The curved upholstery needle is used to sew fabric sections together with blind stitch. Note the use of a strong cord.

own by sewing the same upholstery fabric around it. With a little patience, this can be done with an ordinary sewing machine foot. But if you obtain a welting attachment for your machine, the job would undoubtedly be much easier.

Cardboard strips are used to keep welting along a chair edge straight, and also to provide a straight edge where fabric is folded over on itself. For example, you will note that the top edge of the rear panel is first nailed in place using a paper strip, and the fabric is then folded over the strip. If you leave off the strip, tension on the edge of the fabric would pull wavy dips into the sections between the hold-down tacks. The two side edges of the rear panel are probably blind stitched, using strong cord rather than thread. A curved upholstery needle is a must for this operation (Fig. 25-8). Note that rather long stitches are used.

STITCHING TECHNIQUES

You will get the hang of blind stitching very quickly if you take a good look at the way it was done by the original chair maker.

259

You will find that such stitching can be used in various places on the chair to rectify minor imperfections such as small sags between a fabric panel edge and an adjoining welting.

Although it is wise to stick pretty close to duplication of the original construction methods, there are times when good judgment dictates a change. For example, the original skirt on the chair shown here had a lining. However, the new fabric was much stiffer because of a coating material on the rear, hence the lining was not needed; in fact, the addition of the lining would have made the skirt far too stiff and bulky. You might also want to change the appearance of the chair one way or another by making minor changes. Here the skirt might have been left off because the chair legs were still in good shape.

FINAL TIPS

Remember, clear and complete notes are essential for full success in amateur reupholstery work. To underscore one point, consider one more example. The front horizontal panel of the chair is presewn to a plainer, tough piece of fabric that remains hidden when the cushion is added to the chair. Note that the joined fabrics are also sewn—along the same seam line—to an underlying piece of burlap and/or the springs. When you are ready to install the new seat and front panel combination, your notes should indicate clearly what kind of hidden stitching is used and how far the seam is from the front edge of the chair.

Chair reupholstery certainly is not recommended for those rare individuals who have trouble screwing a light bulb into a socket. On the other hand, method and patience can go a long way to compensate for lack of knowledge or experience if you have any craft skills at all. A woman who is adept at sewing her own dresses would probably handle all the upholstery sewing jobs with ease, although it is a little harder to feed thick upholstery material through a sewing machine than to sew see-through dress fabric. On the other hand, a man may be a bit better at nailing and stapling parts together because he has more strength in his hands. All this adds up to one final observation: reupholstering a chair is an ideal team craft project for a husband and wife.

All about Antiquing

ANTIQUING IS DEFINITELY "in" the home scene these days and thanks to the magic of the antiquing kits available, it's possible to make an old piece of furniture that you've had lying around the basement or attic look brand new—or give a new piece you've just purchased the charming appearance of age.

There are several steps you can take to assure a professional-looking result. First of all, be sure to remove all handles, knobs, or other hardware because it is far easier to work on a smooth surface. It is not necessary to remove old finishes, varnish, or enamel, unless you want to reduce the surface to the bare wood. In that case a paint and varnish remover will do the job.

Cleaning is done by scrubbing all surfaces with trisodium phosphate, ammonia, and water, or an abrasive household detergent using a small brush—such as a toothbrush—to get into hard-to-reach areas. Wash off all traces of the cleaning agent with clear water and allow the surface to dry.

SANDING

The final results of your antiquing job may depend on whether or not the piece of furniture you are working on is sanded properly. To obtain the best results you should use three different grades of sandpaper, starting with the coarsest of the three, and applying the finishing touches with the finest one.

You can make the sanding process—which ensures adhesion of the paint—much easier by using a wooden block covered with the sandpaper, course side out. Any deep cuts or abused areas need not be sanded smooth, since they will absorb more of the toner, producing a "distressed" effect.

If you want to fill any scratches or mars, a plastic wood filler will accomplish this job, and these areas can be sanded smooth after thorough drying. If you wish, these fillers can be colored to match the natural wood tones of the furniture and chalk-like color mixtures can be bought with the filler at most stores.

When all sanding is completed, dampen a cloth with mineral spirits, and clear all the surfaces of dust.

UNDERCOATING

Once the piece is dry and clear of all dust you may apply the undercoating. Read the label instructions carefully, making sure that the coating is stirred thoroughly so that there isn't any pigment collected at the bottom of the can.

If you use a spray-gun to apply the paint, you should add two tablespoons of mineral spirits to thin the mixture enough to ensure an even flow of paint. Remove all drawers and doors, place them on a flat horizontal surface—to avoid streaking—and you're ready to begin.

Use a flat, wide brush for the larger surfaces, painting one side of the piece of furniture at a time. By applying long, even strokes with the grain of the wood you will produce the best results (Fig. 26-1). For any piece with prominent legs, turn it upside down and paint the legs first, followed by the top and work downward.

Apply only enough undercoating to cover the surface well. And then let it dry for twelve to twenty-four hours. Then sand lightly, and you're ready for the toner.

APPLYING TONER

After you have stirred the toner thoroughly with a wooden paddle, read the label instructions carefully, applying a thin coat of the toner in the same manner as suggested for the undercoating

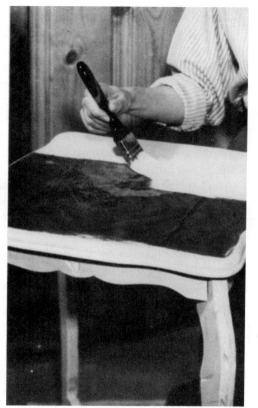

Fig. 26-1. The first step in application is the undercoating. Use long, even strokes and allow the coat to dry at least twelve hours.

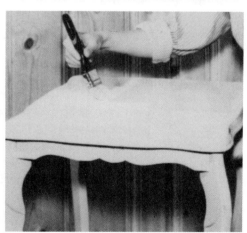

Fig. 26-2. The second step is to apply a thin coat of toner in same manner as the undercoating. Let it set 10 to 30 minutes before rubbing.

(Fig. 26-2). Be sure to pay special attention to any carved trim and crevices, painting them first to allow more absorption of the toner. Let the color toner set for ten to thirty minutes before beginning to rub.

RUBBING

Here you can use your imagination along with a cheese cloth, dry brush, and steel wool. Just be sure to step back and check your progress every so often to make sure you aren't overdoing it.

Rub large, flat areas in long, even strokes, starting with a light touch and apply more pressure as you go along (Fig. 26-3). If you discover you've allowed the toner to set too long, simply dampen your rub cloth with mineral spirits. If the reverse is true and you haven't permitted the toner to set long enough, you can apply another coat and wait again for the application to dry.

The difficulty in rubbing intricate carved trim can be overcome by using a cotton tip in those hard-to-reach areas. After rubbing, allow at least twenty-four hours for the paint to dry thoroughly.

If you want to add a protective coat of clear varnish, it can be applied as soon as the toner has dried. But if you wish to wax the surface, it is best to allow the paint to dry for at least a week before applying.

SPECIAL EFFECTS

After the coat of toner is applied, there are several methods which can be used to achieve interesting special effects:

Grain. For a wood-grain simulation, use a dry brush for your rubbing. Place a small amount of toner on a piece of tin foil or glass, touching the tip of the brush lightly in the color. Apply in long, even strokes, with the grain of the wood, but in irregular lines.

Splattern. For this artistic touch use a stiff bristle brush, such as an old toothbrush. Dip the ends of the brush into the paint,

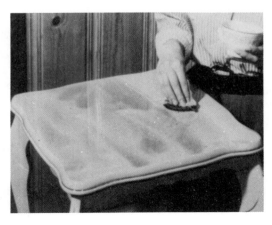

Fig. 26-3. The third step is to rub large, flat areas in long, even strokes. You can also create various interesting special effects.

and "spring" the bristles with your finger to throw a fine spray of toner over the undercoated surface. Check the desired effect by practicing on a piece of paper first, remembering that too much toner on the brush could result in splotches.

Water Stained Wood. This interesting and traditional look is accomplished by first rubbing the toned surface, then splattering it with mineral spirits. The toner spreads out in spots where the liquid has fallen, creating an authentic water-stained look.

Marble. Apply a relatively heavy coat of toner to your surface, then lay a large piece of wrinkled, clear plastic lightly on top of the area. Pat the plastic lightly with a cloth, making sure wrinkles and air bubbles are in evidence. Then pick up the plastic quickly and carefully, but be sure not to drag it. Similar effects can be achieved by using a feather, a sponge or burlap, or a combination of these materials.

Tortoise Shell. The best way to create this effect is to work on one small area at a time. Applying a heavier than usual amount of toner glaze, tap the surface lightly with your fingertips, changing the angle of you hand each time. A similar effect can be accomplished by tapping the surface with a short bristle brush, beginning in the center of the area and working toward the edges.

Distressed. If your piece of furniture isn't naturally worn, this popular antiquing effect can be simulated. You can make your own scratches and mars simply by beating the surface with a heavy tool, or a burlap bag filled with chains. After sanding the scratches, apply the artists oil paint "raw umber" straight from the tube, rubbing off the excess paint vigorously.

Distressed Paint. To achieve this effect apply two layers of contrasting colors to your furniture, allowing each to dry thoroughly. Using a coarse grade of sandpaper, lightly sand the surface until the initial color is in evidence. Do this only in those spots where normal wear would occur.

Working with Moldings

THERE ARE QUITE A FEW different styles of molding available. Each, usually, has a particular purpose or purposes. Base molding, for example, is designed to protect the end of the wall from scuffing and cleaning materials. At the same time, like other moldings, it is also decorative.

But many moldings can be used for purposes other than what they were designed for (Fig. 27-1). The following is a roundup of some common types, and some suggestions on other ways you can use them. They're sure to spark other ideas.

HARDWOOD AND SOFTWOOD

Most molding comes unfinished in either hardwood or softwood. Softwood is, by far, the most predominant material; indeed, many lumberyards don't carry hardwood and it can be considered a specialty item. Softwood is usually pine, fir, larch, hemlock, or cedar, depending on what's native to your area.

By length, moldings usually start at 6 feet and go up in two foot increments to 16 feet. Some lumberyards, however, carry odd-size material, 7, 9, 11 foot, and so forth. Width and thickness vary

Fig. 27-1. Because of the base which is made out of ordinary moldings, the lamp that is pictured here achieves a handsome look.

according to the molding shape or pattern. In theory there are a tremendous number of different sizes, although your lumberyard usually will only stock what has proven to be most popular.

Normally, stock molding is one continuous, unjointed piece. You can also get molding that is put together with finger joints— clear pieces of lumber that have been cut and then finger jointed. However, since the joints do show, it's not the material to get unless your intended finish is opaque paint. Finger-jointed molding, as you might suspect, costs less than unjointed material.

NOMINAL SIZE

As with regular lumber, molding has a nominal and actual size, like a 2 × 4 nominally is a fraction smaller in actuality, due to planing and finishing at the mill. For example, if you order a 3-inch-wide crown molding, you will get a material only $2\frac{5}{8}$ inch wide.

It is crucial, if your project involves joining pieces of the same style and size molding, to get all the material from the same lumberyard. Make sure it's not only from the same mill, but from the same run of lumber. Molding that varies fractionally in size is extremely difficult to join accurately. To check to see if it is the same size, hold the ends of pieces together. They should be exactly the same size.

OTHER MOLDINGS

In addition to stock material, there are a few other moldings to know about. One is embossed moldings. These are usually

267

available in 8-foot lengths and have a sculptured, machine-carved surface. You can get them unfinished, or finished in a wide variety of colors, including silver and gold. A good variety of patterns is available.

At least one company puts out a prefinished hardwood molding. It's available in walnut and oak. Another company has moldings specially designed for making picture frames (a special use we'll talk about later) with corners that are premitered.

While not, strictly speaking, a molding, there is also a large group of ornamental plaques made of wood, plastic, or a composition material. They come in a wide variety of sizes and styles and are a good accent material.

TYPES OF MOLDINGS

There are many different types and various styles of available moldings for standard use. Perhaps a dozen patterns are the most popular.

Cove. In the larger sizes, cove molding is designed to cover the wall-ceiling joint. In the smaller sizes, they're commonly used for wall-corner joints. Unlike the larger cove, smaller pieces have no space behind them when installed, but fit snugly into the corner.

Crown/Bed. These are like cove moldings. Crown is designed to cover the wall-ceiling joint and bed is normally used outside the house to hide the gap between shingles and soffit.

Quarter Round. This is another molding for finishing off corners. In cross sections it is a quarter circle.

Shoe. This is a close cousin to quarter round. It's used at the base of the baseboard and is nailed to the floor (or should be—some carpenters nail it to the base molding). Its purpose is to close the natural gap between base molding and the floor which occurs as a house shrinks when green lumber becomes seasoned.

Half Round. As the name implies, half a circle in cross section, at least in the smaller sizes. In larger sizes it's an oval. It is used to give a blank wall a paneled look and as cabinet decoration.

Base. The main purpose of this type was mentioned earlier. It is often used in concert with other moldings for decorative effect.

Casing. This is normally used around doors and windows. Usually, it harmonizes in style with the base molding. Available are ranch, round edge and traditional styles.

Mullion. This is designed to cover the gap when double hung windows are installed next to one another.

Base Cap. In the old days, molding used to be formed by nailing ''1 by'' to the wall, then installing base cap on top for decoration. Base cap still has the same purpose.

Picture Molding. Originally, this style was installed some distance from the ceiling line (the area above was prepared or finished in some other way) and pictures were hung on it. Today it is primarily used as wall decoration.

Wainscot. This is designed to separate different wall treatments, such as wallpaper and paint.

Ply Cap. If you install plywood on a wall, this is the molding used to finish off the top edge.

Panel Mould. For hiding panel seams. Installed, it makes the paneling look inset.

Chair Rail. This was originally designed to protect a wall against scuffing by chair backs. It has since become largely decorative.

Corner Guard. Outside corners are especially susceptible to damage. Corner guard fits snugly over corners and protects them. Also available are corner guards designed for inside corners.

Screen Molding. This was once used to cover the raw edges of screening, but today its main purpose is to give a framed look to panels, as shelf edge, and as a delicate decorative accent on cabinet doors. Glass-bead style is similarly used.

Astragal. This functions the same way as mullion—hiding that gap between double hung windows. It is also frequently used to cover seams on heavy-board planks. Batten is similarly used, often outdoors.

Stop. Every time you close a door you come into contact with this material. It's the molding the door closes against and stops it from going through the other side—and off the hinges.

Round. For a variety of purposes, including building dividers.

Handrail. Just what the name says—used as a handrail on banisters inside and outside the house.

Squares. This is mainly used as a handrail, usually on porch railings.

Lattice. These are simply flat strips of wood. Originally, they were used to block the area leading to the crawl-space so cats and dogs couldn't get in. Now it has no single purpose.

OTHER USES

The craftsman's ingenuity can really be seen at work when it comes to uses for molding other than their main purposes.

Picture Framing

Molding is a natural for making picture frames (Fig. 27-2). Indeed, you can make frames for about one quarter of what you would pay for them at a custom woodworking shop *and* they are just as handsome.

Picture frames normally have a rabbet to accept the matted picture, painting, or what have you. To make your own frames you can use either molding that has a rabbet, such as ply cap or back band, or make a frame with a rabbet. In the latter, you first make a subframe of flat stock, say "1 by," then assemble molding on it that's ¼ inch narrower all around. The overlapping part of the subframe is your rabbet. (There is also a cove-like molding with a rabbet especially sold for picture framing.)

A few tips on making picture frames. You can use any kind of wood you wish—pine is a good choice—but be absolutely sure that it is straight with no bows or warps. (Sight down it to check.) Miter joints, the kind used in making picture frames (and many other things) are not very easy to cut, but bows or warps can make a snug, accurate fitting miter impossible. Also avoid sappy woods which won't accept finish well.

Be sure to use good tools. A good miter box and backsaw are essential for cutting molding to the required 45-degree angles. You'll also need a good clamp to hold the mitered pieces together as you nail them. A number of companies make clamps especially designed for this purpose. Our advice is to get them.

You can use just about any molding pattern you wish in order to create the frame. Many are composed of a variety of moldings.

Fig. 27-2. The careful cutting of miter joints can produce good-looking, but inexpensive picture frames. Use any wood you wish.

Flush Door Decoration

Any interior or exterior flush door is a candidate for a face-lifting with molding (Fig. 27-3).

Carefully plan the arrangement of the molding on the door. You can outline it on a piece of Kraft paper as big as the door, draw a sketch to scale, or use masking tape on the door to visualize your pattern. Taking the door down makes it easier to work on. When the arrangement is set, glue and nail (use hobs) the molding.

If the style of the house permits, here might be a good place for one or more of the many wood plaques and ornaments available.

Customizing Furniture

There are many things in the house which have flush surfaces and can be decorated with moldings—things like dividers, bed headboards, garage doors, and cabinets.

A favorite use of many woodworkers is to dress up unfinished furniture. It can really transform a bare piece.

In general, you can attach molding to these items with brads and glue. If the molding is particularly thick, use screws. If possible, run the screws in from the backside of the item. In this way, you won't have to counterbore or countersink for them.

Hiding Edges

While plywood is a great do-it-yourself material, it does present one problem—the plies, or layered edges, are not attractive

Fig. 27-3. Here a simple wood front door takes on a new appearance with the aid of some molding trim—neat exterior for homes.

271

Fig. 27-4. Shown here are three steps in making framed wallcovering panels which can dress up walls. It's done with a piece of plywood edged with base cap molding to hide rough ends. (above left) Molding is first glued on, then secured (above right) with nails. Blind nailing (left) hides nails by securing them under a sliver of wood.

and must be covered. One way to cover them is with a flexible wood tape secured with glue. But moldings can also serve this purpose (Fig. 27-4). Just select material—favorites are lattice and half-round—cut it to length, and glue and nail it in place. Countersink nails, fill holes, and sand smooth for finishing.

An even purer way, from a woodworking standpoint, is to blind nail the molding in place. For each nail gouge up a sliver of wood. Drive the nail below the sliver, sinking it the last fraction of an inch with a nailset, then glue down the sliver, holding it until dry with a piece of masking tape. Finally, sand smooth. It's be hard to tell the wood has been disturbed.

You can also use molding as described above to protect edges of various items—shelves, for example.

Building Material

While you can't expect to build a house with molding, there are some small things you can make with it. For example, you can use base and some other types to make narrow shelves. A shadow box goes together nicely using wide lattice strips ($\frac{5}{16}$ inch × $2\frac{5}{8}$ inch); lattice is also great for making spice racks.

If you install shelves, quarter round is a handy cleat for holding it up. Quarter round also has another good use if you're constructing drawers. Tacked around the front edges it helps make the drawer dustproof. For making drawer pulls, you can use any suitable molding (cut into small pieces) as drawer handles.

How to Buy Cabinetmaker's Supplies

HAVE YOU EVER WONDERED where to match authentic antique hardware, or to get rare woods your local lumberyard never heard of, or tools the corner hardware store doesn't stock? The cabinetmaker's supply houses are your answer.

RARE WOODS

If you have any doubts when matching wood in the repair of a choice antique, or in the duplication of a museum treasure, real wood samples are available. These are not small chips, but pieces large enough to allow you to make a thorough study of the wood tone, grain pattern, and texture. After they have served their purpose in helping you make your selection for that project at hand, they can be used to advantage in inlay work with other woods.

Large houses provide such a sampling; they have woods from all over the world, such as rosewood in different species from the East Indies and Brazil, ebony from India, harewood from England, Carpathian elm burl from France, to name just a few. Unless otherwise stated, these fine veneer woods are cut $\frac{1}{28}$ inch thick, and are available in lengths from 36 inches up. You can order just the amount your project requires.

How do you apply these beautiful veneers to the surface of your table or chest as the case may be? A simple-to-operate veneer press does the trick. You may buy the parts and assemble one to suit your own shop, or buy a ready-made unit, both from the cabinet supply house. A new contact-type glue for use without a press is also available.

INLAYS

Many period pieces owe their distinction to the use of inlay work. This aspect may intimidate the amateur craftsman when he first looks at some of the lovely but intricate designs used by the old masters of this art. But, here again, ready-made inlays in almost limitless variety are available with colored woods and motifs to enhance and beautify almost any project you can name.

Designs range from simple geometric forms that can be used on contemporary pieces as well as the classic type of project to charming and delicate floral patterns suited to a lady's desk or a formal coffee table, all executed in real wood, ready to be fitted into the work. One supply house has over fifty, and the only difficulty is deciding which to use!

Inlays may come to you linen-backed or paper-backed. Linen-backed come with the finish surface up. Paper-backed are the reverse; the finish side is covered with paper. To keep them intact during shipment, they are held in a frame. Follow the instructions for releasing the inlay from the frame.

How to Apply Inlays

Inlays can be used in two ways. One is to simply glue the inlay over the finished surface, but this is not quite as elegant as a true inlay job. To do this, outline the inlay on the surface, and rout out the project to a bit less than the thickness of the inlay. This gives you a little leeway in your final sanding of the project. However, you may rout to a flush fit and sand and finish the entire surface in one operation.

After fitting the inlay dry, remove it carefully and use the glue recommended by the supply house. It takes about an hour to harden, but permits you to push the inlay into place with finger pressure. Apply weights until it is firmly set.

After glue is hard, sanding is the order of the day, and then the final finish.

Important Note: If you use a colored or toned finish on the area surrounding the inlay, protect your inlay with a coat of clear shellac to prevent discoloration of the different woods.

Inlay Borders

Inlay Borders, which are ordinarily sold by the yard, are amazingly inexpensive and beautiful. They may be applied the same as the regular inlays, by routing, and their varied colors can change a simple tabletop into a conversation piece. Follow the same general instructions for this type of work.

For a truly different and unusual effect, use inlay borders instead of the tape type so prevalent nowadays, to conceal the raw edges of plywood surfaced tables, or where end grain presents a finishing problem. Since they are all wood, they blend or contrast with pleasing effect.

CARVED TRIM

Don't think that hand carving on furniture is beyond your skill, time, and budget. Cabinetmaker's supply houses stock it ready-made. All carved from kiln-dried hard white maple, it can be matched to any type of finish. It can transform a simple open bookshelf by its use as an edging. With tasteful gilding treatment, period elegance can grace an otherwise dull project. This carving is also a boon in panel work on cabinet fronts that would otherwise be lackluster.

MOLDED WOOD CARVINGS

Less expensive than actual wood carvings, molded carvings fill the bill when economy is a factor. Usually supplied with brad holes, they are easily applied with brads and glue. When non-grain-raising stains are used, it is a simple matter to match the wood used in the main body of the piece. They can be machined just like wood, and come in a great variety of designs, from simple, dignified borders to elaborate floral and leaf patterns to inspire the designer in his home shop.

FURNITURE FINISHING MATERIALS

A wide selection of polishes, stains, bleaches, cleansers, and thinners, as well as fine brushes, are available at the supply houses.

When the corner paint store cannot fill your needs keep this in mind.

READY-MADE LEGS

Ready-made Legs for all sorts of furniture projects have been on the market for quite some time, but they have a limited appeal until you turn again to the cabinetmaker's suppliers. Here you can match period style in wood or metal to the project in the works.

There is a superb collection of metal legs of exquisite beauty of design and workmanship. Ranging from ultra-simple modern design to the more elaborate and baroque styles, all easily attached by means of integral flanges, they open the way for the craftsman who wants to be different.

With a choice of finishes from polished brass or English bronze to antiqued black or white on brass, these legs can be used with almost any wood finish, depending on the result desired. Some are reeded, others fluted and decorated in more elaborate style.

Round and square tapered legs of wood in the modern manner are also available, as is a set of Empire wooden legs. Most of the legs are to be had in an assortment of sizes, ranging from 6 inches in a simple wooden set to be used on a bed to 28 inches for table use.

Period and modern legs are also to be had in selected hardwoods to be finished as you choose. In addition, tea wagon wheels are on hand, fitted with rubber tires, nickel plated hub caps, and oil-less nylon bearings. Although generally called tea wagon wheels, their uses are almost limitless in the nursery, for patio furniture and anything else where mobility is a help.

WORKING HARDWARE

Hardware that takes the work out of everyday living can be purchased at these supply houses, too. Turntables for everything from a lazy susan to a TV chair to rotary shelves for hard-to-reach corner cabinets in the kitchen make life easier and more enjoyable. The cabinet units can be had with or without a center pole, depending on your installation. (Examples of hardware are shown in Figs. 28-1 through 28-5.)

Folding legs for tables used occasionally, then stored away, can be had in a variety of styles. There are also folding brackets for tabletops that are suspended from a wall and drop to a flat vertical position when not in use.

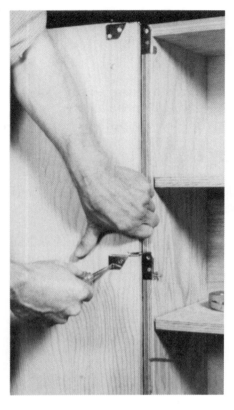

Fig. 28-1. Semi-concealed pin hinges have the advantage of allowing all the screws to go against the grain in flush plywood. Only the barrel shows when the cabinet doors are closed.

Typewriter supports for a desk make it possible to conceal the machine on the desk door when not in use. Ballbearing rollers and an adjustable spring to offset the weight of the machine make for ease of operation of the unit.

It is now possible for the home craftsman to buy platform rocker springs that convert an ordinary chair into a rocker without having rockers that protrude into the room and become a safety hazard. These units come in several sizes, according to the size and weight of the chair on which they are to be installed.

MATCHING OR DUPLICATING ANTIQUE HARDWARE

The cabinet hardware used by the homecraftsman is as important as the fine fit and finish of the wood parts. Whether it is as modern as tomorrow or a faithful reproduction of a period piece, compatible hardware is a must. There is a tremendous selection of these items. Pulls, knobs, hinges and key escutcheons in Early American, English Antique, French Provincial, and Louis

Fig. 28-2. With a touch-type catch, such as the one being mounted here, a door can be opened at a touch. Other catches available are magnetic, roller catch, and friction catch.

Fig. 28-3. Concealed pin hinges offer the advantage of allowing the door to fit flush with no hardware left showing when the cabinet doors are closed. Notching is required when installing middle hinge.

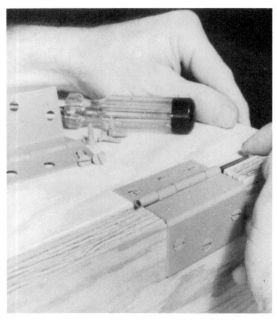

Fig. 28-4. Overlapping (lipped) doors can be hung with semi-concealed hinges with angle bends. These are especially suitable for plywood doors because the screws can be driven against the wood grain.

Fig. 28-5. You may want to use ornamental surface hinges, which not only look good, but also require no mortising. A combination of H and HL hinges provides enough support for the door.

XVI are but a few. The antique brass galleries found on delicate little tables are also available from these houses in a variety of patterns, both simple and elaborate. There also are solid brass moldings used as edgings for tables and desk tops, in designs that are matched to the pulls and hinges.

Two sources of materials mentioned in this article are:
William Hunrath Co., 153 E. 57th St., New York, NY 10022.
Craftsman Wood Service Co., 2729 S. Mary St., Chicago, IL 60608.

Index